*For Scott,
My oldest Grandson,*

*Grandpop
July 29, 2017*

The
FIRST YEAR
of
PACE MUSINGS

The
FIRST YEAR
of
PACE MUSINGS

DALE K. PACE
May 2017

XULON PRESS

Xulon Press
2301 Lucien Way #415
Maitland, FL 32751
407.339.4217
www.xulonpress.com

© 2017 by Dale K. Pace

All rights reserved solely by the author. The author guarantees all contents are original and do not infringe upon the legal rights of any other person or work. No part of this book may be reproduced in any form without the permission of the author. The views expressed in this book are not necessarily those of the publisher.

Unless otherwise indicated, Scripture quotations taken from the Holy Bible, New International Version (NIV). Copyright © 1973, 1978, 1984, 2011 by Biblica, Inc.™. Used by permission. All rights reserved.

Scripture quotations taken from the English Standard Version (ESV). Copyright © 2001 by Crossway, a publishing ministry of Good News Publishers. Used by permission. All rights reserved.

Printed in the United States of America.

ISBN-13: 9781545607800

Contents

Foreword ix
Alphabetized Topic Index xi

Musing 1: Wisdom (initially posted April 26, 2016) 1
Musing 2: Truth (initial posted May 2, 2016) 3
Musing 3: Trump (initially posted May 7, 2016) 5
Musing 4: Tolerance (initially posted May 10, 2016) 7
Musing 5: Racism (initially posted May 13, 2016) 10
Musing 6: Complexity (initially posted on May 18, 2016) 13
Musing 7: Biblical Parallels (initially posted May 27, 2016) 16
Musing 8: Virtue (initially posted June 1, 2016) 18
Musing 9: Good People (initially posted June 3, 2016 20
Musing 10: Guns In America (initially posted June 8, 2016) 22
Musing 11: Priests (initially posted June 9, 2016) 24
Musing 12: Belief (initially posted June 11, 2016) 26
Musing 13: Good Sense (initially posted June 15, 2016) 28
Musing 14: Unbalanced Emphasis (initially posted June 19, 2016) 31
Musing 15: Labels (initially posted June 19, 2016) 34
Musing 16: Rights (initially posted June 23, 2016) 36
Musing 17: Depravity (initially posted June 26, 2016) 39
Musing 18: Silliness (initially posted on June 26, 2016) 41
Musing 19: Miracles (initially posted June 28, 2016) 43
Musing 20: Change (initially posted July 2, 2016) 45
Musing 21: Never Posted 48
Musing 22: Bible (initially posted July 4, 2016) 49
Musing 23: Hebrews (initially posted July 5, 2016) 52
Musing 24: Gossip (initially posted on July 7, 2016) 55
Musing 25: Secondary Blame (initially posted on July 9, 2016) 58
Musing 26: Victims (initially posted July 11, 2016) 61
Musing 27: Unions (initially posted July 12, 2016) 63
Musing 28: Lives Matter (initially posted July 15, 2016) 66

Musing 29: Reasonableness (initially posted July 17, 2016 68
Musing 30: Thought Experiments (initially posted July 20, 2016) 71
Musing 31: Economic Realities (initial posted July 23, 2016) 74
Musing 32: Race Relations (initially posted July 24, 2016) 77
Musing 33: The Bible (initially published July25, 2016 80
Musing 34: Contrarian Perspective (initially posted July 30, 2016) 83
Musing 35: Political Immorality (initially posted July 27, 2016) 86
Musing 36: Repentance (initially posted August 1, 2016) 89
Musing 37: Whole Truth (initially posted August 3, 2016) 92
Musing 38: Reality (initially posted August 6, 2016) 95
Musing 39: Discrimination (initially posted August 12, 2016). 98
Musing 40: Fame (initially posted August 22, 2016) 101
Musing 41: Playing God (initially posted August 23, 2016) 104
Musing 42: Apostles (initially posted August25, 2016) 107
Musing 43: Consequences (initially posted August 28, 2016) 110
Musing 44: Audacious Proposals (initially posted August 31, 2016) . . . 113
Musing 45: Mental Balance (initially posted September 2, 2016) 116
Musing 46: Jews (initially posted September 6, 2016) 119
Musing 47: The World Is Wrong (initially posted September 9, 2016) . 122
Musing 48: Blasphemy (initially posted September 16, 2016) 125
Musing 49: Democracy (initially posted September 19, 2016) 128
Musing 50: Government (initially posted October 2, 2016) 131
Musing 51: Plain Talk (initially posted October 3, 2016) 134
Musing 52: Hard Thoughts (initially posted October 4, 2016) 137
Musing 53: Christian Agnostic (initially posted October 5, 2016). 139
Musing 54: Unasked Questions (initially posted October 6, 2016) 142
Musing 55: Juvenile Media (initially posted October 8, 2016) 145
Musing 56: American Stupidity (initially posted October 12, 2016). . . . 148
Musing 57: Realism (initially posted October 14, 2016) 151
Musing 58: Unborn Souls (initially posted October 15, 2016) 154
Musing 59: Presidential Election (initially posted October 18, 2016) . . 157
Musing 60: Election Choice (initially posted October 19) 160
Musing 61: More On Miracles (initially posted October 20, 2016) 163
Musing 62: Poor Mary (initially posted October 21) 166
Musing 63: More About Mary (initially posted October 22, 2016) 169
Musing 64: Judicial Activism (initially posted October 23, 2016) 172
Musing 65: Prayer (initial posted October 25, 2016) 175
Musing 66: Offensive Language (initially posted November 23, 2016) . 178
Musing 67: Ethical Perspective (initially posted November 25, 2016) . . 180
Musing 68: Stupid People (initially posted November 26, 2016) 183

Musing 69: What Is Wrong With The World? (initially posted November 29, 2016) 186
Musing 70: Sensible Economics (initially posted December 9, 2016) . . 189
Musing 71: Big Problems (initially posted December 17, 2016) 192
Musing 72: Caution Needed (initially posted December 24, 2016) 194
Musing 73: Limited Perspective (initially posted January 21, 2017) . . . 197
Musing 74: Scumbags (initially posted January 23, 2017) 200
Musing 75: Does It Matter (initially posted January 31, 2017) 203
Musing 76: Surprising Facts (initially posted February 5, 2017) 206
Musing 77: Good Of The Country (initially posted February 8, 2017) . . 208
Musing 78: Miss Marple (initially posted February 10, 2017) 211
Musing 79: Presidential Evaluation (initially posted February 11, 2017) . 216
Musing 80: Toxic Communications (initially posted February 17, 2017) 216
Musing 81: Divine Insights From Nature (initially posted February 21, 2017) 218
Musing 82: Diversity and Intolerance (initially posted February 24, 2017) 220
Musing 83: Persons (initially posted February 24, 2017) 223
Musing 84: Special Focus (initially posted February 28, 2017) 226
Musing 85: Immigration (initially posted March 2, 2017) 229
Musing 86: Stoapl (initially posted March 4, 2017) 232
Musing 87: Bad Guides (initially posted March 6, 2017) 234
Musing 88: Benefit Cost (initially posted March 8, 2017) 237
Musing 89: Curiosities (initially posted March 10, 2017) 240
Musing 90: Need For Clarity (initially posted March 13, 2017) 242
Musing 91: Advantage-Disadvantage (initially posted March 16, 2017) 245
Musing 92: LXX Reflections (initially posted March 18, 2017) 248
Musing 93: Before Moses (initially posted March 20, 2017) 251
Musing 94: Insights (initially posted March 23, 2017) 254
Musing 95: Abortion Chaos Part One (initially posted March 26, 2017) 257
Musing 96: Abortion Chaos Part Two (initially posted March 27, 2017) 260
Musing 97: Abortion Chaos Part Three (initially posted March 28, 2017) 263
Musing 98: The Demise of R&B (initially posted March 31, 2017) 266
Musing 99: Sensitivities (April 1, 2017) 269
Musing 100: Stupidities (initially posted April 3, 2017) 272
Musing 101: Truth (initially posted April 6, 2017) 275

Musing 102: The Big C (initially posted April 8, 2017) 278
Musing 103: Rumination (initially posted April 10, 2017) 280
Musing 104-Why? Part One (initially posted April 11, 2017) 283
Musing 105: WHY? Part Two (initially posted April 12, 2017) 286
Musing 106: WHY? Part Three (initially posted April 13, 2017) 288
Musing 107: Publication of Pace Musings (initially posted April
    14, 2017) 291
Musing 108: A Small Concept of God (initially posted April 15, 2017) . . 294
Musing 109: Easter (initially posted April 16, 2017) 297
Musing 110: Folly (initially posted April 16, 2017) 300
Musing 111: Secular Humanism (initially posted April 18, 2017) 303
Musing 112: Biblical Inerrancy Perspective (initially posted April
    19, 2017) 306
Musing 113: Religious Labels initially posted April 20, 2017) 309
Musing 114: Stingy Liberals (initially posted April 21, 2017) 312
Musing 115: The Early Church (initially posted April 22, 2017) 318
Musing 116: First Christian Ministry to Prisoners (initially posted April
    23, 2017) 318
Musing 117: Coerced Morality (initially posted April 24, 2017) 321
Musing 118: Trump Opponents (initially posted April 24, 2017) 324
Musing 119: Biblical Mysteries (initially posted April 25, 2017) 327
Musing 120: Balaam (initially posted April 25, 2017) 330
Musing 121: The Return of Christ (initially posted on April 26, 2017) . . 333
Musing 122: Is It Racism? (initially posted April 27, 2017) 336
Musing 123: Rest (initially posted April 28, 2017) 339
Musing 124: Spiritual Carelessness (initially posted April 29, 2017) . . . 341
Musing 125: Publication of The First Year of Pace Musings
    (initially posted April 30, 2017) 343

Foreword

In the spring of 2016 I decided to write short essays (each less than a thousand words) that I would call "musings." For hundreds of years **musing** has been defined as *thoughtful abstraction*, the act of meditating or pondering. I compose a musing when the mood strikes me, usually a couple each week. I started posting the musings on my Facebook account, and gave permission for others to share them as long as they attributed them to me; that permission was included with each musing when it was posted initially. I do not include that comment for this collection of musings. In the past year (April 26, 2016 to the end of April 2017), I have written 125 musings (a glance at the table of content shows their variety as does the alphabetized topic index after this Foreword) and managed to keep each of them within the thousand word limit I imposed on myself.

This book contains the first year of my musings; each was posted on my Facebook account between April 26th of 2016 and the end of April 2017. I believe they contain insights worth your consideration. Some ideas may challenge your perspective. I believe I'm realistic; if you find my comments challenging, it could be worth your while to give the topic serious thought. It's possible your perspective is unrealistic in some way, and you might benefit by becoming more realistic in how you look at things. Of course, it's also possible that I'm the unrealistic one. If you believe that, I ask you to let me know because I want to deal with reality honestly and candidly. I try to do that in my musings; if I'm off base, I want to know it so I can modify my perspective. Your help in correcting my perspective will be much appreciated.

I confess that publishing this collection of musing is challenging. I had to decide to publish as originally posted (with just typo corrections) or to modify the musings where my thinking had progressed or changed since I originally posted a musing. I decided to do the first option. So these musings, with a few typo corrections, are the same as I posted originally. That makes them something of a record of my thinking over time. Of course, being an old coot before I started these musings means that most of my evolution of ideas and concepts had occurred long ago.

Some have commented on my musings, and some have shared them with others. Some even indicated they liked a particular musing, using the Facebook like indicator. I appreciate the attention given to the musings and hope all readers received benefits from their ideas.

If I continue to produce musings, I'll probably publish collections of them in annual batches. If I publish them electronically I can charge a modest price for each collection of musings, which is what I am doing with this publication. Others may find my musings helpful. The publisher also provides a print edition for those who wish to have a paper copy of my first year musings.

The topics addressed in my musings were topics of interest to me at the time I first posted the musing. Some were stimulated by contemporary events, such as my comments about the presidential election and my suggestions about how people should decide for whom they would vote. Other topics were stimulated by things I read, my interactions with others, or just something of interest to me at the time.

Perhaps a sense of who I am will enable you to appreciate my comments better. I'm a college drop out with no technical degree who taught for a decade in a graduate technical management program of the Johns Hopkins University engineering school; I also developed an elective graduate course used at the Naval War College that I taught there a few times as an Adjunct Professor. Over a decade ago I retired from the Applied Physics Laboratory of the Johns Hopkins University as a member of its Principal Professional Staff. I have a couple of graduate theological degrees (B.D and Th.D.) and have been involved in Christian ministry to inmates since 1971, having established and led programs in more than a dozen jails and prisons. I received the 2017 award from the Institute for Prison Ministries of the Billy Graham Center for Evangelism at Wheaton College. Hence I have been exposed to both technical and religious perspectives on reality as well as to a broad spectrum of society. For example, one day I was involved in a morning meeting at the White House with the President's Chief of Staff and that evening I led a Bible class in a county jail; this provides an indication of the span of social conditions to which I have been exposed. However, you should be aware that I'm neither the sharpest cookie around nor the most talented wordsmith; in spite of such I believe my musings may be useful for you by insights they provide.

Alphabetized Topic Index

The Alphabetical Topic Index below lists the topics of my musings alphabetically and indicates which musing addresses a topic; some topics may appear in more than one musing.

Alphabetical Topic Index

Topic	#
A Small Concept of God	108
Abortion	58, 95, 96, & 97
Advantage-Disadvantage	91
American Stupidity	56
Apostles	42
Bad Guides	87
Balaam	120
Before Moses	93
Belief	12
Benefit Cost	88
Bible	33
Bible on Immigrants	22
Biblical Inerrancy	112
Biblical Mysteries	119
Biblical Parallels	7
Big Problems. Big Thinkers.	71
Blasphemy	48
Cancer (The Big C)	102
Caution Needed	72
Change	20
Christ's Return	121
Christian Agnostic	53
Coerced Morality	117
Complexity	6
Consequences	43
Contrarian Perspective	34
Curiosities	89
Democracy	49
Depravity	17
Discrimination	39
Diversity and Intolerance	82
Divine Insights from Nature	81
The Early Church	115
Easter	109
Economic Realities	31
Election Choice	60

Topic	#
Emphasis (Special Focus)	84
Ethical Perspective	67
Fame	40
Folly	110
Free Will and Neuroscience	104, 105, & 106
God	75
Good of the Country	77
Good People	9
Good Sense	13
Gossip	24
Government	50
Guns in America	10
Hard Thoughts	52
Hebrews	23
Immigration	85
Insights	94
Jews	46
Judicial Activism	64
Juvenile Media	55
Labels	15
Limited Perspective	73
Lives Matter	28
Mary	62 & 63
Me (Never Posted)	21
Mental Balance	45
Ministry to Prisoners	116
Miracles	19
Miss Marple	78
More on Miracles	61
Need for Clarity	90
Offensive Language	66
Persons	83
Plain Talk	51

Topic	#
Playing God	41
Political Morality	35
Prayer	65
Presidential Evaluation	79
Presidential Election	59
Priests	11
Publication of Pace Musings	107 & 125
R&B Demise	98
Race Relations	32
Racism	5, 122, & 125
Realism	57
Reality	38
Reasonableness	29
Religious Labels	113
Repentance	36
Rest	123
Rights	16
Rumination	103
Scumbags	74
Secondary Blame	25
Secular Humanism	111
Sensible Economics	70
Sensitivities	99
Septuagint (LXX) Reflections	92
Silliness	18
Spiritual Carelessness	124
Stingy Liberals	114
Stoapl (Sad Tale of a Petty Life)	86
Stupid People	68
Stupidities	100
Surprising Facts	76
The World Is Wrong	47

Thought Experiments	30
Tolerance	4
Toxic Communication	80
Trump	3 & 118
Truth	2, 37, & 101
Two Audacious Proposals	44
Unasked Questions	54
Unbalanced Emphasis	14
Unions	27
Victims	26
Virtue	8
What Is Wrong With The World?	69
Wisdom	1

Musing 1: Wisdom
(initially posted April 26, 2016)

A meaningful definition of **wisdom** eludes me. It has too many aspects for any definition I have seen to capture the fullness of its essence.

Not only has a definition of wisdom been beyond me, but wisdom itself has often been absent from my actions and attitudes. In the nitty-gritty of life, many of my thoughts, words, interactions with others, as well as my deeds have not been wise. They have hurt me; they have harmed others; they have made life more difficult than it needed to be.

Given the confession above, why continue reading? That's a good question. The point it makes is valid; but there are two reasons to continue reading. First, even a foolish dimwit such as I can understand some basic truths. Second, smart people can learn from the mistakes and folly of others as well as from insights of the wise.

What ideas do I have about wisdom? What have I learned from my folly?

First, **wisdom is realistic**. It deals with reality, not some partial imitation of reality that an ideologue might propose. The annals of philosophy are full of such ideologies, many of which have some valid perspectives but which only address part of reality. History records how various ideologies have been popular and then become discredited by their failure to address reality fully. I will mention just one that is prevalent today. I call it "scientism;" it is the perspective that says there is nothing beyond the material world, ignoring the spiritual aspects of reality and denying the Creator and His involvement in our universe.

Second, **wisdom is comprehensive**. It addresses both positive and negative aspects of an attitude, a concept, an action. Too often analysis of something only addresses its benefits and largely ignores its costs and potential consequences. Think of the arguments put forth by many of the one-issue advocates, such as those concerned about preservation of a particular animal. Do they ever discuss consequences of the cost of preserving the specified animal and identify the point where the cost of such preservation would be too great? I have not seen such; perhaps others have.

Third, **wisdom is practical**; it works. It is well known that many beautiful theories (ideas, hypotheses, etc.) have been demolished by "ugly" facts. Numerous notables have said that in the past few centuries; several of whom are often credited with originating its articulation. Some claim the idea can also be found in writings from antiquity. Practicality provides wisdom with a distinctive characteristic. It is consistent with the facts. That is why wisdom works.

The question is, where does one find wisdom? How does one become wise?

Religion, science, education, and a host of other suggestions have been put forth as the answer to those questions. Certainly one can find benefit in each of those suggestions; but not one of them can ensure that you will be wise all the time. That takes desire and determination from you. Stick-to-it-ness.

I recommend following the example of the magi, the ones we call "wise men." They sought and after a long trek found the promised One from God. Connection with Him always helps one who seeks to be wise. The story about the magi can be found in the Bible.

Musing 2: Truth (initial posted May 2, 2016)

Most of us have a hard time dealing with truth. Unfortunately the casual attitude that the Roman Governor of Judea in the First Century, Pontius Pilate, showed toward truth abounds. His famous quip, "What is truth?" was Pilate's response to Jesus' statement that He came into the world to testify to the truth; Pilate's quip was said just before Pilate condemned Jesus to death, a man Pilate said was innocent. Truth was not important to Pilate. Many today seem to have a similar attitude about truth.

The truth is important: If you ask for directions, you want to be told the truth about how to get to your destination, not something other than the truth since that would make it more difficult to get where you are going. If you are about to drink something, you want the truth about what it is because you do not want to drink poison or something else that would harm you. If you visit a doctor and are examined, you want to know the truth about your condition so you can deal with things properly.

Determining the truth can be hard work; often people are unwilling to expend the effort required to discover the truth. They are willing to live with something less than the truth, or they decide the truth is unknowable. They may even contend that everyone's view on a subject has equal validity. That is a popular approach. It appears to demonstrate tolerance, a perspective praised by many today. Unfortunately living with untruth can cause many problems.

False claims are made about truth at times. Sometimes Jesus is quoted as saying "The truth will make you free." It is a fact that Jesus said those words. They appear in verse 32 of the 8th chapter of the Gospel of John. However that statement is not valid UNLESS you include the condition that Jesus stated as a prerequisite for His comment that the truth will make one free. That condition is found in the previous verse in John's Gospel: "To the Jews who had believed him, Jesus said, "If you hold to my teaching, you are really my disciples." Then, Jesus said, you will know the truth and the truth will make you free. The truth only brings freedom when certain conditions are met.

Truth is sometimes unpleasant. Many people have a hard time accepting the truth about themselves. They may deceive themselves and others about their motivations and about their responsibility relative to consequences to others of their words and actions. This problem exists for common folk as well as for those in leadership and other responsible positions. Diogenes was not the first to note the widespread lack of honesty in his futile search with a lantern in daytime for an honest man in ancient Greece. Five hundred years earlier Solomon said something similar about the difficulty of finding someone he could trust (Ecclesiastes 7:28).

Truth problems are not restricted to religious and moral issues. Information found in the leading scientific peer-reviewed publications is usually considered reliable and trustworthy, yet serious questions have been raised about widespread failure of such publications to act in ways that ensure their material is valid. A number of analyses have noted substantial failures in that regard for a significant portion of the publications analyzed, perhaps a quarter or more of material analyzed had significant problems. Issues noted included such things as inappropriate conclusions from statistics used, inappropriate selection of data used in the report, hiding information inconsistent with conclusions presented, etc. If truth problems exist in such peer-reviewed publications of science, it is very likely they are also present (and likely to be even more numerous) in areas whose credibility is lower. Only a very foolish person expects truthfulness from those involved in politics or social advocacy.

Truth is required from good people. Good people tell the truth. They do not lie, nor do they distort the truth by only presenting part of it or presenting it in an unbalanced way. At the same time good people are wise enough not to expect that everything they are told or hear is the truth, the whole truth, and nothing but the truth. They understand the reality in which they live. I hope you will strive to be a good person.

Musing 3: Trump (initially posted May 7, 2016)

It appears that Donald Trump will become the Republican nominee for president of the United States. That is something few people thought possible six months ago. I present my perspective and how that came to be. I make no claim to special understanding of the political process and have no inside knowledge about any of the primaries. Nor have I spent a huge amount of time studying this issue. Instead I simply share my perspective; it is the perspective of one who has been a registered independent (not aligned with any political party) since I started voting about 1960. Perhaps you will be amused by my naivety, or stimulated by my insight. That is something which only you will know.

A significant portion of Americans are distraught by our dysfunctional government. They feel that the political establishment, which is dominated by professional politicians from the two major parties, cannot correct itself and probably does not want to even try; trying to do that might put their cushy livelihoods at risk. Hence many of those distraught Americans supported and voted for the one candidate who was outside the political establishment: Donald Trump.

What distresses the distraught Americans? **Entitlement expectation is a leading concern.** Instead of promoting self-reliance and personal responsibility, there has been a tremendous increase in expectation that the government will take care of every need and satisfy every interest, regardless of what the individual may or may not have done in terms of providing and caring for him or herself. Such growth in entitlement expectation creates an unsustainable situation. For example, during the current administration's tenure, federal debt held by the public (ala data from the Congressional Budget Office) has doubled when measured as a percentage of GDP; basically the government has been buying public favor at the expense of our nation's future.

Another leading concern is America's dysfunctional government. The two major political parties are so polarized that serious problems are not dealt with in a timely or rational fashion. For example, Congress seldom produces a budget on time, and continues to pack the budget with stuff to appease special interests at the expense of most of us. Likewise the administration tolerates non-functionality and bad behavior, such as that repeatedly demonstrated by the VA in its abuse of vets.

Donald Trump presented himself as the only one who was not obligated to the political establishment and as one who talked straight to the public instead of being a namby-pamby professional politician concerned about political correctness. He has positions that he knows are unpopular, but he does not try to hide them. He is very public about his positions. Trump embodies four characteristics associated with America's ascent to greatness. 1) He's smart and tough. 2) He can focus and achieve his objective. 3) He's flamboyant, a superb showman. 4) He's greedy; his life has been devoted to making money.

The Republican Party contributed a great deal to Trump's success in the primaries. The huge field of candidates initially, about twenty altogether, so dispersed votes among the candidates that the cohesiveness of distraught American support for Trump made Trump the easy leader of the pack initially. Egomania seemed to have precluded moderate Republicans from coalescing about an alternative to Trump until it was too late to stop him. Party leadership and those numerous candidate are to blame (or to praise) for Trump's advance to the nomination. Of course, the media helped Trump too. As the flamboyant front runner, Trump got far more media attention than anyone else. Likewise the media encouraged debates among the candidates to be personality clashes instead of serious policy discussions since that attracted bigger audiences. The public prefers to be entertained over being made to think seriously.

This fall I expect America will have to make a choice between a Democratic nominee who as part of the political establishment will continue to move America toward increased entitlement expectation and continued dysfunctional government OR a Republican nominee who might change the direction in which America is heading. Whether Trump could achieve what he and his supporters hope, or whether he might do something crazy is unknowable in advance. Distraught Americans appear to feel that America's situation is dire enough to warrant that risk. It will be interesting to see what the rest of American voters do.

Musing 4: Tolerance
(initially posted May 10, 2016)

Tolerance has become an elevated virtue; now tolerance is legislated in many areas and there seems to be desire by some to expand the scope of legislated tolerance. Tolerance is an oxymoron; at least as it is practiced at times because promoters of tolerance about some things are most intolerant of those they consider to be intolerant.

Tolerance is promoted as respect for the rights of others. In itself that makes tolerance something admirable, similar to the Golden Rule – an ethical practice of treating others as you would like to be treated. The concept appears in most religions and ethical teachings. Jesus mentioned it (Matthew 7:12) in the Sermon on the Mount. Unfortunately those emphasizing particular rights they want respected sometimes fail to recognize or appreciate rights which might be compromised or infringed upon by what they seek. Every right has limitations, and those limitations usually come from conflict with other rights.

The classic example of that kind of limitation on rights concerns free speech. Free speech is one of the most important and honored rights that Americans cherish, even if they often fail to honor it by tolerating speech from others which they find objectionable. This intolerance of free speech is illustrated by speech codes at America's universities. They abridge freedom of expression in many ways. Some abridgements are proper, such as forbidding one to yell "Fire!" in a crowded theater when there is no fire. Such frivolous speech is dangerous; it could cause physical harm to people if panic ensued from the shout of "Fire!" However, I consider abridgements to be inappropriate which merely protect various people from embarrassment or limit expressions of vulgarity, racial and ethical slurs, and sentiments which do not accord with contemporary political correctness. Freedom of speech tolerates verbal nastiness and its associated unpleasantness. Unfortunately speech codes at some universities are guilty of such inappropriate restrictions on freedom of speech. That is shameful behavior for institutions which should be at the forefront in freedom of thought and expression as well as in expanding knowledge.

Currently an example of the complexity of conflicting rights related to tolerance has created conflict between one of the states and the federal government. The state enacted legislation to protect women in its state from potential exposure to male genitals (i.e., penises) in public restrooms. The logic for such is similar to laws throughout the country prohibiting public exposure of male and female sexual organs. The federal government (with the concurrence and direction from the president) has sued the state for passing the law and is trying to prevent its enforcement, claiming it discriminates against those born male who have been legally classified as female in gender. Obvious there is a conflict in rights here; one right is based upon long standing accepted principles to protect women from sexual harassment; the other right is based upon a choice by a person to be something different gender-wise than he or she was physically at birth.

Life produces people who are different. Occasionally a person is born with fewer or more fingers or toes than the normal five at the end of each limb. Some people are extremely tall or short. Some have a variety of physical or mental issues from birth. A few are born blind, or with severe mental limitations. In the past, life was much harder for these folks than it is today. Often they were ridiculed, labeled as freaks, or abused; labels related to their condition, such as dwarf, often were used and many did not live to old age.

Some are born with a gender orientation mentally and emotionally that is different from the gender of their physical sexual apparatus. In the past such people often experienced the same kinds of problems as others who were different. Now tolerance for this particular class of people has been promoted and legislated. Currently laws have been passed whose impact on society is unclear in various ways, especially when rights of this particular class of people conflict with rights of others.

One point seems very clear from much of the rhetoric that I have heard about the current conflict between a state and the federal government. Those promoting tolerance for this class of people have no tolerance for any who disagree with them.

Contrary to popular mythology, you cannot have everything. Freedoms, such as that of speech, at times are incompatible with a society's security, tolerance, and stability. One is emphasized at the expense of another. Likewise resource limitations, something that always occurs in finite reality, can preclude things that sometimes are desired. For example, some contend that every person (regardless of economic circumstance) should have a right to the best possible medical care. However, there are not enough medical resources (doctors, nurses, hospitals, funds, etc.) for that to happen anywhere; not even in the part of the world with the greatest wealth and more medical resources than anywhere else.

Unfortunately advocates for many things cannot be bothered by such realities; they both ignore them and lambast those who mention them. They manifest attitudes similar to those shown by proponents of tolerance who are most intolerant toward those with a different perspective.

Musing 5: Racism
(initially posted May 13, 2016)

Racism is dangerous to discuss. Many people have such strong opinions about racism that comments not fully in agreement with their own perspective might cause them to have a negative attitude toward another without paying attention to what the person says, or to what reality may be. A willingness to ignore facts is a problem in many areas about which people have strong opinions.

The word "racism" is relatively new (less than a century old), and there is ambiguity about it. The Oxford English Dictionary (OED, which many consider to be the most authoritative English lexicon, cites the initial time a word is known to have appeared in writing – for some words in the OED that was more than a thousand years ago) has a neutral connotation for the word, defining *racism* as "the theory that distinctive human characteristics and abilities are determined by race" (noting its 1936 first appearance in print). *Racialism* is a word with the negative connotation of preference toward or antagonism to people of a particular race (its first use in print was 1907).

However the on-line version of the Merriam-Webster Dictionary indicates the simple definition of *racism* is "poor treatment or violence against people because of their race" and "the belief that some races of people are better than others," a negative connotation and says it was first used in 1933 but does not provide a citation for such.

These definition differences illustrate racism is an ambiguous and difficult topic. People are likely to have very different connotation by what they say even when they use similar words. Hence a comment not intended to be inflammatory might light the fuse of some who hear or read it. That might even happen with this short piece.

A touchy subject is the possibility that one's physical traits, behaviors, intelligence, etc. are a function of one's race. Everyone knows that these characteristics vary widely. Some people are tall; others are short. Some are smart; others are not. Etc. Both simple observations of people and detailed studies of genetic information (such as produced by the Human Genome Project) make it clear that there is more variation of these factors among members of the same race than between races. However, it is also true that some traits and characteristics are more prevalent among some racial groups than they are in other racial groups.

This can be seen in obvious physical characteristics such as skin color, hair color and texture, etc. However, when characteristics such as intelligence and behaviors are discussed, the subject becomes very contentious. Instead of calm and careful consideration of evidence and reasoning, discussions may become raucous and abusive. It is not unusual for some to apply derogatory labels and slurs to those with views different from their own. Such an approach to discussion does no one any good.

In many areas, cherished ideas and theories have often run afoul of facts. Sometimes people have a hard time accepting reality. This seems to be the situation for many on every side of discussion about racism. Contemporary technology makes it possible to begin to have facts about impact of genetic composition on thinking and behavior; at the same time we are beginning to understand how one's environment and experiences can modify the wiring of one's brain, even over-riding its previous inclination based upon one's genetics. The old debate about the impact of nature versa nurture (i.e., genetics versa environment) on a person's thinking and behavior is more complicated than had been known previously.

Hence caution is needed in claiming or denying that people of a particular race are more prone to criminal behavior, possess higher intelligence, or have more of particular characteristics than do those of other races. Identification of real racial causation of traits is much more difficult than we used to think. That is widely understood for an individual, given the great variation in physical traits and behaviors. Likewise, given the current limited state of knowledge in this area, we should be just as cautious about drawing conclusions statistically about racial causation of traits.

I close these brief comments with a question for the reader. While there is widespread condemnation of racism when it involves negative attitudes toward members of a particular race solely because of membership in that race, should there likewise be condemnation of a positive attitude toward members of a particular race such as shows in pride of one's racial heritage? Functionally there is no difference in the character of the discrimination involved; the only difference is in the direction (positive vice negative) of the discrimination resulting from such racism?

The reason for raising that question is simple. Such positive attitude toward a group brings some level of negative impact on others. This was illustrated by legislated preference for members of some groups in programs like Affirmative Action (for example, in applications of people from those groups to elite academic institutions, analysis reveals that such preference essentially gave applications of those in a preferred group a 200-plus SAT score advantage which made it likely that applicants not from those favored groups with higher SAT scores would be rejected by the schools). Some bristle at calling such things racism, although functionally that is what it is from Webster's definition of the term.

In this discussion, "race" applies both to biological heritage and ethnic identification.

Musing 6: Complexity
(initially posted on May 18, 2016)

Human relations are complex; they have many interacting aspects. Such complexity makes it difficult to account properly for *all* aspects of human relations. This is especially true for an issue that is getting a lot of attention in America currently. **That issue is the proper way to deal with transgendered people.**

Aspects of this issue include 1) conflicts between rights of different groups, 2) murky laws whose unintended consequences may not have been adequately considered, 3) analyses and arguments about the issue which fail to approach it comprehensively, and 4) ideological conflicts. History has shown repeatedly that failure to deal properly with complex issues often creates far larger and more serious problems; that has been true politically, socially, economically, and scientifically. This short piece cannot provide examples in each of those areas, but my comments illustrate the truth of what I said.

Consider the importance of multiple perspectives on time frames for an issue. Whether dealing with provision of electrical power, staffing for an endeavor, or laws and regulations, things most important in the short-term usually are not the most important things in the long-term, or even in the middle-term. Failure to appreciate such can prevent an endeavor from getting started or later to become a disaster. Remember the rocket rise and spectacular collapse of the dot.coms bubble. Likewise consider extravagant projections of promised cheap electricity from nuclear power made in the 1950s and 1960s; then compare them with the horrendous costs and problems now facing the nuclear power industry as it desperately seeks locations for its spent radioactive fuel.

A complex issue requires that all significant aspects of the issue be properly addressed for a lasting solution that does not create extensive problems. Let me illustrate some of the complexities in regard to the issue of proper treatment of transgendered people (i.e., those whose gender preference/choice is at odds with their sex determination at birth).

The first complexity: Who qualifies as transgendered? Any who claim that they want to be a different gender than their birth sexual identification? Or only those who have been designated as transgender by the court or other government authority? Who specifies qualifications for legal identification as transgendered?

The second complexity: Should transgender identification be permanent, allowed to be made only once? Or can one change their gender preference subsequently?

The third complexity only applies to those seeking transgender classification before becoming an adult: Who can make the decision to be or seek transgender identity? Is this something that a parent or guardian has to do for a minor? Or can the minor make that decision? Most laws restrict minors in many areas. They cannot marry, join the military, or get a bank loan without parental approval; likewise they may not be allowed to drive or drink because of their age. Does the legal system give minors who wish to be transgendered a kind of self-determination not allowed minors in other areas?

The fourth complexity is the one getting a great deal of attention at present: What access to public accommodations such as restrooms should transgendered people have? Should they be permitted to use facilities according to their gender preference? Should they be restricted according to their physical sexual identification at birth? Or should they be restricted to facilities designated for transgendered people (such as a one person restroom used by all genders and sexes)?

It is easy to understand desire for access to the more numerous facilities because, as they say, dogs have to run faster in Spain because the trees and fire hydrants are farther apart. However, the right of women not to be exposed to a penis in the restroom they are using, and the right of men not to be exposed to a vagina in the restroom they are using should not be ignored. How to properly resolve the conflict between rights of the transgendered and those of normal men and women can only be determined by a comprehensive consideration of *all* aspects of this issue. Unfortunately, that does not seem to be something that the government (i.e., the president or the courts) is trying to do. They seem bent on pursuing an agenda designed to please and accommodate the LGBT community.

A fifth complexity is religious: Freedom of religion is explicitly guaranteed in the Constitution; yet the government currently is willing to deny citizens that right if their religious beliefs contradict what is deemed politically correct. The Bible, which is the source for religious beliefs of Christians and Jews, groups who constitute the majority of Americans, says that homosexuality is wrong. Other religions also identify homosexuality as wrong. Most agree that transgender would be included in sexual activities that the Bible says are wrong. Yet the government says that now its civil religion (i.e., what its laws says are legal) has to be considered right regardless of what one's religious convictions may be. In essence this denies many their Constitutionally-guaranteed right of religious freedom.

Complex issues such as that related to the transgendered require comprehensive consideration of all aspects of the issue for it to be addressed properly. That is not happening currently. We should expect serious problems to result from the current way this issue is being addressed. ***Unfortunately that is what I see as our future.***

Musing 7: Biblical Parallels (initially posted May 27, 2016)

It is wise to try to obey Biblical commands, even when the command is at odds with our natural inclination as it is in things that Jesus provides as guidance for His followers in what we call the Sermon on the Mount. For example, He said instead of hating your enemy, we should love our enemies and pray for those who persecute us (Matthew 5:44).

However, sometimes people want to go beyond explicit commands in the Scripture and also use Biblical parallels for guidance. For example, some will use the parallel of what happened to the Jewish nation in the Old Testament when the people and their leaders turned from following God as a warning for what may be the future of our country if it persists in attitudes and behaviors contrary to Biblical guidance. For the Jewish nation in the Old Testament, the nation was attacked and conquered by other nations as a consequence for turning away from God and indulging in evil. Those using such a parallelism warn of danger to our nation if it continues what it currently is doing. Unfortunately, some also want to use the example of the way Jewish leaders used violence to eliminate worship of gods other than Jehovah as a guide for actions against those with different religious beliefs.

This raises an important question. **Is it appropriate to use Biblical parallels for such guidance?** That is the issue addressed in this musing. If it is, we should clearly understand how to identify an appropriate parallelism from an inappropriate one.

Experiences and examples of others are widely accepted as valid means of instruction. Early in the 20th century, philosopher George Santayana wrote in his *Reason in Common Sense* that "those who cannot remember the past are condemned to repeat it." Of course, this idea was not new with Santayana; it had been expressed long before him by many others, such as the 18th century British political theorist, Edmund Burke. Those who want to learn how to do something often watch someone do it as a way of learning.

Thus, using Biblical parallelism for guidance can be appropriate *IF* done properly. I suggest the following three ideas will help you to do it properly and avoid erroneous guidance.

1. The most appropriate use of a Biblical parallelism is to help one better understand an explicit Biblical command. If the guidance from a Biblical parallelism is not providing insight about an explicit Biblical command, you should be very cautious about that guidance – it could lead you astray. For example, Abraham is used in the New Testament as an example of trusting God (i.e., believing in Him) for His grace, forgiveness, and righteousness. The point of being acceptable to God by faith/trust is explicitly stated in both the Old Testament (e.g., Habakkuk 2:4) and in the New Testament. So use of the Biblical parallelism of Abraham's righteousness based upon his trust in God is appropriate.

2. There must be a pertinent parallel, not just incidental parallelism, for the guidance to be valid. For example, it would be inappropriate to assume someone is a traitor or likely to betray others simply because the person is named Judas. There are seven different people named Judas in the Bible; only one of them is a betrayer. Nothing adverse is said about any of the other six men named Judas in the Bible. So mere parallelism of one's name is incidental and should not be the basis for guidance of any sort simply based upon that parallelism.

Sometimes it is hard to determine if the parallelism is pertinent. I tend to be cautious in this area and will only consider guidance from a Biblical parallelism when the pertinence of the parallelism is very clear. Others are not so cautious in the parallelisms that they turn to for guidance. A prime example of extensive use of Biblical parallelism is done by many who are involved with Biblical numerology (the idea that many numbers found in the Bible carry significance beyond indicating quantity; symbolic significance may be attached both to individual numbers and to numerical values assigned to words based upon letters in the word).

3. Ignore "guidance" from Biblical parallelism that is contrary to explicit Biblical commands. Many Biblical Scriptures warn of false teaches who distort the meaning of God's Word. These warnings come from Jesus, John, James, Peter, and Paul as well as also being found in the Old Testament. This is application of a basic principle of sound Biblical interpretation: more emphasis should be placed upon ideas from clear passages than upon ideas from unclear or ambiguous passages. We should always let ideas in clear passages help us to interpret unclear passages correctly.

If a person simply applies these three principles, benefit can be expected from insights of Biblical parallelism with little risk of being misled because these principles keep one within the bounds of clear Biblical commands. The more fully we understand Biblical commands, the more completely we can apply their guidance in our lives.

Musing 8: Virtue (initially posted June 1, 2016)

Virtue has been used in English for nearly 900 years to express the value and goodness of a person or thing. The earliest *OED* citation for virtue is from 1225 A.D. referring to conformity in life and conduct with moral principles. Persons or things without virtue, i.e., virtueless, are worthless or immoral (or so usage of the word shows as far back as Chaucer in the 14th century). Thus virtue, as a word, is truly English since there are no citations for it in the *OED* from "Old English" which is also known as "Anglo-Saxon" and covers the period from about 600-1150 A.D. Of course, the word "virtue" is thought to have come into English from the related Latin word, either directly or via its French, Spanish, or Italian derivatives.

In the current time of confusion about what is right and good, any discussion of virtue has to begin with consideration of how one knows what is right and good. Otherwise, how can virtue be determined since virtue is conformity with moral principles? This musing only has enough length to touch on that aspect of the subject.

There are three possible sources for moral guidance: 1) what is right and good can be determine from the perspective of the individual; 2) what is right and good can be determine from the perspective of the group (e.g., society); or 3) what is right and good can be determine from an authority (that authority might be divine — many look to the Bible for guidance about morality, or it might be political authority as many in communist countries know from their personal experiences). Most of us draw upon all three of these sources for our perceptions of what is right and good.

Before we explore virtue more, it is well to remember that any virtue carried to excess becomes a vice. This point has been articulated by many. Three thousand years ago, Solomon advised not to be overly righteous in Ecclesiastes 7:16. The same point comes across from Aristotle's *Nicomachean Ethics* and from many contemporary wits.

If what is right and good is determined solely from the perspective of the individual, then no one should sacrifice himself for others. No brave soldiers facing the enemy to protect the homeland from foes. That kind of good and right cannot be based upon morality derived from the perspective of the individual. From this source (perspective of the individual), getting caught is the only bad aspect of lying, stealing, cheating, etc. I have met many in jail whose morals are based upon the individual perspective; getting caught is the only thing they think they did wrong.

If what is right and good is determined solely from the perspective of the group, then we become like ants and the individual has no value except as that person contributes to the well-being of the group. Carried to extremes, this means that the weak, the sick, the lame, and others who drain group resources should be eliminated so the group can be enhanced. This kind of attitude has been demonstrated at times in ethnic cleansings and genocides (where members of an ethnic group are perceived as harming or corrupting the dominant group), euthanasia, forced sterilization of those with severe mental limitations, etc. Last century this kind of thing was done many times, such as to Jews by Nazis in the holocaust and to Armenians by the Turks.

If what is right and good is determined by some authority, then it is important to know that the authority is both competent and good. Those who have lived in communist societies know the havoc and agony that comes from morality, identification of what is right and good, which is determined by fallible and corrupt government officials. Those who turn to a divine authority, such as the sacred writings of a particular religion, need to know that the divine source is both competent and good, that guidance from that source has not been corrupted, and that the guidance is properly interpreted. Both history and contemporary events, such as actions by ISIS and the Taliban, show the dangers of this approach to morality.

Even those who turn to the Bible for such guidance get it wrong at times, as illustrated by atrocities of the inquisition, religious wars, and the mass murder-suicide tragedy in Jonestown, Guyana in 1978. In the Gospels, Jesus criticizes Pharisees for distortion of Old Testament guidance about the Sabbath by prohibiting people from doing good on the Sabbath. Jesus showed that even the explicit words of God, such as the commandment about the Sabbath, had to be properly interpreted and applied.

That leads to my bottom line, which I state but cannot within my space limitation fully describe how I reached that bottom line. For our nation and for us as individuals, what should be considered right and good comes from a mixture of things from the three sources mentioned. The Bible is a reliable guide to right and good, but requires care in its interpretation and application. Because there can be conflicts between what is right and good from the different sources, at times it can be difficult to determine in some situations what should be decided to be right and good in particular situations.

Musing 9: Good People
(initially posted June 3, 2016)

One who saw my second musing (the one about truth) said, "Perhaps you will muse on 'good people' and whether there are any." It has taken me a month since that comment to come to this point, but here is my musing on that subject.

Diogenes is famous for searching Athens for an honest man in daylight with a lantern and never finding one; perhaps his problem was that he did not know what to look for since he had been run out of Sinope, his hometown, for debasing currency, i.e., counterfeiting. I hope you do not view my musing about "good people" in that way.

In one sense, it is easy to say there are no "good people." The New Testament makes it clear that no human (other than Jesus) can satisfy God's standard of righteousness; every one of us has fallen short (Romans 3:10, citing Psalm 14 & 53 as well as Ecclesiastes 7). We all are condemned because of our sin, our failure to live up to the level of light we have about God from His creation, from our conscience, and from what we have heard about Him from the Scripture and from others. Every one of us is guilty of failing to comply with the great commandment: to love God with our whole selves all the time, and most of us have also failed to satisfy many other aspects of God's requirements for righteousness. The New Testament also tell us that breaking the least of the commandments brings the whole weight of God's law upon the person (James 2:10).

In another sense, there are many "good people" around in a social sense. These are people who are respectful and considerate of others. They deal with others honestly and help others when they are in need. Such people may be found in most or possibly all strata of society. Some are religious; others are not. Unfortunately such people are not as numerous as we would like, and some who are not so good may pretend to be good in that way. Such hypocrisy has been around for a very long time.

Of course the standard for this kind of "good person" is very different than God's standard. For God, being a good person requires perfection, no failure in loving Him totally at all times. The only way a person can achieve that is by God's grace, by accepting His gift of forgiveness and spiritual cleansing because Jesus the Christ died to make that possible. Then God will see the person who turns to Jesus for that salvation in Christ with the righteousness of Christ imputed to the person. That is the only way a person can become a "good person" in God's eyes, whether or not the person is a good person in the social sense.

While many people in every strata of society are not "good people" in the social sense, we should ask what causes a person to be a good person in the social sense. Unfortunately, there does not seem to be a simple correlation between economic status, educational level, personality type, or even genetics (as reflected by family relationships) and being one of the good people. Nor does being a good person seem easily correlated with political beliefs and other ideologies; unfortunately the correlation of religious beliefs and practices does not seem as strongly correlated with being a good person as I wish it were. All who have been saved by Jesus should understand that the great commandment to love God totally is followed by a second commandment to love others as you love yourself and to do to them as you would like to have done to you. Those who take such commandments serious are likely to be good people in the social sense.

I suspect most of us know some of the social "good people;" they bless our lives, our community, and our society. I urge you to let those that you know who are "good" in that sense that you appreciate the way they behave and act. You should tell them that what they do makes life better for all of us. Such encouragement can help them to stay motivated to be good people because I am sure that every good person gets tired and discouraged at times. Perhaps you may even start thinking and acting like a good person, and join their ranks.

Musing 10: Guns In America
(initially posted June 8, 2016)

Personal possession of firearms is a very sensitive subject, and there are many aspects about this issue that people have strong, even sometimes violent, feelings about. I do not intend to enter the fray about constitutional rights to bear arms or the various arguments about the impact on society and national well-being of firearms in the hands of private citizens. There are numerous proponents and opponents on all sides of the many aspects of the issue. Some positions are presented intelligently by informed and thoughtful presenters, and other positions are ravings of loud-mouths with strong opinions, some of which are not supported by facts. Unfortunately, meaningful discussion of the complex aspects of the gun control issue is far less than would be good for us.

Instead this musing is about a few things related to firearms that I do not think most people know. I only found out the facts I will present recently; they came to my attention while I was browsing periodicals at the library. The facts I discovered are the number of annual deaths in the U.S. from firearms during a recent five year period (2010-2014), sorted in a particular way.

Four categories of deaths by firearms were presented: 1) those caused by police, 2) those caused by accidents (such as when a loaded weapon is dropped and discharges), 3) those in homicides, and 4) those causing suicides. For the first three categories, there was essentially no change in the number of deaths per year from 2010 to 2014. In suicides, the number of deaths in a year grew about 20% over the five year period. I will only present the numbers for 2014.

I was amazed at the number of shooting deaths caused by police (464 in 2014). That number includes both those killed in gun battles with police or in police protecting people from perpetrators, and also any situation in which police are thought to possibly have used excessive force. For a twelve month period, fewer than five hundred shot and killed by police in the entire nation is amazingly small. It is a very different impression from that one gets from the rhetoric of those who make a living off of protesting. Think of the armed assailants that police have to confront in a year; such limited use of lethal force by the police amazes me.

The next largest number killed by a firearm in 2014 accidentally was just 586. That's less than one accidental death from firearms per month in a state. Again, an amazingly small number, especially when compared with other "accidental" death causes (such as the number of people killed in auto accidents caused by drunk driving: 9,967 in 2014).

The first big number of firearm deaths in 2014 comes from homicides (10,995). Yes, guns in the hands of criminals and those involved in lethal arguments with family members and friends are deadly. Most of the talk I hear about gun laws only addresses access to guns by lawful citizens; little of the talk has meaningful suggestions for keeping guns from criminals. Better background checks of gun buyers to preclude purchases by those with criminal histories just moves their purchases underground; they will buy from other criminals. The hypocrisy of many protesting police violence against certain ethnic groups is shown by their quietness about the ethnic proportion of such groups among perpetrators of homicide. One does not often hear criticism from protestors of such murderers even though such ethnic criminal perps kill many times more (perhaps more than a hundred times as many) of the ethnic group of concern to the protestors than the police do, even when both rightful killings and the questionable ones by the police are considered.

The final category of deaths by firearms is by far the largest. It is suicides (21,334 in 2014)! This number has grown substantially (about 20%) from 2010 to 2014 (the rate of increase in suicides by gun during this period is more than twice the rate of increase in suicides overall). I do not remember hearing this problem being extensively addressed in talks that I have heard about gun laws. Those who are really concerned about dealing with misuse of guns in America should be concerned about this since it causes more deaths each year than all the other categories combined; suicide by gun causes almost twice as many deaths in a year as do all other kinds of gun use in the U.S.

Perhaps failure to discuss this issue much comes from reluctance to attack current sacred cows: the increasing social nastiness of the commercial media, the growing anonymous harassment on the internet and social media, etc. My impression of some gun law agitators is that they are very captive to contemporary political correctness and deliberately avoid many real issues.

The next time you hear someone express an opinion about gun laws, ask that person what he or she suggests should be done to deal with the problem of suicides by guns. Tell the person that because this problem is so much worse than any other kind of gun use that until he or she has meaningful suggestions about how to deal with it that he or she should keep their trap shut and not waste air in just making noise. Perhaps that barb will stimulate useful ideas.

Musing 11: Priests
(initially posted June 9, 2016)

It is quite possible that some will be offended by my noting that the belief and practice of some is not consistent with what the New Testament says. I hope those who are offended do not think I speak from malice. I simply present what I believe the New Testament teaches.

The word priest has many connotations in its common usage. Generally it means some kind of religious official. Some groups restrict application of the term to particular officials, such as those who consider a priest as lower than a bishop in authority but higher than a deacon. Others have different connotations for the term "priest."

Because of varied connotations for the word "priest," it is not possible to identify functions and activities which would apply to a priest in every religious group. For some groups, the priest has a two-fold role of mediation: the priest both presents God to people through preaching and teaching, and presents people to God by officiating at religious services and being the one to offer such sacrifices as required for people to enter the presence of God. I believe many practices of priests and beliefs about them in contemporary Christendom are wrong because they are at odds with what the New Testament tells us.

The New Testament says that God has given followers of Jesus a variety of gifts to equip the church to tell people about Jesus and to guide those who believe in Jesus so that they grow spiritually and can serve Him in a pleasing manner. A number of different terms in the New Testament are applied to these gifts and those given them: apostles, elders, pastors, teachers, evangelists, etc. However, none of these are called "priest" in the New Testament. That word is used only of the Jewish priests and of the unique priestly role of Jesus, the one the New Testament says is the ONLY mediator between God and man (1 Timothy 2:5).

Peter uses the term "priesthood" to describe ALL believers in Jesus (1 Peter 2:5, 9). He says that as such every believer (whether male or female, rich or poor, free or slave, of Jewish or Gentile descent) is expected "to offer spiritual sacrifices acceptable to God through Jesus Christ" (the Apostle Paul explains such sacrifice is a life dedicated to pleasing God, Romans 12:1-2) and to proclaim the praises of God to others. This dual role of this universal priesthood of Christian believers, offering spiritual sacrifices and proclaiming God's praise, is not something restricted to a special subset of believers but is what EVERYONE who believes in Jesus and trusts Him for salvation is to do.

The New Testament never uses the term priest as mediator for any individual in the church other than Christ, our great High Priest Who is the only One to Mediate between us and God. The other terms in the New Testament describing functions and leadership activities of those in the early church (apostle, pastor, elder, teacher, deacon, etc.) are used a number of times in communications to churches and Christian leaders, but never for one to be a mediator between people and God.

It seems obvious why the term "priest" for religious leaders entered church vocabulary a couple of centuries after the last of the Twelve official witnesses of the life and teachings of Jesus had died. Having an earthly human church official who serves in some way as a mediator between people and God provides a mechanism for more effective control of those claiming to believe in Christ. Their access to God can be restricted by such priests so those not complying with instructions from the priests are denied things available to those complying with what the priests say; church history certainly illustrates such being done repeatedly.

Attention to the Scripture, especially the New Testament, provides protection for the church from erroneous beliefs and practices; such erroneous ideas have often been promoted by prominent individuals in church history. Sometimes basing their ideas on visions and what they claim is revelation from God as well as upon their own thoughts. Also efforts to reform and correct aspects of the church often have been stimulated by reference to what the Scriptures actually say; unfortunately such corrective endeavors often have been very partial and left many things in church practices and teachings that are at odds with what the Bible says. Such erroneous ideas and practices can persist for centuries in the church as church history has shown. Ideas about priests and their roles as a subset of believers in most churches is a prime example of such.

I have a suggestion for those upset by this musing and for those wanting to check things out for themselves. Get a concordance (or use one that is available free on line) to simply look at passages about priest(s) and priesthood in the New Testament. Simply reading those passages should provide insight about the subject. By not suggesting more than that, I avoid any charge of biasing your perspective and conclusion. I have clearly claimed that my perspective is based simply upon what the New Testament says. This suggestion will enable the reader to determine if that claim is valid or not. I give my best wishes to and pray for God's blessings upon all who read this musing.

Musing 12: Belief
(initially posted June 11, 2016)

Belief is a difficult topic. I knew a lady who said she believed airplanes flew safely, but she would not trust an airplane enough to take a flight in it. How should one classify her "belief" in a plane's safety? I think many of our beliefs are like hers. That is what makes belief such a difficult topic.

When is belief real? And when is it just words, even if spoken with sincerity at the time?

Perhaps I should start with an easier aspect of this topic and ask, Does it matter whether or not belief is real? Please notice that I am not asking about the truth or validity of a belief. It is obvious that such can matter a great deal. For example, if one believes wrongly that a beverage is safe to drink, but in reality the beverage is poison, it will matter a lot. That mistaken belief could cost a person his life.

If the belief in airplane safety stated by the lady I mentioned had been real, she would have taken a few hour trip on a plane to visit her first granddaughter's birth instead of spending more than a day on the train traveling to be there. Her belief was merely words to reduce her embarrassment socially when people laughed at her for being behind the times. People often say things they do not really believe in order to be more acceptable socially. This is especially true in the area of religious beliefs.

For example, many would say they believe the Bible to be God's Word, which presumably makes it a reliable guide to truth about God, His character and behavior; yet it is clear that many of those saying they believe that actually have very different conceptions of God than what the Bible says. For example, the Bible is very clear that at least since the time Jesus was on the earth that the only way to be accepted by God (i.e., to be saved and spend eternity with God) is through faith in Jesus Christ. However some claiming to believe that the Bible is God's Word will tell you they expect to see family members and other loved ones and friends in heaven EVEN though some of them have never expressed faith or trust in Jesus for salvation.

For example, I know a man whose grandparents were active Muslims, but who as an adult graduated from an Episcopalian seminary and serves in some capacity in an Episcopal church. Although he knows New Testament passages about salvation only through Jesus (and I assume that he recites the Apostles and Nicene Creeds at times in religious services), he has said that he cannot imagine God condemning "good" people like his grandparents to hell.

Perhaps the proverb "actions speak louder than words" is a way to identify a person's real beliefs: they are ones demonstrated by the person's life, not just proclaimed by the person's words. This proverb, first noted in this exact form in English dates back to 1736 (*Melancholy State of Province in Colonial Currency*), has been found in many languages, including ancient Greek, for many centuries.

Jesus was clear about this point. He said that those who truly believe in Him both hear and obey His words. The 8th chapter of the Gospel of John has an interesting discussion beginning in verse 31 between Jesus and "the Jews who had believed in Him." In that discussion, Jesus says that instead of obeying His teachings the Devil is their father and they try to kill Him. Certainly in this situation their actions showed their real beliefs better than their verbal claims initially of belief in Jesus. Hence it is quite clear, beliefs do matter, or at least they can.

Likewise in our days, as in the first century, our actions show what we really believe. The Apostle John in his first letter succinctly states that reality: "Whoever claims to love God yet hates a brother or sister is a liar. For whoever does not love their brother and sister, whom they have seen, cannot love God, whom they have not seen." (1 John 4: 20) An interesting exercise is to speculate what one would say you believe if that person only saw what you did and never heard anything you said. Would such a statement of your beliefs be anything like what you say you believe?

If you are bold, or perhaps more correctly to say if you are insane, you might ask three people who know you a bit (one a friend, a second perhaps someone that does not like you very much, and the third just an acquaintance) to write what they think are your beliefs based upon what they have seen you do in five areas of life: religious perspectives, financial dealings, truthfulness and accuracy in what you say, respect of people outside your circle of friends, and your contributions to a better society. Encourage them to be candid.

You probably should be sitting down when you read what they say, and perhaps that should be in private too because it is possible you will be quite upset by their assessments of you. I think that might be the case for most of us.

Our real beliefs do matter and they show in our lives.

Musing 13: Good Sense
(initially posted June 15, 2016)

Thomas Payne's *Common Sense* had considerable impact during the American Revolution. He meant "good sense" by the title; good sense deals with reality honestly and carefully. Good sense seems rare today, but is much needed.

A news article said women hold only 1 in 5 seats on corporation boards. That was used as an indication of sexism in the corporate world based upon assumption that board seats should reflect gender distribution in the population; the article did not use good sense. This musing is not a male tirade against sexual equality in the workplace; instead it urges use of good sense instead of simply promoting partisan ideology about inappropriate processes in the corporate world.

The 1 in 5 statistic noted is as meaningless as saying every mother is a woman or that every father is a man. Significant statistics about representation on corporate boards should deal with the number of qualified members of a particular gender, not just the number of a particular gender. Most activities have nominal qualifications; e.g., typically university professors have doctorates in pertinent subjects. Simply comparing the number of women and men in professorships would not be a good sense approach; instead the number in each gender of people with appropriate doctorates should be compared. This is why statistics (such as the 1 in 5 mentioned earlier) even when factual may not represent a good sense approach; statistics should address *fully* pertinent information, not partially pertinent data.

I do not know whether the number of women on corporate boards is less or more than appropriate because I do not know what nominal qualifications (intelligence, education, work experience, etc.) for board members are and I have no information about gender statistics regarding such. Nor have I seen news articles purporting to present such information in good sense discussion of the issue (of course I do not have expert awareness of what information exists in this regard).

American reporting is lousy; much of it lacks good sense. This reflects badly on the quality of journalism and of public tolerance of such; we simply act stupidly in accepting such twaddle as abounds in the media, public and social.

Reflect on things you see in the news and hear from others about issues. Ask yourself, how many bring a good sense approach to the issues? A good sense approach starts with consideration of fully pertinent information, not just partially pertinent information. The good sense approach does not imitate Sherlock Holmes with his exceptional capabilities for observation and jump to a *possible* explanation concluding that it is the *actual* explanation. Arthur Conan Doyle, creator of Holmes, allowed Holmes to get away with that fallacious approach in his stories because it made Sherlock interesting to read about, but reality is not so accommodating and good sense does not assume it is.

Your reflection may lead you to the same dismal conclusion as I: good sense is a rare commodity today, and few discussions of issues demonstrate good sense.

This is illustrated by the idea that equal work deserves equal pay; many note that women are paid far less than men. However statistics cited seldom are comparisons of compensation for the same job by people with the same level of experience, and expertise. Also discussion of equal pay usually ignores differences in employee cost other than pay that may vary by type of worker (facilities required by building codes, insurance rates, sick leave taken, actual hours worked, etc. are simply ignored). Even the best peer-reviewed scientific journals have often been criticized for presenting statistical analyses and conclusions based upon them that are not valid (some analyses of this show a third or more of such material in the journals is faulty). Thus it is not surprising to find similar sloppy use of data and statistics in the general public media and on social media.

Unfortunately science is often like Sherlock's deductions: a possibility taken as a certainty. For example, conservation laws (e.g., energy, momentum) are fundamental realities upon which the rules that govern physical behaviors are based are applied not only to closed systems not interacting with other systems but also to the entire universe. The question of whether that is the only possible explanation for what has been observed usually is ignored.

Contemporary science has no answer for where matter and energy come from. Some accept creation by God; others postulate matter and energy have always existed. Observation cannot answer that question scientifically. In recent decades scientists realized that what can be observed directly represents only a small portion of the energy and matter in the universe. Dark matter and dark energy are terms used to describe things that cannot be observed directly, but which produce noticeable impact on what can be observed.

These things about science illustrate that good sense may be limited in many arenas, including the arena of science. Please use good sense and encourage others to do so also. Look for information fully pertinent to the issues; do not blithely assume a possible explanation is indeed the true explanation; and try to be sure to consider an issue from all (or at least most of the more significant) perspectives. Society, as well as you, will benefit.

A final thought: God desires that we trust Him (have faith) since merely observing reality does not always bring a correct understanding of Him; a good relationship with God comes from believing in Him according to the Bible, His Word.

Musing 14: Unbalanced Emphasis (initially posted June 19, 2016)

Recently there have been a number of mass killings and lethal terrorist incidents; and much attention has been given to the incidents. Public officials have condemned them, promised increased efforts to ensure all perpetrators are punished, and appeared in ceremonies commemorating victims. Many others have expressed sympathy for those hurt and provided funds and other help to victim families and to survivors of the attacks. Such is commendable; but it is sad that similar attention is not given to the far more numerous victims of another kind of heinous activity. This musing is about that unbalanced emphasis, the failure to give appropriate attention to something that unnecessarily takes many more lives and leaves many more sorrowing families and loved ones without comparable support from political leaders and the rest of us.

In the US from 2009 through 2015, just 199 people were killed in mass public shootings and another 197 were wounded in the attacks but survived. A total of 396 dead and wounded casualties, an average of 66 a year. Most people are aware of the tragedy recently in Orlando, Fla., where 49 people were killed and another 53 were injured. However, the 248 people killed in mass public shootings in the US since 2009, six and a half years, is about the same number as killed by drunk drivers in the US during little more than a week! And drunk drivers keep killing that many people week after week.

Officials do not show the attention to deaths from drunk drivers that they show to mass killings. The public does not take umbrage at such or pour out sympathy and help upon victim families as they have done for those hurt by mass killings. Such certainly shows unbalanced emphasis given the relative number of victims from these two different kinds of unnecessary slaughter of people.

What are the facts about drunk driving? According to comparisons of self-reported drunken driving and arrests for driving under the influence, only about 1% of drunk drivers are arrested. This dangerous activity, impaired driving, is abundant in part because law enforcement personnel do not consistently enforce the laws against it vigorously and because the public tolerates those whom they know do it. Good people fail to shun those whom they know drive at times under the influence.

About 10,000 people a year (about 1/3 of all traffic fatalities) die in accidents attributed to impaired driving. I have been unable to find reliable estimates of the number injured who survived vehicle accidents caused by impaired driving; that the number is possibly more than the number killed by drunk drivers since many are injured in non-fatal accidents caused by drunk drivers. It has been estimated that costs related to drunk driving are about 200 billion dollars a year (far more than any costs associated with mass killings or a terrorist activity – e.g., cost estimates for 9/11 were about $100 billion, about half the estimated annual cost of drunk driving).

More facts illustrating the unbalanced emphasis shown by our lack of attention to the heinous activity of drunken driving. About 25-30% of those arrested for drunk driving have been arrested previously for impaired driving; a significant portion of whose licenses had been suspended or revoked. Good lawyers and official leniency allows many arrested for impaired driving to avoid imprisonment. I could not find reliable statistics about sentences given to those convicted of manslaughter in lethal accidents caused by impaired driving, but my impression is that usually such sentences are light – at most a year or two behind bars. How different that is from what is expected to be done to any surviving perpetrator of a mass killing or a terrorist incident. The longest sentence I saw in the cases I could find a record of on line for a dunk driver whose accident killed people was seven years in prison.

Too many officials have friends and loved ones who drive impaired at times, and some officials themselves also do that at times. Hence they are unlikely to approach this heinous activity with the vigor and attention they give to mass killings and acts of terrorism, even though impaired driving kills more weekly than mass killings or terrorists normally kill in a year or more. Likewise the public accepts the horrendous damage to lives from impaired driving as just part of life and does not give it attention because it is so much with us; the perpetrators may be our pals and at times our very selves.

Ultimately each one (the perpetrators, officials, and the rest of us) will have to stand before One Who will hold us to a true standard of justice. We will have to account for what was done in causing harm, in efforts to prevent harm, and in care for those who were harmed. That experience is not likely to be pleasant. Perhaps it would be wise now to change and to stop being so unbalanced in our emphasis about some heinous activities while largely ignoring other heinous activities which hurt far larger numbers of people. Instead we should give appropriate attention to all forms of heinous activity and to helping all who have been harmed by such activities.

What do you think about my criticism of our leaders and the public for unbalanced emphasis in largely ignoring the heinous activity of drunk driving?

Musing 15: Labels
(initially posted June 19, 2016)

Labels are assumed to be a short-hand expression about ideas and activity, but usually I think they are merely a substitute for careful thought. This is a serious allegation, and I should have strong reasons for saying such if I do not want to be known as a loose talking lame brain.

First the meaning of a label is like beauty, in the mind of the individual. To find the meaning of a word one turns to standard dictionaries or to the web (where one has to be careful because one finds as much misinformation from that source as reliable information). However, one is likely to find a wide variety of descriptions associated with a label if one turns to the web or even to books claiming to be authoritative descriptions of labels. You can see that my comment is true by looking up political terms such as conservative, liberal, extremist, or traditionalist; the same will be true of religious terms such as Christian, Muslim, atheist, or spiritual. I suspect that you would find similar uncertainty about the precise connotation of any label you are likely to encounter. Just think how many aspects are captured by a label such as "management" or "labor."

Careful thought seeks clarity and removal of possible ambiguity about what is being considered. Labels cannot provide such. It takes more than a single word (or even a phrase) to clearly express an idea unambiguously.

Second a label tends to have significant emotional baggage which obscures an idea as much as the label may communicate an idea. People frequently use a label to castigate or to praise. Instead of taking the time and effort to carefully explain exactly why someone or something should be rejected or avoided, a label is used to demonize or to create a hero. Instead of explaining exactly what someone did to merit praise, a label is used. Hence the hero's clay feet are kept out of sight, as are kind deeds and generous actions of a villain. Labels are a common way of passing part truth off as whole truth.

Careful thought, by contrast, strives to ensure a balanced perspective is communicated; the whole truth and nothing but the truth as required from witnesses in court. Often we are too lazy or too emotionally committed to a particular perspective to take the time and put forth the effort to think carefully and then to communicate careful thought; instead we resort to using labels.

Third labels are bad for society. Labels tend to polarize people unnecessarily. I believe that America's dysfunctional Congress is in part a byproduct of a society addicted to labeling. The abundance of our communication means (over the air, via cables, on line, etc.) makes our connectivity ubiquitous, and induces us to become addicted to labeling. It is so easy for people to be divided and set upon one another when people do not take time and effort to clearly state what is believed and why (facts and reasons) so that areas of possible agreement and areas of disagreement are understood exactly as well as the evidence, reasoning, and assumptions upon such are based are known. Calling positions left and right easily ignores the possibility that more than half of the beliefs of one are also held by the other; such labels tend to focus on the extremes of a position, not the core of the position.

Given human laziness (few will put forth the effort for careful thought) and the natural tendency to want one's own way more than what is best for all, can anything helpful be done? That is an excellent question, and, unfortunately, I do not have a good answer to the question.

I have a tendency to be cynical, and my knowledge of history gives me little hope for reasonable solutions to this problem, especially in societies as multicultural as the U.S. is today. History, both recent and ancient, tends to suggest that societies are not torn apart or do not fall apart only when some aspect of the society has adequate power dominance that its will can be imposed upon all aspects of the society. The reader can check that out; I will not even suggest contemporary or past examples one might consider. If the reader investigates this seriously and comes to a different conclusion than I state above, please let me know so that I can consider revising my perspective because I prefer to line my ideas and beliefs up with reality rather than simply hold to views because I previously espoused them.

I consider labels very dangerous, and I try not to use them if I am permitted to say fully what I think about someone or something. I also do not have a very high opinion of the ideas of anyone who uses labels when they have time to explain clearly what they mean about someone or something. I wish more people would behave this way; it would benefit everyone.

Musing 16: Rights
(initially posted June 23, 2016)

The *Declaration of Independence* says "We hold these truths to be self-evident, that all men are created equal, that they are endowed by their Creator with certain unalienable Rights, that among these are Life, Liberty and the pursuit of Happiness." This is correct, but there are limits and boundary conditions on those rights.

Liberty can be taken from those failing to obey the law; they may be imprisoned. Sometimes disregard for the law might even cost a person's life. Many feel that those shooting others in a church, school, or club should be executed. Similar limitations also apply to pursuit of happiness.

I discuss driving rights to provide insights about issues related to rights. Unfortunately these insights seem to be ignored in much of what I hear and see about rights that currently stimulate intense emotions.

Most acknowledge government propriety in establishing age, knowledge, physical capabilities (such as vision acuity), and skill demonstration (i.e., driving test) requirements for those authorized to drive on public roads, requirements that may vary with vehicle type and function.

Some find pleasure in driving fast and claim a right to pursue that pleasure, even if it means driving ten, twenty, or thirty miles per hour faster than the speed limit. Most do not think the "unalienable right" to pursue happiness authorizes such behavior; it is appropriate to punish one who did such a thing (fine, or even confinement in egregious situations).

Often desirable parking locations are reserved for the handicapped. A person is not qualified to use parking locations simply because the person declares that he or she is handicapped. Instead information from competent medical personnel is used by authorities to determine if a person qualifies to use such reserved parking locations. Those using such parking locations without handicap qualification are subject to penalty.

I used handicap reserved parking locations a number of times when I transported a friend whose medical condition qualified her for handicap authorization. I did this when I drove her to see the doctor, to go shopping, and to attend church. Other times when I drove the same car to the same places that I used when transporting my friend, I could not use parking reserved for the handicapped because she was not with me. I did not have appropriate authorization for handicap parking. This was true even on those days when my hip was uncooperative and I had to use a cane when I walked.

The above discussion illustrates that even "unalienable rights" such as life, liberty, and the pursuit of happiness have restrictions. That is also true in regard to rights that are the center of emotionally intense controversy at present. Those are LGBT rights.

Government authorities have been woefully deficient in this area. Various government decisions have been made about LGBT rights without providing a comprehensive conceptual structure for the decisions. There is no standard identification of process or location of authority re deciding that a person's gender is different from that indicated physically by one's genitalia at birth. Some assert the individual can make that decision, or that parents or guardians of a minor can make the decision for the minor. Others put that decision in the hands of medical experts, and others would restrict it to government authorities based upon information from medical personnel. Government failure to establish a comprehensive conceptual context for transgender issues contributes to the current controversy, as does the absence of clarity about permanence of a change in gender determination.

Restrictions of rights usually arise from overlapping rights. For example, in transgendered use of restrooms and changing facilities such as gym locker rooms, their claimed right to use of public facilities overlaps the right of others to use such without exposure to the genitalia of the opposite gender. Reasonable ways to accommodate both kinds of rights may exist, but unfortunately the emotional intensity with which many approach such situations often precludes reasonable action.

In the restroom use situation, simply making exposure of genitalia of the transgendered to others in a restroom an instance of sexual harassment would permit the transgendered to use facilities in the privacy of a restroom stall while protecting others from exposure to genitalia of the transgendered in the restroom. That kind of reasonable approach would allow many of the issues in current controversies to be defused and progress to be made. Those on all sides of such issues need to approach the issues with consideration of *ALL* rights involved and to calmly seek reasonable solutions. That approach to issues would benefit us all.

Things change with time. For example, franchise (the right to vote) in the U.S. has expanded from a privilege restricted to a select few, mainly propertied Caucasians during Colonial times, to most adult citizens today.

While the increase in franchise is approved by many, I am not aware of solid evidence indicating better government has resulted from the larger pool of those allowed to vote; on the contrary, there is evidence that quality of people elected has actually decreased. Given the record of totalitarian communistic countries in having much higher percentages of the population voting than ever experienced in a democratic nation, it appears that greater franchise is no guarantee of better government. Reality is not always popular or appreciated, as may be illustrated by comments in response to this musing.

Musing 17: Depravity
(initially posted June 26, 2016)

According to the *Oxford English Dictionary (OED)*, the word "depravity" started being used for perversion of moral faculties, corruption, and viciousness about 1650 A.D. From the time of Jonathan Edwards a century later, it also began to have a specific theological connotation as "the innate corruption of the human nature due to original sin," as in "total depravity."

Many things previously considered as instances of depravity are no longer viewed as such by many Americans; acceptance of some such things is not only tolerated but encouraged by our society and its leaders. Some things previously considered depraved have even been made compulsory by law. Many contemporary Americans seem to have degenerated to the level of the Jewish people in the generations before establishment of the Jewish monarchy under King Saul. Twice the book of Judges in the Old Testament describes this low moral level as "everyone did what was right in his own eyes." That occurred once in Judges 17:6, at the end of a story about a man who robbed his own mother (certainly a low moral ebb), and again in Judges 21:25 at the end of the book of Judges, just after describing how Jewish men connived with the men of Benjamin for them to kidnap daughters of Shiloh and force them to become their wives something some might describe as abduction and sexual slavery, another low ebb morally). Several hundred years later, King Solomon warned that "A person may think their own ways are right, but the Lord weighs the heart." (Proverbs 21:2 NIV) It is dangerous to put one's own opinion above the assessment that God places on something.

In the time of Abraham, the Bible describes a particular city as wicked and sinning greatly against the Lord. Of course I am referring to Sodom, assumed to have been located somewhat east of the Salt Sea, now called the Dead Sea. Abraham thought he had saved the city when he asked God not to destroy the city if ten righteous people were in it. Unfortunately, there were not that many righteous people in the city. Only four fled from its destruction, and one of them was killed because she did not obey the instruction to flee without stopping to look back. It is possible that God used an earthquake in the area about 2050 B.C. (geological records suggest there was an earthquake in the region about then) to spew out bitumen, sulphur, and hot gases to destroy Sodom and cities in the plain with fire falling on them from above. Both Old and New Testaments use Sodom as an example of God's judgment on wickedness. Parallels between behaviors described of the men of Sodom and our own time are appalling (much of the story is found in Genesis 18).

Lot's wife was turned to a pillar of salt for stopping to look back at the destruction of Sodom. It is possible that stoppage caused her to be covered with hot tar, and then subsequently coated with salt, which abundant in that area may have been thrown up by the earthquake so that she became a salt pillar.

God's righteous and forgiveness was illustrated by Nineveh, as reported by the prophet Jonah. Nineveh was a wicked city God said He would destroy; but God spared the city after it turned away from wickedness, seeking God's forgiveness. In contrast, Sodom's people persisted in their wickedness, and God brought destruction upon them as He said He would do.

Contemporary American society behaves in many ways that are contrary to what the Bible says pleases God. That concerns me because I love my country, and I would hate for it to be destroyed by God. We should not foolishly think godliness of our people in the past will protect us from consequences of contemporary depravity. This point is clearly stated in Jude, a very short book near the end of the New Testament (it is next to last).

Some will dismiss my comments merely as religious talk. Others may excoriate me, alleging I am guilty of bias, prejudice, intolerance, and other negative behaviors. Some might even make reasoned statements presenting evidence and arguments for why people should not accept my view.

Unfortunately the fact remains. Much occurring in America today is contrary to clear teachings from the Bible, a source that has been trusted for reliable guidance about morals and ethics as well as insights about God since the founding of this country. A reasonable intelligent person should insist upon very sound reasons for abandoning something that has proven itself so helpful for many generations. Much of what I hear and see that is counter to Biblical guidance qualifies more as rabble rousing than anything else.

When people turn to their own ideas as the ultimate source of guidance and willingly turn away from guidance of proven reliability, then bad results are likely to occur, for the nation as well as for individuals who behave that way.

The prophet Hosea in the Old Testament warned people that they would reap the whirlwind because they sowed the wind (Hosea 8:7); this is generally taken as a warning that we should expect to suffer serious consequences as the result of our own bad actions. I hope that my fellow citizens will become as concerned about our present dire situation as I am.

Musing 18: Silliness
(initially posted on June 26, 2016)

It is often said that insanity is doing the same thing over and over, but expecting different results. Albert Einstein, Mark Twain, Ben Franklin, Narcotics Anonymous, and many others have been attributed as the source for this witty-ism, but in fact who first said it is unknown. In any case, that kind of behavior is silliness. It is the silly kind of thing a drunk might do by looking under the street light for keys he lost half-a-block away in the dark; his rationale for looking under the street light is that the light is better there.

There's that kind of silliness in much of what I hear about gun control.

Let me mention a few things that most discussions of that subject are likely to leave in the dark while harping on their usual litany of ideas (the equivalent to the drunk looking under the street light for his keys).

Tight gun control laws in other countries are associated with lower rates of deaths by guns, but most of those countries allow their citizens far fewer liberties than we enjoy in the U.S. There may be a tradeoff between liberty and gun laws that usually is not noted by either side of debate about gun laws. Perhaps more relevant than experience abroad might be experience in the U.S. of such tight gun control laws that they were struck down after being in place for two decades. Such an example occurred in Washington, D.C.; the tight gun laws were in effect from the mid-1980s to early this century. During the two decades that extremely tight gun control laws were in place in D.C., its murder rate was substantially higher (over 70% higher!) than it had been prior to the onset of the gun control laws. It should also be noted that murder rate for the U.S. as a whole during that period decreased slightly. Isn't it strange that those advocating stricter gun control laws seem to ignore such a notable example of the impact of tighter gun control laws? After the extremely tight gun control laws in D.C. were struck down, the murder rate in D.C. came back down to the level it had been before the laws were enacted. To me, an example such as this in the U.S. with the level of freedom and liberty we enjoy as citizens is far more relevant than information about the impact of gun laws in countries that do not grant their citizens such freedoms and liberties.

Perhaps it is appropriate to ask why tight gun control laws might result in an increase in murders? Pertinent evidence exists. Various surveys have noted that a significant number of those with firearms have displayed or used them to deter intruders striving to enter their homes or to protect themselves or others from attack (some of the information suggests that such may occur as many as a million times a year in the U.S.). Surveys of imprisoned inmates have shown that a significant proportion (more than a third) of the thousands of inmates surveyed had been deterred from a crime or prevented from completing a crime by the presence or use of a firearm by the intended victim or someone aiding the intended victim. Tighter gun control laws reduce potential for people to deter attacks or protect themselves and others when attacked. This explains why more people may be hurt when gun control laws are tight.

It is obvious that availability of guns has an impact on the number of gun-related deaths, especially when a gun is used by its owner in suicide or against a family member or friend. Tighter gun laws might reduce such, but how much that reduction might be is unknown. It could merely change the suicide method used from a gun to poison or jumping out of a window high in a building. I know of no reliable information about the likelihood of such. I discussed only the suicide element because of space limitations in my musing and because suicide is at least ten times more likely to cause a gun death than the other gun uses noted in this paragraph.

The probability of tighter gun control laws reducing the likelihood that a stranger, especially a repeat criminal, will use guns in crime is unknown as far as I can tell. Some information suggests that perhaps half of guns known to be used in crimes were used by people who had not acquired them legally; the guns were stolen, bought from the black market, or borrowed from someone inappropriately. Whether tighter gun control laws would have any impact on deaths from such is unknown.

My hope is that this musing might stimulate people to demand that discussions of gun control issues move from being like the drunk under the street light, merely repetitively parading the party line of the speaker, to grappling carefully and realistically with issues in the murky darkness of the real problem. Only then is there hope of progress, of doing things that in fact actually help and make our society safer and better without removing our freedoms and liberties. Of course, some would say that such a hope is indeed insane; it requires people to be sensible

Musing 19: Miracles
(initially posted June 28, 2016)

Many people do not think or talk clearly about miracles. Some define a miracle as something not explicable by natural or scientific laws; and then declare miracles impossible by assuming that everything which happens must comply with scientific or natural laws. Such people assume that things which cannot be explained by current knowledge of those laws will be explicable by future understanding of those laws. Others define miracles more loosely and simply mean something very unusual, but usually restrict that unusual something to things that are beneficial, such as surviving a natural disaster. Yet others accept the possibility of miracles, positing a cause (often supernatural) beyond natural and scientific laws.

My musing with its length limitation will not address miracles except in a very cursory way. It is obvious that those who deny the possibility of miracles are most unscientific, or at least hypocritically inconsistent in what they consider scientific. No current widely-accepted scientific theory can explain creation (where matter and energy came from); postulates that such always existed totally lacks any observational evidence – such ideas are just bald assumptions, and as such certainly should not be called scientific. Such an assumption-based approach is often labeled superstition by some claiming it is based in science, although bias is shown by those who use that label since they mainly apply it to religious folks and fail to use it on the non-religious.

What scientific evidence exists that creative activity only happened once (as postulated in the "Big Bang")? Could not a Creator from time to time insert a tiny bit of matter and energy into the universe during what might be called a miracle such as an unusual healing, restoration of life to a dead body, dividing of waters, change of a substance (such as water) into a different substance (such as wine), increasing the amount of oil, fish, or bread beyond what was available initially, etc. The magnitude of matter and energy added in a miracle such as these would be so minute compared to the matter and energy brought into existence at Creation that it would be impossible for observation to ever discover such if it were not observed and measured at the time it occurred. Historically the observation mechanism for most miracles has been people, most of whom died long ago.

Unless those denying the possibility of miracles can conclusively prove that such creative activity is impossible, those denying miracles should fess up honestly and admit their position is simply a matter of their bias and prejudices, driven by their assumptions; it is not any more a scientific approach than is a plain confession of belief or faith in the reality of the miracles reported in the Bible.

Modern science has come to realize it does not know much about the majority of the matter and energy in the universe, and cannot even tell if we live in a multiverse or simply a universe. Honest scientists acknowledge that belief in or denial of God (and the possibility of miracles caused by God) is a matter of faith, not something provable by science.

The Bible identifies more than a hundred events that most would consider miracles. For some of them, God may have used natural means to accomplish His purposes; many have speculated about ways God might have caused things to happen (e.g., some think the fiery destruction of Sodom described in Genesis 18 was caused by an earthquake releasing bitumen and hot gases in the plains just west of the Dead Sea, possibly about 2050 B.C.). In other instances, something more than natural means was involved (e.g., as when 185,000 Assyrians were killed in one night by the angel of the Lord, 2 Kings 19:35).

It is unlikely that the record of a miracle, or even observing one, will cause a person to have the kind of faith in God that brings one to righteous acceptance by God; instead it is more likely that the kind of faith in God that brings one to righteous acceptance by God will make a person more likely to believe that the living God is capable of performing miracles if He chooses to do so.

What is the bottom line I suggest? For the sceptic about miracles, I recommend a focus on the more basic issues of Who God is, What He is like, and How one should relate to Him. One's attitude about miracles will take care of itself when those primary issues are addressed. If one is intimidated by negative attitudes about miracles from peers and perhaps from teachers and others in authority, realize that such people can talk foolishly through their hats in ways similar to the ignorant and uneducated. Often people claim much more authority and credibility for their ideas than they actually deserve. The simple comments above may help you if you find yourself in such a situation. You, too, just like the sceptic, should focus on the more important issue of your relationship to God; it is far more important than your attitude toward miracles.

Thank you for reading this muse. I hope it was helpful. I believe this musing is based upon the same fundamental premise as I hope all my musings are. That premise is that calm and careful consideration of issues with an open mind will benefit both the individual and our society.

Musing 20: Change
(initially posted July 2, 2016)

Change happens. Sometimes change makes things better, and sometimes it does not. In the material world, one aspect of change is that things run down. The amount of usable energy decreases. Things become more chaotic and less ordered.

In society, change may come from technology. People can travel faster and communicate more extensively today than in the past. More food can be produced now than in the past. Materially the world is richer (more goods are available now than previously) and people are living longer; yet we continue to have many poor and multitudes are malnourished.

This musing asks about changes in our society during recent decades, Are they improvements? Or are they the other kind of change?

The U.S. has been an independent nation for two and a half centuries. Many social analysts and historians describe ideas and behavior of America's leaders in government, business, and society during the first two-thirds of that time by the WASP work ethic, a label some use as degrading. WASP work ethic has nothing to do with a flying insect; instead it is an acronym from White Anglo-Saxon Protestant, similar to "Puritan" for describing social and economic attitudes during the colonial period.

That social and economic perspective among most American leaders in government, business, and society for more than a century and a half was a major factor in the country becoming the most powerful nation on earth. That perspective about work, responsibility, ethics, and society was so dominant that it was not confined to its Protestant religious origins, but was mainly held by those of all religious persuasions in leadership positions during that time. This is illustrated by famous words from a Catholic when he became president of the U.S. "Ask not what your country can do for you — ask what you can do for your country." John F. Kennedy Inaugural Address, January 20, 1961.

For the past several decades, America has been changing from what it had been in that era. It is now far more multicultural; its standards also have changed dramatically. Things long considered despicable and wrong are now tolerated and in some cases even required by law. I suspect any president who might be so foolish today as to proclaim what Kennedy

The First Year of Pace Musings

said half-a-century ago would get jeered because of the way our society has changed.

Not all of the changes have been good. Today there is much greater dependence upon the government and less on individual self-reliance than was the case in the earlier era. Today's society is much more oriented toward getting, to being a recipient of government largesse, than was so in the earlier era.

In the earlier era, multitudes came to America from elsewhere, but most came legally and they acclimated to our ideals and standards. In contrast, maintaining the cultures of those coming to the U.S. is now emphasized by many, ignoring that problems many of those coming here fled are by-products of their cultures. If such cultural aspects are brought here, America will change into what those coming fled. Change can be bad as well as good.

Some even say those coming here illegally should be accepted and given privileges of those who were born here or those who immigrated legally. It is foolish to ignore the wrong illegal immigrants have done.

Some things long considered despicable are now said to be acceptable because they are just natural behaviors. So is hitting someone who makes you angry. It is also natural to take something belonging to another if you really want it, as we see in the way young children behave. Most people are not so foolish as to say despicable behavior should be acceptable simply because it is a natural behavior; unfortunately others, including America's courts, are not so wise.

Our country has never been perfect. There are many bad things in its history. Our nation's horrible exploitation and abuse of Native Americans is a prime example of such bad things. It is good to try to correct bad things that our nation has done or continues to do, but it is important to remember the old medical adage about the possibility of a cure being worse than the disease. We should be careful not to make changes that create more harm than whatever good they may be.

Wise people recognize when they have made a mistake, and then take corrective action. America needs to be wise like that and undo some of the changes that have been made.

It helps to look at things functionally. Forget labels; just look at what is done. For example, in efforts to correct wrongful discrimination, the courts ordered new discrimination (the court-ordered discrimination just favored different groups than those previously favored). Two wrongs do not make a right, not even when ordered by the Supreme Court. Such simple functional analysis often can reveal whether a change is good or bad.

Sometimes a change focuses only on rights of some involved, and basically ignores rights of others. That approach is bad. All rights should be given appropriate attention.

Please do not presume to read my mind. Only what I say explicitly expresses my perspective. Do not presume I consider a particular change I did not name to be good or bad. Such a comment just shows your bias, not what my attitude is.

Musing 21: Never Posted

This musing was about me. I could not decide if I should post it. The few friends who saw it suggested that I keep it private and not post it. Therefore no Musing 21 is included in this book. I share review the draft of musing 21 (which I first drafted in early June 2016) from time to time, and possibly I will post it; but until that happens it will continue to be a private musing that I do not share with the public.

Musing 22: Bible
(initially posted July 4, 2016)

"Perhaps you might muse on what the Bible has to say about how to treat immigrants" was a comment on my recent musing about Change. This musing is in response to that comment. It strikes me as an appropriate topic for Independence Day. I hope you and your family have a delightful celebration.

This topic (proper dealing with immigrants) is addressed abundantly in the Bible. There are many passages in the Old Testament that explicitly address how the Jews are to treat non-Jews. Such are essentially Biblical ideas about how immigrants should be treated. These passages include more than 150 verses in the Old Testament about strangers (most of which deal with non-Jews living among the Jewish people), references to treatment of the various peoples in Canaan after the Jews entered the land under Joshua, and about thirty references in the Old Testament to Gentiles (the New Testament has about three times that many verses with the word Gentile). This collection of passages provides the core of Biblical teachings about proper dealing with immigrants.

This topic is very complex. Much in the Old Testament about relations between Jews and the non-Jews living among them relates to God's preparation and maintenance of the Jewish people as a chosen, peculiar people through which the Messiah would come to make salvation available for all peoples. After Jesus the Christ came and fulfilled God's plan for salvation of people, some of the requirements specified in the Old Testament no longer applied to God's people on earth (now they are the church, i.e., those who accept Jesus as the Christ and trusted in what He did for them as the reason God accepts them as His people). This was illustrated in Acts 10 when the Apostle Peter was given a vision that showed Old Testament restrictions on food and interactions with Gentiles no longer were binding on Jews or Christians. The Apostle Paul makes the same point in the second chapter of Colossians. The challenge comes in determining which aspects of guidance in the Old Testament about dealing with strangers living among the Jewish people continue to be pertinent today as guidance for Christians about dealing with immigrants.

The New Testament has no specific guidance for how government leaders should deal with immigrants since it was written by and for people living under the control of a single government (the Roman Empire); those for whom the New Testament was written had no control or authority over that government. Thus, there is nothing like the Old Testament passages telling Jewish leaders how to deal with such things; the New Testament has no counterpart of such direct guidance for political leaders.

Unfortunately I am not aware of a standard substantial theological examination of what the Bible says about dealing with the strangers among us. Personally I have not seen anything addressing Biblical teachings about immigration comparable to the comprehensiveness of material about the nature of God in a standard systematic theology; nor have I come across a reference to such in materials that others have written which I have seen. If others know of such substantial theological works related to immigration, I would be delighted to hear about such so I can consult the material for myself.

Many writers use *some* Bible passages to support a position that the writer espouses (I do not believe any I have seen claim to have addressed every pertinent Biblical passage). I have seen this kind of writing from all sides of immigration issues. It is done both by those opposing immigration and by those seeking amnesty for illegal immigrants. It has been done by both those espousing liberal theologies and those with conservative theologies.

I have not personally examined Biblical materials on this subject sufficiently to come to a conclusion about the scope and limitations of Biblical guidance about immigration. That is something that I may feel led to do in the next month or two since this subject is likely to be a prominent issue in the coming presidential election. As a Christian, I should seek Biblical guidance about such issues when I think such might be found.

Unfortunately, I confess that my present attitudes about immigration have been based more on common sense and simple logic rather than on Biblical guidance, other than guidance of the most general sort. I understand general Biblical guidance about the importance of all people (that is clear from the fact that Jesus was willing to die to save us!), that Christians are expected to help the poor and needy, and that Christians should show love to others, especially those who believe in Jesus for salvation. Also I understand that Christians are to deal with situations honestly (not distorting the facts of a situation) with careful consideration of the views of others, and seek to bring glory to God by doing good. However this general guidance by itself does not reveal clearly how I should deal with the complex reality of immigration in the U.S.

One point, though, has become very clear. Perhaps it has also struck you too. That point is this, how to deal with immigration Biblically is far too complex for it to be addressed satisfactorily within the space limitations of my musings. Hence, I will not try to address that topic (beyond what I have said here) in one of my musings.

Musing 23: Hebrews
(initially posted July 5, 2016)

Hebrews is an unusual book in the New Testament. It is the only letter of the New Testament whose sender is not explicitly identified within the letter. It is the only letter in the New Testament addressed specifically to Jewish believers. I had a new insight about its possible author recently when I read the last few chapters of *Hebrews* in my devotions. This musing shares that insight.

As most people know, the book of *Hebrews* does not identify its author. Many have thought that the Apostle Paul wrote *Hebrews*, but that is not as common today as it was in the past. In everything else that Paul wrote he clearly and explicitly identified himself and the location or identity of those receiving his letter. The list of those suggested as the person who might be the author of *Hebrews* is long; it includes Barnabas, Luke, Clement of Rome, Silvanus, Apollos, Philip, Jude, and Priscilla.

Which group of Jewish Christians were intended as the initial recipients of *Hebrews* is also unknown. Speculated locations for them include Alexandria or elsewhere in Egypt, North Africa, Palestine, several locations in modern Turkey, and Rome. No single one of these, or anywhere else, is generally agreed to be the most likely; it seems that we have no way of knowing exactly to whom the author was writing.

The above synopsis is something I have known for many years. Personally I had thought that Priscilla (the only woman suggested as a possibility) was the most likely because the identity of the author of *Hebrews* was unstated. Such would be likely simply because of her gender and prejudices of the time. The book of Acts explained how she and her husband had corrected a prominent Jewish Christian, Apollos, in his understanding of the good news about Jesus in light of the Old Testament. The fact that her name is mentioned first half the times she and her husband are named in the New Testament suggests that she had a unique place of prominence in the early church (no other wife is mentioned in that way).

The insight I mentioned came from *Hebrews* 13:23 ("I want you to know that our brother Timothy has been released. If he arrives soon, I will come with him to see you." NIV) as I read the last several chapters of *Hebrews* in my devotions. That insight was very simple: the writer of *Hebrews* was someone associated with Timothy. Previously I had not approached the authorship of *Hebrews* by considering those known to be associated with Timothy.

This verse indicates that Timothy had been locked up (there's no other Biblical indication of Timothy being confined). It is likely that Timothy would go to someone he knew upon his release from confinement; possibly someone with resources and connections to help Timothy get re-established. Paul's words in his last letter to Timothy might suggest that kind of relationship with Priscilla and Aquila (2 Timothy 4:19). So I checked to see who Timothy might have known well from what the New Testament says about him.

Unfortunately the only person it is explicit about that Timothy spent a lot of time with was the Apostle Paul; but the New Testament implies that Timothy was with Paul during time that Paul lived and worked with Priscilla and her husband in Corinth for more than 18 months (they were tent makers). And there were other times and places that Timothy was where Priscilla and her husband (Aquila) were at the same time.

Thus it seemed possible that Timothy might go to Priscilla and Aquila upon release from confinement. If that had happened, it would fit well with the comment about Timothy in *Hebrews* 13:23. This just gave me an additional reason to think that Priscilla might be the unnamed author of *Hebrews*.

Paul had Timothy, the son of a Jewish mother and Gentile father, circumcised so that he would be fully accepted as Jewish as well as Christian by those in synagogues and elsewhere that he went with Paul when they were on Paul's missionary journeys. Thus Timothy would be most appropriate to accompany the author of *Hebrews* in a visit to those who received this letter. Timothy was particularly qualified to meet with Jewish Christians and talk with them about their faith in Jesus.

This insight means a lot to me; however, it may not have the same significance for you. The insight has not "proven" something about the Bible I had not known; it merely adds a layer of possible explanation to something that I thought might be true. The significant point for me was that the insight caused me to appreciate the help I could get in understanding Scripture from things just hinted at in the Bible. Everything did not have to be explicit and crystal clear to help me increase my understanding of God's truth.

I believe that in the future I will pay more attention to such hints than I have in the past. Of course I know that such hints never should be allowed to contradict things clearly said in the Bible; the hints, however, can help to flesh out situations that are not fully described. As *Hebrews* says in the fourth chapter, the Word of God (the Scripture) is alive. It keeps stimulating me with additional aspects of its truth after many years of Bible study.

Musing 24: Gossip
(initially posted on July 7, 2016)

America is a nation addicted to gossip, and that is bad for us individually and as a nation.

What is gossip and why is it so bad? For the past 500 years, the primary meaning of the word "gossip" in English has been "To talk idly, mostly about other people's affairs, to go about tattling" and the person who is prone to "idle talk; trifling or groundless rumour; tittle-tattle" (for the first couple of centuries the word "gossip" was applied mainly to women, although that gender has never had a monopoly on gossip); gossip also came to mean "in a more favorable sense: easy, unrestrained talk or writing, esp. about persons or social incidents" (material in quotes from the OED, the *Oxford English Dictionary*, perhaps the greatest authoritative source for meanings of English words).

There are numerous warnings in the Bible about the spiritual harm to the person doing it and the harm to others from careless and loose talk. The book of James in the New Testament warns about the danger of the tongue as does the book of Proverbs in the Old Testament. Literature is full of stories that illustrate the harm that gossip has done to others.

Why do I allege America is addicted to gossip? Simple observation of how people I know behave and of the media, both public and social, make it evident. For example, think about how much time a network news program, whether national or local, spends on things that are basically gossip instead of information that has major impact on how government performs, things that might impact you economically, physically, or legally. Romantic interactions between celebrities and reporting the nasty name calling among politicians certainly fall in that category as do emotion grabbing images of people hearing shocking news, whether good or bad. In the limited time of a nationally oriented network news program, one would think such gossip things would have little place. At times the majority of time not devoted to advertising seems to be spent on such gossip materials. Think of how much important and useful information you were not given because of the time devoted to gossip material.

This behavior by the public media is one reason I watch it or listen to it so little; and I am tempted to abandon it completely, which I do for a few weeks at a time sometimes.

I participate so little in social media that my impression of it is questionable, but the little I have dipped my toe into its waters indicates it is as gossipy as the public media, and possibly even more gossipy than the public media.

Why do intelligent people tolerate the huge presence of gossip in our society? Greed and desire for attention are major factors in the answer to that question. The public media makes money by getting public attention, and they know people want gossip. It gets their attention far more than many kinds of important and useful information. So they feed the public the slop we want. It is good business from their perspective. Hypocritically they mouth more noble intentions, but their actions show what really drives them.

The attention one gets by delivering gossip is an important factor in personal relationships and in what is done on social media and by many celebrities. A quip that captures the attention seeking attitude, "there is no such thing as bad publicity," has been around for more than a century; it is believed by some to have originally come from Phineas T. Barnum, a 19th century showman and circus owner.

Some think interest in gossip and desire for it is hard-wired in the human brain. Those who take this view think humans are evolutionarily set up to judge and talk about others, no matter how hurtful it might be. Baboons groom each other to keep social ties strong. Humans use gossip as social glue. Both are learned behaviors. Studies have found gossip establishes group boundaries and boosts self-esteem. The goal of gossip is not truth or accuracy. What matters is the bond that gossiping can forge, often at the expense of a third party.

Whether such is true or not, I do not know; but it does not matter. If one is not careful to speak only the truth and to deal with others, whether directly or in reference, with respect and love, then one does not act in ways that please God. Ultimately that will matter a lot. God's judgment will come to each of us.

People tend to be short-sighted, focused on immediate interests and benefits (or costs). That short-sightedness often causes one to ignore long-term consequences of what one does. Think of unwanted pregnancies from a night of pleasure, of tragic deaths from driving after over-indulging in drink at a party, or of other calamities that might come from ignoring possible adverse consequences because of over-focus on satisfying immediate interests or desires.

The need to restrain our participation in gossip, both as a producer and as a consumer of such, is the same as the need to restrain other harmful impulses we have. We understand that when it comes to things like forcing attention on another sexually, taking things that do not belong to us, giving false testimony in court, cheating in games, etc. We also need to apply the same kind of restraint in regard to gossip.

Musing 25: Secondary Blame
(initially posted on July 9, 2016)

People are upset by maliciousness, especially mass killings and misconduct by police. Some quickly cast blame for the incident, often before facts of the case are established. Such blame casters seldom acknowledge or apologize when it turns out they blamed wrongly; but they protest loudly if anyone blames them before the facts are clear.

Sensible people know to be cautious about blame because things may not be what they first appear to be, as illustrated in every magic show. It takes time to make sure what really happened and why. I know better than to apply the term "sensible people" to the motley crowd of professional protesters – people frequently engaged in protest to gain notoriety, celebrity, influence, or pay from being a protester. It is their career path; they behave similarly to another motley crowd, professional politicians.

Those doing the maliciousness mentioned above deserve blame and punishment, but I will not say more about them here. Instead I address a related topic that does not get the attention it deserves. That topic is secondary blame.

Secondary blame applies to things which contribute to maliciousness such as mentioned above. This musing cannot discuss all kinds of maliciousness; I focus on just one which has gotten a lot of attention recently: police misconduct with lethal consequences. These are inappropriate killings by police.

Angry mobs, large protests, and harsh accusations before facts of the situation are clear are obviously wrong; all guilty of such evil behavior should be ashamed and soundly criticized by others. Some lash out in such protest because of pain from losing a loved one. Others express frustration at what they see as bias and prejudicial treatment. In either case what they are doing is wrong. They should always wait until the facts are clearly established.

I mention just two secondary blame factors: police training and behavior of the victim's race. Space limitations preclude discussion of other factors or fuller discussion of these factors in this musing.

For the past half century police training has been strongly influenced by military training methods. Much of the equipment now used by police, especially with its SWAT and riot-control units, is similar to that employed by the military. Principles taught police are similar to those used by the military (such as emphasis on "overwhelming force," a marked contrast with the "one riot one Ranger" attitude from the early days of the Texas Rangers). Police are exposed to many ways that bad guys might act, and are taught to take preventive action. This can make police more aggressive than Sheriff Andy Griffith would be in Mayberry. Police training might be a secondary blame factor in some instances of police misconduct which have lethal consequences. Those responsible for police training should review their training and remove any inappropriate emphasis or perspectives that might encourage inappropriate excessive use of force.

Many instances of lethal police misconduct alleged in the public media in recent years have had black victims, which some claim is a result of racism. Police generally are aware of characteristics of those who commit crimes; they know some people are more likely to commit crimes than others. That awareness comes from a combination of their personal experience in law enforcement, their training, and information derived from studies of the topic. They know that age, gender, race, and other factors have crime implications; some crimes are more likely to be done by certain kinds of people. For example, a skinhead covered in tattoos who had been drinking and roaming around bars is more likely to violence than most retail clerks doing their jobs.

Studies show rates of violent crimes (the number by a specified unit of population) by blacks are several times (3-6) greater than similar rates for other ethnic groups (white, Hispanic, Asian, etc.) in the U.S. Such facts are based upon numbers of those convicted of violent crimes; such facts are correlated by statements about perpetrator race by surviving victims of the crimes. This higher violent crime rate for blacks is a secondary blame factor contributing to police misconduct because it makes police more likely to over-react in an encounter with a black person.

Those condemning police for lethal misconduct fail to likewise condemn the black community for its excessive tendency to violent crime. That tendency also causes blacks to be victims of violent crimes from other blacks at a rate several times greater than other ethnic groups suffer from all criminals. The number of blacks killed every year by black murderers is far larger than the number killed by police misconduct this century (a period of more than 15 years). Silence about this tendency of the black community belies belief that black lives matter.

Secondary blame factors also need attention, which often they do not get.

Promoters of political correctness (PC) will condemn my saying this, whether my comments are factual or not. Many PC promoters are embarrassed that studies do not show excessive black criminality comes from social or economic conditions since other races in comparable circumstances do not show such increased criminality.

Sensible people deal with problems realistically; they do more than rant and rave. Sensible people make sure of the facts; then they act. They deal with those deserving primary blame and also with secondary blame factors. Both have to be addressed if problems are to get solved. Fixing things so that things are better in the future is what sensible people want.

Musing 26: Victims
(initially posted July 11, 2016)

Some victims get a great deal of attention, such as those killed by mass murderers or police misconduct; there are perhaps a hundred or two thus killed annually. Other victims, though far more numerous, such as those killed by drunk drivers (there are about 10,000 such victims each year) get little public attention even though their loved ones suffer as much heartache and loss as others. Such lavishing of attention on some while largely ignoring others seems very wrong to me, especially since part of the reason for such unbalanced attention seems to be a consequence of media greed. Of course, what we the public seek from the media also is a major part of the reason for this egregious wrong.

If we want to be sensible, we should strive to be sure that we know pertinent facts. Our media leaves the impression that the U.S. is a deadly place to live; facts give a different impression. For example, comparison of the death rate per million people from mass public shootings during a recent six year period (2009-2015) for the U.S. and European countries has the U.S. as number 11. Ten European countries have higher death rates from mass shootings than the U.S.: Norway, Serbia, France, Macedonia, Albania, Slovakia, Switzerland, Finland, Belgium, and the Czech Republic. That kind of fact surprises most Americans, in part because of an erroneous presumption – they expect the media to present information in balanced perspective.

Other mundane facts also surprise most Americans. The death rate per 100,000 population in the U.S. for all murders is about 4.6 (in 2014 there were nearly 12,000 murders in the U.S.). Such a death rate is less than half the death rates for either falls or accidental poisonings. It is also less than half the death rate for dying in a vehicle accident. Of course, about a third of 2014's 32,000-plus vehicle related deaths were caused by intoxicated drivers (roughly the same number of victims killed by drunk drivers as by murderers); and shamefully many of those drunk drivers were not punished harshly for causing deaths.

Most people in the U.S. do not have realistic perceptions of hazards we face; and that contributes both to their tolerance of such shameful unbalance in the attention given to victims of various tragedies and to their contribution to the unbalance in attention to victims. I think it is time for us to grow up; to do as the Apostle Paul urged Christians at Corinth to do by putting away childish attitudes because life should be approached with an adult perspective.

Not just those excessively publicized by the media, but the families and friends of every victim of lethal tragedy needs our sympathy and concern; they need to know that we understand their loss and that the death of their loved one is a detriment to our society. The public, the government, and various organizations have provided survivors and families of those killed or injured in some tragedies a great deal of material help as well as attention and sympathy; yet a far greater number of other victims and their families basically have simply been ignored by the public, the government, and various organizations. Nor has such material been given them. How can this shameful situation be changed?

I will not bother with comments for the media or public officials; they would be unlikely to heed my words. Instead I hope ordinary people will think about what I say and do what they feel is appropriate.

When you see the media, officials, or others lavishing excessive attention on some victims and their loved ones while ignoring others, complain to them about their inappropriate unbalance in what they do. Tell them that they should treat all victims and their families more even handedly.

Look at yourself. Have you been unfair by helping some and ignoring others? If so, change! You have power to control what you do. Show the same level of concern for all victims and their loved ones. Help each in the same kinds of way and with similar levels of help. Explain to others why you act the way you do when knowledge of tragedies come your way. You might be surprised at how much effect what you do may have on others.

This musing has only addressed victims of some kind of malicious activity; I have not talked about victims of natural disasters such as wild fires, floods, or storms. Sometimes such disasters are worse than they might have been if people had behaved prudently before the disaster (such as cleaning out brush in areas to reduce the amount of combustible stuff, not building or living in regions where flooding is likely, etc.); but in any case you might want to think how you react to such disasters so that you avoid wrongful unbalance in your response to different disasters.

Life is never easy. Hard choices have to be made, and sometimes those choices concern how we respond to news of trouble experienced by others. I hope you will provide others with a good example of proper balance in your response to news of tragedies and disasters.

Musing 27: Unions
(initially posted July 12, 2016)

I expect that my discussion of unions may generate hate and discontent. If it does, I am sorry. That is not my intent; concern about such caused me not to share my thoughts on the topic earlier.

The union movement originated in the 19th century with the goal of reducing some of the horrors in treatment of workers as industrialization spread. I was first exposed to such horrors through the muckraking novels of Upton Sinclair, especially *The Jungle* with its description of conditions in the U.S. meat packing industry. The union movement in the U.S. began to bloom after FDR's *New Deal*. A couple of decades later union membership reached a peak of about 1/3 of U.S. workers, but in the past half-century union membership has fallen to just a bit over 11% of wage and salary workers (an even lower percentage of all workers). Currently about half of union members are government workers, so that the percent of unionized government workers is several times greater than the percent of unionized workers in non-government jobs.

The above simply states facts and should not upset anyone. The question is, Are unions helpful or harmful for America at this time? That is the focus of this musing. So you know where I come from: I am not now and have never been a member of a union, nor have I been in a business position where I had to interact with union leadership. Politically I have been registered as an independent (i.e., no political party affiliation) since I started voting more than half-a-century ago. I have worked in both blue collar and while collar positions; at times I worked alongside people who were union members, some of whom were union activists.

Problems of worker abuse as industrialization spread that unions try to counter certainly need to be prevented and corrected. That is not the issue. The issue is, Did unions correct such problems? Did unions bring other benefits, and did the unions bring problems?

Union demands contributed to improvements in work conditions for many wage and salary positions; but how much such improvement owes to union endeavors and how much the improvements owe to other reasons is not clear. For example, a number of sociological work-related studies in the early 20th century gave many insights about worker productivity and factors impacting it. Changes in work conditions to make workers more productive (not because of union agitation) seem to have occurred in many industries; many of those changes made working conditions far better than they had been previously. Some of the changes were ones that unions also demanded. It is unclear whether most of the changes came from union demands or from business seeking to be more efficient.

A phrase originated during World War II, a time when few government workers were unionized: "good enough for government work." Originally it meant something met high quality standards required by the government, especially the federal government. Since WWII, the unionized portion of government workers has increased to over 35% (Bureau of Labor Statistics 2015 data). During that time, connotation of the phrase "good enough for government work" changed from commendation on work's high quality to exactly the opposite. The phrase now describes low quality work that no one respects. Could there be a correlation between increase in the percent of unionized workers in the government and the quality of government work? I know many who think there is, and I have not seen studies contradicting that perspective. For example, Vets I know blame poor quality VA care largely on the difficulty in firing inept unionized government employees.

Media, and literature abound with stories of union corruptness and their harm. Sometimes union harm is portrayed in comedy, such as Peter Sellers acting as a union shop steward in the 1959 British comedy *I'm Alright Jack*. Other portrayals show a more vicious side of unionism, such as in the 1954 Marlon Brando movie, *On The Waterfront*. These movies are from the time of highest union membership by American workers. I do not know how much corruptness and inefficiency actually exists because of unions, but its abundant presentation in literature and film would be unlikely if there were none.

Another way of looking at union's social impact is to compare teacher effectiveness in public schools (more than 2/3 of teachers belong to unions) with teachers in non-public religious and other private schools (where few teachers are unionized; about 10% of high school students in the country attend such schools). In 2014, average SAT scores for public school students was 5% below the average for all students; religious school student scores were 3% above the national average and other private school student scores were 7% above the national average. Such suggests that teacher unionization does not correlate with better student performance; other factors also impact such performance differences.

My bottom line: unionization does not seem to correlate with better products (such as student performance or work quality and efficiency); unionization probably means more pay and more job security for union members (plus political influence and possibly lavish life styles for union leaders). That bottom line seems bad for the country; it causes me to examine very carefully ideas and programs promoted by unions. Such are likely to be self-serving for the union and possibly bad for the rest of us.

Musing 28: Lives Matter
(initially posted July 15, 2016)

All lives matter. That fundamental point seems to elude some in groups that are concerned about inappropriate actions against particular kinds of people. Certainly that seems to be the situation with the Black Lives Matter folks; some of whom make comments about killing whites and police. The situation is similar for LGBT supporters who so focus on getting recognition and proper treatment for that community that they seem oblivious to rights and concerns of anyone else.

Certainly those who turn violent in protests and hurl rocks at police or burn and loot businesses do not act as if all lives matter since they are willing to physically harm others and damage the livelihood of others. Those objecting to all in such protests being blamed for the evil actions of a few, as is often done, fail to appreciate that such wrongful blame is the very kind of thing that the protesters are doing in their condemnation of police for misbehavior by a small portion of the law enforcement community.

It would help everyone if each one of us would treat others the way we want to be treated. If you think it is wrong to blame all protesters for the actions of a few, then do not cast blame on all police for the actions of a few of them. The basis for that is that All Lives Matter. Black, white, brown, yellow, and red. Also true for both police and private citizens, poor and rich, educated and uneducated, suave and uncouth. All Lives Matter.

Because all lives matter, every inappropriate action, whether by the police or by private citizens, needs to be addressed, but they need to be addressed in a proper way. The police should not use excessive force in their law enforcement endeavors, and private citizens should not use violence, destruction of property, or disruption of the lives of others to get what they want; both kinds of behavior are wrong and hinder progress toward improvement of our society.

There was an old adage about a pot and kettle that criticized accusing others of something one is guilty of himself, but it cannot be used any more without someone claiming it was intended as a racial slur. However, the point made by that adage is quite valid. You should not criticize others for behaving the way you do. Jesus gave a similar warning in the Sermon on the Mount. He warned that you will be judged in the same way you judge others (Matthew 7:2).

I spent many years as an analyst addressing complex problems related to national defense issues and systems. One of the things I learned from that was the importance of identifying the factors which have the greatest impact on the problem so that the greatest attention could be given to them. This is the way to have the biggest impact on the problem. It was unwise to spend most of your effort on factors with little impact on the system.

Unfortunately that approach to dealing with problems is not being applied by those in the Black Lives Matter community. For example, essentially all I have seen on the web and in the media from that community is focused on inappropriate police actions, especially actions which have lethal consequences. From everything I have seen, the number of black lives that are lost in a year from inappropriate police actions is no greater than a few dozen. Yes, every such life lost is a tragedy and should be addressed appropriately so that wrong-doing by the police is punished.

However, there are far more black lives lost every year, thousands of them, to other causes that those proclaiming Black Lives Matter seem to ignore, or at least I have not seen that community give attention to them or to how such loses might be reduced. I would think that those truly concerned about black lives would give as much attention to factors causing thousands of black deaths a year as they do to the factor causing a few dozen such deaths a year.

What factors cause such large numbers of black deaths? I will mention just three. First, there are avoidable medical mistakes. It is now estimated that hundreds of thousands a year die in hospitals from avoidable medical mistakes, and I suspect that at least tens of thousands of the ones losing their lives are black. Second, drunk drivers kill more than ten thousand people a year; probably at least a thousand or two of the ones killed are black. Third, there is an ethnic community that produces far more murderers per unit of population in the group than any other ethnic or racial group in the U.S.; the rate of murders by members of that group is several times greater than that of any other race or ethnic group. Murderers from that ethnic group kill about 4,000 black people a year. Helping that group change its behavior could save many black lives a year. That might merit much more attention from the Black Lives Matter community than it currently receives.

Those who truly believe black lives matter will give attention to all who kill black people, not just to misbehaving police who kill only a few dozen a year. Also, those who truly believe that black lives matter may want to ask themselves, Do only black lives matter? Or do all lives matter?

Musing 29: Reasonableness (initially posted July 17, 2016)

There have been a lot of instances recently of black people telling of the emotional hurt they felt when others, especially white people, seemed to be concerned about being in their presence. Even the President of the U.S. recited an instance when he was a youngster of a white lady getting off the elevator so she would not be alone in the elevator with him.

The implication from the way such incidents have been presented in the public media is that the white people behaving this way were acting shamefully simply because of the other person's color and had no reasonable basis for such behavior. The question that this musing addresses is simple: Is such really the situation?

Some will react emotionally to that comment and simply relegate my comments to the litter bin for stupid expressions of racial bias. I hope others will be more sensible. Sensible people try to be sure they understand the situation, and are not content with a caricature representation of it.

It is true that some people unreasonably shun others. People of a different race, those who dress in certain ways, or some who have various physical conditions are just shunned by some folks. For examples, some women will not date bald men. Others avoid the presence of those seriously handicapped. Some ignore people from low social or economic classes. And some whites are simply uncomfortable in the presence of black people.

Some have reasons for behaving in ways just like the unreasonable ones. For example, people of various sorts have reputations. Sometimes such reputation is a valid indication of how many people in that group behave; other times it is not. For example, consider the reputation of used car salesmen. Wise people do not simply believe what a used car salesman says; their reputation suggests they may bend the truth at times. Most people do not think a person who is cautious about accepting what a used car salesman says is necessarily showing unreasonably bias against that salesman; they recognize the person is using reasonable caution, even if the particular used car salesman in this case is a very honest person.

Let's ask, Might a similar kind of reasonableness have caused some white people to shun black people in the incidents mentioned earlier? Certainly the color of a person's skin in itself poses no danger to another person; so reasonable behavior would need some other reason. That reason could be the behavior of many black people.

Every group of people has people in it with various attributes. Some are brilliant and others are stupid; some are strong and others are physically weak; some are constantly talking and others are quiet; etc. However, groups also have statistical characteristics. Certain physical ailments are more common in some groups than in others. Certain behaviors also appear more frequently in some groups than in others.

Such statistical differences show in groups identified by sex, age, occupation, activity, and race as well as by other factors. Employers were not unreasonable in pre-automation days to mainly select women to work on assembly lines of electronic equipment because women generally have better fine motor skills than men. Medical people are not unreasonable when they think coal miners may be more likely to have black lung disease than office workers. We understand and accept such reasonable behavior based upon group statistics.

The question is, Are there statistical characteristics of black people that might be a basis for the kind of behavior by whites mentioned at the beginning of this musing? The answer is, Yes, and unfortunately general knowledge about such may be as distorted about such facts as are used car salesman stereotypes.

The criminal rate for blacks is three times the national average; that rate of criminality exceeds rates significantly for any other racial or ethnic grouping. For some violent crimes, such as murder, the number of murders in a given population size is more than six times as great for blacks as it is for whites and other races. Such disparity is widely known, and is at least a partial reason for some of the kind of shunning mentioned at the beginning of this musing.

It is unfortunate that innocent members of the black community are sometimes viewed with caution because of the bad behavior of other blacks, but such caution is not unreasonable. It even shows in black behavior such as the greater interest by blacks in moving out of a predominately black community than any other race shows for moving out of a community that is mainly of that race.

I have seen a number of media presentations expressing the hurt experienced by black people that were shunned by whites, but I do not recall any media mention that perhaps at least some whites who acted that way might have done so because of concern based upon statistical behavior of the black community. This is another example of unbalanced presentation from the media, and failure of the government by and large to correct such unbalanced presentations. Changes in behavior of the black community are needed as much or more than changes by whites. The whites mentioned in the incidents cited did no physical harm to the blacks they shunned. The whites mentioned early simply kept their distance because of caution based on possible harm that might occur, given statistical behavior of blacks. Some people who do bad things dress nicely and speak well; as has long been said, you cannot truly judge a book by its cover. Nor can we properly understand something until all aspects of the situation are considered.

Musing 30: Thought Experiments (initially posted July 20, 2016)

A thought experiment thoroughly thinks through a situation. Scientists use thought experiments to consider hypotheses, theories, and principles so that their results, implications, and consequences can be more fully understood. Sometimes a thought experiment is a precursor to an actual experiment, helping to shape the experiment by predicting what results might be and how various factors may interact. That can identify what needs to be measured during the experiment and how. Sometimes thought experiments address things that cannot be addressed in actual experiments.

I suggest a thought experiment related to a topic of current attention: caution a police officer might use in a traffic stop of a pickup with a rifle rack in its cab or a car the color of one reported to carry armed robbers fleeing the police. Regardless of why the vehicle was stopped, do you think it would be appropriate for a police officer to use extra caution in that situation because a weapon might be in the vehicle? Many would consider such extra caution very appropriate.

That thought experiment had no racial connotation. If the occupants of the car were African-Americans, some jump to the conclusion that the police officer used extra caution in approaching the car because of racial bias and prejudice. Often such assumptions are made before the person knows whether such conditions as noted for the thought experiment existed, and unfortunately there are some who would still condemn the police officer for racial bias even if they knew such conditions (the rifle rack or car color being that of fleeing armed perpetrators) were true. One can only lament that such pig-headed doctrinaire people live among us.

A second thought experiment. What conditions associated with a person's race or ethnic background might give a police officer appropriate reason to use extra caution in approaching them? If the thought experiment cannot identify any such condition, then it would be appropriate to say that any use of extra caution in approaching someone because of race would be wrong. However, if conditions do exist which justify extra caution in approaching a member of a particular race, then police use of extra caution in approaching a member of that race might be appropriate in such conditions.

Many would agree that a police officer should use extra caution in approaching someone with a fire arm; many would say it would be appropriate to use extra caution in approaching someone reported to be armed, even if the weapon could not be seen by the approaching police officer. Some might say that extra caution by the approaching police officer is appropriate if violent actions by the one being approached had been seen, or even just reported.

Now back to the second thought experiment. Suppose someone lives, works, or just is in a particular neighborhood or community which has a much higher incidence of violent crime and weapon use than anywhere else in the jurisdiction. Such neighborhoods and communities exist in our cities. Often the majority of people in such a neighborhood or community belong to a single race. Is that a condition that might make it appropriate for a police officer to use extra caution in approaching a car in that neighborhood with occupants of that race?

A bit more about the second thought experiment. Suppose a racial group has a much higher incidence of certain criminal behaviors, such as violent crimes like murder, rape, and assault, than any other racial group. By much higher, I mean factors of several (at least 3, 4, or 5 times) more than others; not just a few percent more. Also suppose that incidence of those committing such crimes is particularly great for some age and sex groups. Would that give a police officer appropriate reason to use extra caution in approaching a person of that race, age, and sex?

Some might quibble that information about that kind of behavior cannot be trusted because of racial bias by law enforcement personnel. There has been some of that, but if you compare information from law enforcement sources with reports about race of perpetrators by surviving victims of such crimes, you come to the same conclusion about criminal tendency association with race. Victim identification of perpetrator race avoids possible law enforcement bias.

Many would say it is appropriate for a police officer to use extra caution in approaching one known or suspected to be associated with violent crime. The second thought experiment may give you reason to think about things differently than you had before.

For many people, facts and rational behavior is less important to them than their ideas, prejudices, presumptions, pleasures, privileges, and the like. Continuation or initiation of smoking by many in spite of abundant information about its health harm to the smoker and others illustrates that. Unfortunately, such behavior extends into racial areas as well as in unhealthy activities.

My objective in this musing has been to stimulate looking carefully at a particular area of police behavior to ensure our thinking about it is appropriate, and to provide a basis for modifying our thinking if needed. I have not presented facts or recommended how one should perceive things. I have left that to the reader so that the reader's conclusion will his or her own, not something generated for the person by others.

I know that many are too lazy to put forth the effort needed to do the two thought experiments or too pig-headedly doctrinaire to care about facts, but I hope you are not such a person. I hope you are a thinking person concerned about making sound decisions realistically and behaving in a good way.

Musing 31: Economic Realities
(initial posted July 23, 2016)

Snake oil salesmen have a slippery reputation when it comes to the truth; and, unfortunately, so do their first cousins, political leaders. Many economic indicators (such as unemployment rates, borrowing to provide current benefits that the future will have to pay for, etc.) can be manipulated by political leaders, but basic economic realities are more difficult for them to manipulate. Only four times in the past two centuries has the federal deficit (the amount spent beyond current income) reached the 10% or higher level of GDP (Gross Domestic Product); those four times were during the Civil War, WWI, WWII, and the Obama administration.

Great danger to the nation in the three wars justified such extensive borrowing; but the Obama administration indulged in that level of borrowing to provide more benefits for various groups, desiring to attract voters to keep the administration in office. Such economic policies will be continued by that party if it wins the election according to campaign statements by Mrs. Clinton. Such economic profligacy places great economic burden on coming generations without their consent.

The national debt has grown to $13 trillion (about 3.5 times as much as the federal government currently spends annually); that debt doubled since Obama took office (increasing the debt as much in less than 8 years as accumulated in the two previous centuries, including the three wars mentioned).

Wealth of a nation is basically dependent upon its civilian employment. The more people employed in such, the greater the nation's wealth. Government employees typically contribute little directly to the wealth of the nation since they are paid by taxation of civilians. Hence the percent of civilian population employment is a good indication of a nation's financial health. Other indicators, e.g., unemployment rate, are not such good indicators because they can be politically manipulated (e.g., by adding government jobs which may help the current generation, but may increase the debt burden on coming generations since paying those government employees has to come from civilian taxation).

When did you hear political candidates talk so plainly about economic realities? It probably has been a long time since they were that honest with the public.

Bureau of Labor Statistics (BLS) data show about 63% percent of the U.S. population (16 and older) were employed before Obama took office; during his administration that percentage has dropped 3-5%. Comparable numbers of the civilian labor force employed was 66% before Obama took office; since it has dropped to about 63%. Such has resulted from bad economic policies by the administration.

The bottom line economic reality from the above is simple: administrative policies of the Obama administration (which Mrs. Clinton says she plans to continue) have increased benefits for people (expanding the number of those receiving benefits and striving to increase the benefits of those receiving them) while reducing the percent of the population producing the nation's wealth; such benefits have been paid for by doubling the national debt. It does not take a genius to realize that such is a path to economic disaster. That is an economic reality Americans should be very concerned about.

Years ago I heard a witty description of a political liberal; I do not know who is thought to have originated it, but a variety of politicians and commentators have expressed similar ideas, often in comments about socialism. That witty description says "the liberal is someone who seeks to do good with other people's money."

Unfortunately, that description seems to be very appropriate when applied to many leading political liberals in the U.S. who tried to change U.S. law so it provided more benefits for various segments of society; their tax returns (made public because of their positions in government) showed that many of those political liberals contributed a smaller percentage of their income to charitable purposes than did the average tax payer. The liberals were eager to use other people's money (i.e., from taxes) but not so eager to use their own money to help the needy and others.

I think that witty description of a political liberal is a fair description of what the Obama administration has been doing, and what Mrs. Clinton says she will continue doing.

Calamities often occur when people do not deal with economic realities. Those who bought more expensive homes than they could afford often experienced economic disaster. The whole country has suffered from economic follies of large financial firms. And we have seen the turmoil that follows when countries go into economic default, as illustrated by Greece and Venezuela.

People need to deal with economic realities, whether at the personal level or at the national level. In this musing I mention a few economic realities that greatly concern me and I have indicated those primarily responsible (in my opinion) for the problems I identified. I urge you to think hard about economic realities and consider what you believe could be consequences of ignoring them. Then I trust you will make good decision for yourself and urge others to also do that.

It has long been recognized that living within one's means is prudent, both for nations and for individuals. The problems indicated by the economic realities I mention in this musing are examples of failure to live within one's means (which is how I view doubling the national debt in less than 8 years instead of calling upon the citizenry to live within our current means, even if it required austerity – the Obama administration seems to lack the courage and integrity to do that, instead they have dumped a huge debt burden on coming generations).

Musing 32: Race Relations (initially posted July 24, 2016)

For roughly a decade before Obama took office as President, a number of polls and surveys showed more people of most races felt race relations were good than felt they were bad.

During Obama's presidency, that changed. Now numerous polls and surveys report a majority of all races (black, white, Asian, Hispanic) believe race relations are bad.

What might have caused such a radical reversal on racial attitudes during the administration of a black president? Race relations should improve with a black man in the highest political office. Instead race relations deteriorated more during Obama's administration than in any other eight year period of my lifetime. I share a few thoughts on the subject.

The first thing I note is growth in both wealth of Americans and their expectations. In the 1950s, 60s, or 70s, not every family had a car, a TV, or even was connected to others by phone. Today even the poorest is likely to have a cell phone and a TV, and many families have multiple automobiles. Some families even have more than a car per person. This simply illustrates how the wealth of Americans has increased.

Expectations have also grown. Now many people think everyone is entitled to far more than was thought when I was young. Growth in expectation brought a broad sense sense of entitlement, the idea that others should provide things for you regardless of who you are or how you behave. Emphasis upon entitlement has reduced emphasis on self-reliance. Now many are not satisfied with simply being given opportunity, they desire assurance that their wants will be satisfied; that attitude comes from their sense of entitlement.

The switch from emphasis on self-reliance and opportunity to an emphasis on entitlement and satisfaction of wants is bad, both for individuals and for the nation. Who is to blame for this?

Greed plays a major role in blame for this situation. As American wealth increased, many more people who are susceptible to unrealistic claims by advertisers presented repeatedly by the media could be exploited for their money. Greedy scoundrels shamelessly emphasized that everyone deserved to have whatever one wanted, and should get it without having to save for it or even pay for it immediately. The young, many of the less educated, and some not so bright made such scoundrels rich.

Obama facilitated this situation with emphasis on increasing benefits for people (which enhanced their sense of entitlement) and deferred paying for such benefits by doubling the national debt (his 8 years in office will have spent 10 years of annual federal expenditures – he's dumped a ton of debt on future generations). Only the Civil War, WWI, and WWII previously had required the federal deficit level of the Obama administration. During those wars, the future of the nation was seriously at risk. Obama has stolen from future generations just to expand current benefits for Americans. Many of the people benefiting from Obama's largesse do not seem to care that someone else has to pay for their benefits; such callousness is a byproduct of entitlement thinking.

Many people have been concerned about needs of those low on the social-economic scale; some approaches to meeting those needs take the entitlement approach instead of the opportunity and encouragement approach. Hence we have a number of people in our society now who are physically and mentally able to work and provide for themselves, but who choose to live off benefits provided instead and perhaps also indulge in idleness, substance abuse, and the like.

Appropriate provision should be made for those physically or mentally unable to provide for themselves, but the rest should do without if they choose not to avail themselves of opportunity. In my youth, that was much more the approach taken than today. Today it appears that entitlement thinking dominates. Certainly that seems so from policies and practices of the Obama administration, policies that are likely to continue to if Mrs. Clinton were elected president.

I grieve for future generations of Americans if we, beneficiaries of current benefits, do not shoulder the responsibility of paying for what we get. I'm shamed by the moral turpitude of our political leaders who dump debt for our benefits onto future generations. It may be justifiable to dump debt on a future generation when faced with the dire threat of world war, but there is no such moral justification for doing such so the current generation can enjoy benefits it is unwilling to pay for while leaders use such debt to buy votes from those getting benefits to stay in power as Obama has done.

I think the sense of entitlement also makes people bitter that they do not get more, no matter how much they get. That is why attitudes toward race relations have turned so sour during the Obama administration. Blacks feel they should have more, and whites think their clamor for more is inappropriate; hence all think race relations are bad.

The media magnify race relation issues to increase ratings, and ignore sensible information such as from a black professor at Harvard whose study of the subject (the most extensive and credible to date) revealed that blacks were no more likely to be shot or killed by police than whites. It takes a source more careful about facts than most American media to report such, as was done by a recent issue of a well-respected publication, *The Economist*.

Some will react to this musing with partisan bias, pro or con depending upon the person's persuasion. However, I hope others will think hard about race relations, the topic of this musing.

Musing 33: The Bible
(initially published July 25, 2016)

Sometimes my musings have addressed things of current interest, like some of them which touched racial or political topics. Others have addressed general characteristics of people and our behaviors, and some, like this one, have dealt with religious topics. Certainly the Bible is a religious topic, although it is also something that has significantly impact on both our literature and our culture.

In general, most Americans ignore the Bible. Many have not read a significant portion of it. This is even true of a number who attend church. Others pick and choose which parts of the Bible they give attention to, generally ignoring things that would be inconvenient for them. The Bible is full of such inconvenient things. For example, in the Sermon on the Mount, Jesus said to be good to those who are bad to you; that's very inconvenient. In that same part of Scripture, Jesus also warned of the danger a judgmental attitude brings; that too usually is ignored.

I urge all Americans, whether Christian or not, to read the Bible (at least the New Testament portion) and seriously consider what it says. There are many valuable insights about people and human behavior in the Bible, as well as what it says about God. Those insights can be very helpful.

Most people who take the Bible seriously consider it to be the Word of God. Unfortunately some of them have serious misconceptions about what that means. I mention a few of those misconceptions in this musing.

I will not identify any who have espoused misconceptions I mention, but I hope you realize that I am not making them up. I have heard people say these misconceptions, or I have read such in their writings. I am sure that the reader has also encountered such misconceptions.

First, some act as if what the Bible says can be interpreted however one chooses, and then that interpretation can be claimed to be valid because it comes from the Word of God. Hogwash! Nothing should be more stupidly wrong than that.

Valid insights involve proper interpretation of what the Bible says. Biblical words are understood within the context of the meaning of the words, how people usually communicate, and in consort with other passages of the Bible so that what is said in one passages is understood in the context of all the Bible says on the subject. That approach prevents many foolish ideas such as the silliness that God wants everyone to be rich as some Green Power proponents say.

That approach also prevents the foolishness of reading contemporary ideas into what the Bible says as some have done who want to blur the clear masculine identity for God in the Bible, seeking to replace male pronouns and the words Father or Son which are what the best manuscripts of the Bible consistently read with gender neutral terms.

Second, some who take the Bible seriously make distorted claims about the character and reliability of the Bible in their claims about its inspiration and inerrancy. We do not need to worry that the power of God's Word is limited by human belief or disbelief about it; that power resides in God as His Spirit touches the hearts of people with His Word whatever they may believe or not believe of some doctrine related to the Bible.

The Bible (a collection of books, writings produced by different people over an extended period of time, well more than a thousand years) itself does not contain a list of which books should be included in it. Jesus' reference to the Old Testament as consisting of three parts (the law, the prophets, and Psalms/the writings) fails to identify items specifically. For example, Genesis came before the law; should it be included? Should "historical" books be considered Scripture? Jews call some of them (e.g., 1 & 2 Kings) prophetical; others (e.g., Ruth or Ezra) Jews include in the writings. Peter calls Paul's writing Scripture, but comments in the letters of Paul in the New Testament suggest that he also wrote other letters; are parts of the Scripture missing?

Those who make excessive claims about Biblical inspiration and inerrancy, some going so far as to specify a particular translation of the Bible into English as the exact Word of God, often do not address the reality mentioned above nor explain how their particular view addresses such.

It is obvious that some versions of the Bible have errors; such as the notorious "sinner's Bible" (a 1631 edition of the King James Version in which the printer accidentally left out "not" from the seventh commandment, the commandment about adultery, ten copies of that Bible edition are said to remain to this day).

We need to understand that there are some uncertainties associated with the Bible from possible textual differences in the oldest and best extant manuscripts and in how some passages should be translated or interpreted; but we also need to understand that generally the Bible as we have it today in any of the major translations is a reliable and authoritative expression of God's Word. If one seeks to know what God's Word says and reads the Bible in the ways people normally read things and focuses on things said clearly in a number of places in the Bible, that person can be sure he or she will get valid insights about God's truth.

God also promises that anyone truly seeking Him in that way will be led by the Spirit of God to connect with the living God in a saving manner. Try it and see that I speak the truth.

Musing 34: Contrarian Perspective (initially posted July 30, 2016)

The Oxford English Dictionary (OED) defines a contrarian as a person who opposes or rejects prevailing opinion or established practice; a person who behaves in a contrary manner. Perhaps it is expected that a curmudgeon (i.e., a cranky old man) such as I will have a contrarian perspective. The prevailing opinion that I oppose is the belief that the USA is a Christian nation.

Before I present my perspective, let me state clearly that I am glad I was born in the USA; I am blessed by having been born in the USA. That made my life far better personally, socially, and materially than it would have been had I been born elsewhere.

Some claim American started as a Christian nation because of presumptions about religious conditions during colonial days. Some may claim the USA is a Christian nation in hopes that such will bring God's blessings upon America, making it rich and protecting it from its enemies.

I need to define "Christian nation." I am only willing to apply the adjective "Christian" to a nation if the majority of them believe Jesus is the Divine Son of God Who provides salvation for people and they seriously try to live in ways that the New Testament says pleases God. That sets a high bar for calling the USA Christian.

The USA does not meet that standard today even though for over a century more than half of Americans have claimed Christianity as their religion. Only a third or less of the population attends religious services. The USA judiciary declares legal behaviors that the New Testament clearly identifies as displeasing to God. The levels of substance abuse, criminal behavior, marital infidelity, and other behaviors that the New Testament says do not please God are more prevalent in the USA than in most nations with significant proportions of their populations claiming to be Christian. These are reasons why I say the USA is not a Christian nation.

Was our country ever a Christian nation? During colonial days, more than a dozen Christian groups had significant numbers of adherents in the colonies: Amish, Anglican, Brethren, Congregational (which includes Baptist groups), Dutch Reformed, Huguenots, Lutheran, Mennonite, Moravian, Presbyterian, Quaker, Reformed, Roman Catholic, and Schwenkfelder.

During colonial days formal church membership/adherence was limited to less than 1 in 5 of the population; some estimate it was as low as 5%. However, a larger portion of the population were involved in various religious services; perhaps as many as half the population would be in some "religious" activity during a week as part of a colony's civil or social activities (such as discussion of town business in the meeting house where worship services were held). It may not be appropriate to always consider such involvement as something "Christian."

Many people assume the grand words from the Pledge of Allegiance, "with liberty and justice for all," reflect "Christian" ideas that were widespread in colonial days and during the founding of our nation. Unfortunately those words come from much later (1892) and were originally intended to increase allegiance to the US by the multitude of immigrants arriving in that era.

Do the words from the Pledge of Allegiance reflect reality of colonial days and the founding of our nation? If liberty and justice for all include the right to vote, those words did not reflect reality for women, free black men, Native Americans, or white men who did not own a significant amount of property. Slaves were not even considered people by many in that era. After the American Revolution, there was great debate about extending the right to vote to veterans of the war; prominent leaders such as John Adams, a signer of the Declaration of Independence and the second US president, felt expanding franchise (the right to vote) would be bad for the USA. Based upon history of US politics with expanded franchise, some believe Adams' perspective has proven valid.

Thomas Jefferson, credited with drafting the Declaration of Independence and many admirable statements about human dignity, was a slave owner who refused to accept payment for his slaves so they could be free. Colonial days and the early decades of USA history were not very Christian if measured by the portion of the population seeking to live in ways the New Testament says pleases God.

Those who call the USA a Christian nation do not mean what I mean by the term. The USA has never deserved to be called a Christian nation if that means anything more than a lot of people in the country belong to a church. Only by that could the USA be called a Christian nation; it is the lowest level of possible meaning for the label. The USA has never been Christian in a more meaningful sense.

Some may find the perspective in this musing distasteful, but it is realistic. Our nation is in a situation similar to that of an addict who has to admit addiction before recovery can really begin. Only when we acknowledge how unchristian the USA really is will we begin to do the things that might start to move our nation toward becoming a truly Christian nation; and that is much needed. Repentance is where to start. That changes our perspective so we look at things as God does, and then act in ways that please Him.

American Christians need clarity in their thinking about our nation. Perhaps my contrarian thoughts will stimulate some to act seriously by seeking to help others become Christian in reality, not just Christian in name. Thank you for taking time to read this musing.

Musing 35: Political Immorality (initially posted July 27, 2016)

Immorality by political leaders is nothing new. The immorality may be inappropriate sexual behavior that may be covered up by the media for popular leaders (as they did half-a-century ago) or made a focus of national news (as has been done with Clinton and numerous other political leaders). The immorality may be inappropriate financial activity and lead to prison as well as loss of offices (as has happened to people as high in office as Vice-president). Sometimes immorality is known, but not punished (as happened recently when the Justice Department refused to charge a political star for things an ordinary citizen would have been sent to prison for doing).

Such political immorality is well known and often gets media attention. This musing is not about such; it is about a political immorality that is not given media attention nor addressed by pundits prone to share their views with the public. That immorality is stealing future prosperity from coming generations for benefits of the current generation that we are not asked to pay for.

What in the world am I talking about?

During the 8 years of the Obama administration, benefits for many were created or expanded, but cost of those benefits has been deferred to the future by massive increase in the national debt because the Obama administration was unwilling or unable to make those receiving the benefits pay for them. In just 8 years, the Obama doubled the national debt; he added as much additional debt in just 8 years as had been accumulated in the previous two centuries!

The level of federal deficit (amount spent beyond federal government income) during the Obama years (about 10% of GDP) had been experienced only three times previously in U.S. history: during the Civil War, World War I, and World War II. Those three wars put the nation in such peril that borrowing so extensively was generally considered justifiable. Obama borrowed that simply to give more benefits to the current generation. A cynic might note such was a way to buy votes so the administration could stay in power.

Dumping so much debt on future generations just for benefits those receiving them do not pay for is very immoral. During 8 years in office,

Obama spent as much as the federal government would normally spend in more than 10 years. Future generations will have to pay for Obama's largesse to present recipients of the benefits.

Think what that means. Obama stole from future generations money they will need to fix our aging infrastructure (roads, sewers, public utilities, dams, etc.). He has stolen prosperity from your children and your grandchildren. That is very immoral. He, his administration, and all in Congress who permitted such egregious deficit expenditures are scoundrels and I think they should be run out of the country. They are the most immoral of political rascals.

I am ashamed of the silence about this by American pundits. They deserve exile to Siberia or some other remote unpleasant place for their connivance with the politicians about this. They know as well as anyone but an idiot knows, at some point bills have to be paid. We, current beneficiaries, are not paying them. No magic genie is going to pop up from a bottle with a ton of money to pay that debt. It is going to land squarely on future generations. Their prospects for prosperity are going downhill fast under a mountain of debt.

The Democratic candidate for president is very likely to continue the Obama practice of robbing future generations to provide benefits for contemporaries, and entice folks to vote for that party in hope and expectation that those benefits will be forthcoming. If Democrats think particular benefits are appropriate, the proper thing to do is to convince the country of such so that the current generation is willing to pay for those benefits. Stealing money from future generations to pay for benefits to the current generation is never right. It is always immoral, regardless of which party does it.

Republicans had been guilty of doing that at times, but never to the extent done by the Obama administration. It is hard to believe he was not impeached for creating a federal deficit as large (in terms of GDP proportion) as that necessary during world wars! Where were pundits who help us retain sane perspectives? Why have they been so silent? Who can trust them in the future? They are too inclined to cozy with the political establishment to provide reliable warnings to the public about political stupidities like this immoral behavior. We know politicians have an overwhelming primary motivation: get and keep power, regardless of what it takes. Their behavior repeatedly demonstrates that is the case.

I hesitated posting this; it has so much bitterness in it. However, I am compelled to share it because no one else seems to be beating this drum. This kind of political immorality must stop. We should not continue to rob future generations of opportunity for prosperity by dumping debt of them for our benefit simply because we are unwilling to pay for those benefits.

Don't trust my comments. Check out the data from those reporting on federal expenditures. Look to publications, such as *The Economist*, that are likely to give insightful reports (such as that by a Harvard professor on the long term wage consequences of an influx of immigrant labor, the influx from Cuba three decades ago) than most popular American media. Be vigilant, the eternal price of liberty we are told, for future generations as well as for our own.

Musing 36: Repentance
(initially posted August 1, 2016)

What is repentance? Originally I had an answer in mind that would lead to what I had planned for the musing: our need to repent, i.e., change our way of looking at things so we take God's view of them and act according. That applies to us as individuals, as Christians collectively in our churches, and as Americans because our nation is heading in many bad directions.

Repentance does more than bring one to Christ initially, well summarized in the first of Martin Luther's 95 Theses (credited with initiating the Protestant Reformation in 1517). A thesis is a topic for academic and theological discussion. Luther's first one said: "When our Lord and Master Jesus Christ said, ``Repent'' (Matthew 4:17), He willed the entire life of believers to be one of repentance." We should always look at things as God does.

As I thought about repentance, this musing took a different direction than I planned.

I'm a snob about language. I respect words and try to use them with their primary meanings. Those cursing and using profanity to express anger or hurt instead of more precise words that say exactly what the person means show limited mental capabilities. Such is my snobbery.

Dictionaries define *repent* as "to affect oneself with contrition or regret for something done" and *repentance* as "the act of repenting." Most use the words so. As a Christian, I try to use words used in the Bible with the meanings the Bible gives to them, even when society may give them somewhat different connotations.

In the New Testament the primary Greek word translated by *repent* (metanaoeo, used about 50 times in verb or noun forms) means to change how one thinks about things, i.e., to change one's mind. That is how John the Baptist and Jesus used it. People need to look at things God's way, and act accordingly.

Then I realized I had not looked closely at how *repent* is used in the Old Testament.

A great deal of Jewish literature uses the Hebrew word (teshubah) in discussion of *repentance*. That word is based upon another Old Testament word (shub) with *repentance* connotations; it means a literal change of direction. Forms of this word occur nearly a thousand times in the Scripture, often translated by turn, return, and similar words; but only a dozen or so times is it translated by a *repentance* related word.

The primary word translated by *repent* in the King James Version of the Old Testament (nacham) means to be sorry or to pity and console oneself. Often it describes God's attitude in regard to things He did or planned to do with His people. I focused on the King James Version for exploration of *repent* words in the Old Testament because detailed information about the Hebrew words translated by the individual verses in the Old Testament are more readily available for the King James Version (thanks to *Strong's Exhaustive Concordance*) than for other translations of the Bible.

For the human side of *repentance*, my original intent for this musing applies. We need to change. Our attitudes need to line up with God's. That is something we need to do all the time, not just when a person comes to God initially. The need to look at things God's way all the time applies to us as individuals, as collections of Christians, and as a nation. That is always the best thing for us. Period.

Realizing that *repent* words are used of God more than a dozen times when God was the speaker or it was more than just what a person said or prayed, my thoughts turned to God's *repentance* (e.g., Gen. 6:6; Jud. 2:18; 1 Sam. 15:35; 2 Sam 24:16/1 Ch. 21:15; Jer. 4:28; 18:8, 10; 26:3; 31:19; Ezek. 24:14; Amos 7:3, 6; and Zech. 8:14). This was a direction for my musing that I had not anticipated when I chose to muse about *repentance*.

Several times God says He will not change His plans or actions, i.e., He will not repent. Several times God's sorrow and unhappiness about things causes Him to change what He was doing or planning to do; those changes could be catastrophic, as was the case of the flood in Noah's days. He says He will change His plans of evil on a people or individual if the person or group turns to Him away from evil ways. He says similar things about changing good plans for people who turn away from Him.

God, an infinite and omniscient being, is beyond total comprehension by finite creatures such as we are; yet many find it helpful to try to put *all* the Bible reveals about God in coherent and organized form so we can better understand Him and worship Him as He wants us to (Jesus said God wants us to worship Him "in spirit and in truth," John 4:24).

It is hard to put everything the Bible says about God together, such as how God can be Three Persons in One Godhead, or how passages about

God's *repentance* fit with other things the Bible says about God. Some translations use *relent* or similar words when a Hebrew word applies to God, but use *repent* for that same word for people; that makes it harder to fully understand *repentance*. I'm glad that God loves us and is good. For that, I trust Him; whatever He does, regardless of how it is described, is the proper thing that needs to be done. Trusting Him to be the good God that He is liberates me in so many ways. I just say, Thank you, God.

Musing 37: Whole Truth
(initially posted August 3, 2016)

Truth is important. This has long been recognized for legal proceedings, especially those which might result in execution of the guilty. Since at least the 13th century, in English courts sworn testimony has been a legally binding promise that it is "the truth, the whole truth, and nothing but the truth." American jurisprudence largely follows that tradition.

Whether one swears that oath or affirms it, whether it's in reference to God, etc. are issues at times, the following point is clear: content of testimony that should be trusted has three aspects: 1) the truth, 2) the whole truth, and 3) nothing but the truth.

Let's think about each of these.

What is truth? The Roman governor Pontus Pilate asked Jesus that question, but was not interested in His answer. Many today are as contemptuous and careless about truth as Pilate was.

Truth corresponds with reality. It is how things are. Things may not be how we want them to be or how we assume and expect them to be. Fact and fiction are not the same.

The whole truth is needed because just truth itself does not always leave a valid impression. Think about the example below of two true statements about a prominent person: preacher, doctor, ship captain, or someone else of prominence.

Statement 1: The preacher/doctor/captain was sober today.

Statement 2: The preacher/doctor/captain is always sober.

Would you have a different impression of the person from Statement 1 than from Statement 2? This shows why a true statement can give the wrong impression. That's why the whole truth is needed. Statement 1 is true, but not the whole truth. Statement 2 is the whole truth.

What about the restriction to nothing but the truth? Medicine has shown the importance of avoiding contamination. That's why surgical instruments are sterilized. That's why air is filtered in hospitals. That's why courts do not permit hearsay from witnesses.

Fact should not be confused with supposition. Unfortunately much presented to us by the media so mixes fact with supposition and other fantasies that little we see in the media is trustworthy. That applies to social media as much as it does to network TV. Unfortunately such also seems true of what comes from our educational system. It seldom distinguishes between fact and supposition (which at times is called "theory"). Often theories are presented as scientific laws, and students are seldom informed about that. Mixture of supposition with fact is a problem in hard sciences as well as elsewhere, but less frequently admitted there.

Lazy people are dolts. Thomas Jefferson warned that eternal vigilance is required to preserve liberty. Lazy Americans have frittered away much of our liberty. The vigilance needed to preserve liberty begins with insistence upon the truth, the whole truth, and nothing but the truth.

It is most unlikely that such will come from politicians. No politician of prominence in America for decades has addressed issues that way: dealing with the issue truthfully, looking at it from all perspectives so that the whole truth is evident, and not mixing anything with the truth so that fact is clearly distinguished from supposition and partisan ideology.

Why do politicians behave that way? Some are scoundrels; others understand laziness of the electorate and behave accordingly. The electorate responds more to emotion and party propaganda, with little regard for truth. They're as unconcerned about truth as Pilate was. "Decent politicians" (an oxymoron if there ever was one) play the game so they can be elected.

Is there any hope? Or are we doomed? Is watching America descend into depravity and chaos all we can do?

I don't know. We have to be concerned about truth for there to be any hope, but I don't see much likelihood of that. Perhaps a Money Bag with deep pockets who doesn't want America to destroy itself with indulgence could establish an institute to tell the truth and staff it with people committed to separating fact from fiction (not promoting particular philosophies or political agendas). That might make a difference, but who is likely to spend a few billion on such? If a trustworthy source for reliable information, i.e., information that clearly distinguished fact from supposition and other expressions of ideas, existed, people might pay attention and begin to give less attention to slop from media and politicians.

Even lazy indolent dolts sometimes get serious and make good decisions; at least fiction alleges such can happen in stories. It might not be too late.

Because it means a lot to me, I mention a personal aspect to the concept of whole truth for Christians. There are two different aspects of our lives and BOTH aspects are part of the whole truth. One aspect is the miserable reality of our fallible lives; we are a mess. At least I am and so are Christians I know. Even the Apostles were. Hot headed "sons of thunder" with a privilege-seeking mother, James and John. Christ denying Peter. Etc.

At the same time as we're such messes, the Bible says God sees those born-again in the righteousness of Christ. The whole truth is somehow both aspects are true at the same time. Fortunately, the fallible mess aspect is temporary; it's left behind when the saved enter eternity to be with God.

The truth, the whole truth, and nothing but the truth is important. Let's approach life appreciating the importance of truth and always emphasizing the whole truth, not just part of it.

I wish I could have presented a rosier picture for America's future, but it doesn't look that way to me. I hope I'm wrong.

Musing 38: Reality
(initially posted August 6, 2016)

For me, perception of reality has three components: speculation, supposition, and evidence. Though philosophical, I hope this musing provides insight and perspective.

Reality is where we are: physically, mentally, and spiritually. Speculative aspects of reality arise from imagination and include fiction, whether in what we read, see on TV, or just think. Sanity knows such is fiction and does not mistake it for something else. Fiction includes ideas about how things are, at times correct and at other times inconsistent with physical reality – as in fantasy, science fiction, or untrue history. We realize the fiction of novels, plays, poetry, and TV cartoons is not reality, but ideas and attitudes presented can shape how people think and act.

Supposition explains how we think reality is; supposition may just be an idea or include facts. When a supposition has general applicability, many call it "theory." Sometimes people assume things are facts proven by evidence when actually they are theories. For example, the idea nothing can go faster than the speed of light is associated with the theory of relativity; it's not a fact based upon testing maximum speed of every possible thing. Next to nothing other than its gravitational impact is known about most of our universe (the stuff of black energy and black matter); no meaningful measure-based comment can be made about potential speed limits on black matter.

We know aspects of reality based upon evidence, which we supplement with supposition and speculation to create what we understand about reality. I classify evidence as anecdotal or measured (with three varieties of measured).

Anecdotal evidence says what happens without detailed description of context and conditions under which results are obtained. Anecdotal evidence points in the direction of reality but without precise indication of why or interactions among factors involved. Most evidence aspects of reality people perceive are anecdotal.

In contrast, measured evidence contains substantial information about context and conditions of the measurements such as the range of temperature, pressure, moisture, and radiation pertinent for the measurement as well as estimated accuracy and uncertainties of the measurement.

"Facts" often are presented with limited information about conditions. For example, consider weight of a cubic foot of H_2O. Temperature determines whether the H_2O is ice, water, or steam; weight for a cubic foot of each varies significantly. A computer chip that works reliably in normal room conditions might not work reliably in an instrument orbiting the earth during a solar storm because of exposure to intense radiation. I categorize measurements as limited, substantial, or abundant.

Unfortunately America's education system generally fails to give students appreciation for how supposition is mixed with evidence in what they are taught.

Reality evidence may be based upon limited measurement. A particular item was measured only a few times by a few measurers. Such occurs for much of the information developed by contemporary science. Measurement evidence is limited because the measurements cost too much, take too long, or can only be done by one or two facilities. That creates opportunity for mistakes about the evidence.

More reliable reality evidence is based upon substantial measurements that come from dozens (or even hundreds) of experiments and observations with quality instruments by a number of different measurers. Such replication of results provides a rational basis for confidence in their validity. Descriptions of reality evidence with the greatest reliability come from abundant measurements based upon thousands (or many thousands) of experiments and observations.

It's easy see why perceptions of reality for many people, even well-educated people, are more based upon speculation and supposition than evidence. That kind of perception applies as much to atheists and agnostics as it does to religious people. Comments above suggest much of contemporary science is mainly supposition and those who accept its perspective as reality do so by faith (i.e., acceptance of suppositions in that perspective). Trust in those suppositions is as much a matter of faith as believing in God. The New Testament makes it clear faith is essential to please God: "without faith it is impossible to please God, because anyone who comes to Him must believe that He exists and that He rewards those who earnestly seek Him." Hebrews 11:6 (NIV).

Many are shocked when they realize much of modern perception of reality is supposition. Many things are wrongly presented as fact, such as the speed of light being the fastest possible speed, when actually they are supposition (i.e., theory).

Aspects of suppositions (such as scientific theories) are consistent with many observations and measurements. However, for years people observed things each day consistent with the supposition (theory) that the sun went around the earth. A supposition may be replaced by additional measurement-based evidence and a more correct supposition, as happened with the theory the sun circled the earth.

Christians have an advantage over others. Christians believe Jesus has given eternally reliable information about God and what pleases Him. Thus their beliefs have durability because they conform to reality, even though our present understanding of that reality is supposition (i.e., faith) based. What Jesus revealed about God will endure. PTL.

That is not the case for materialists. They have to keep changing basic ideas. For example, there was no idea of relativity two centuries ago, or of dark matter and energy a mere century ago. Who knows what will be next?

Not only do materialists have to keep changing their ideas, the Bible warns that rejection of the evidence from nature about God brings dire consequences (Romans 1:18-32) upon both the rejectors and their society. May God open the eyes of all to wisdom and reality.

Musing 39: Discrimination
(initially posted August 12, 2016)

My perspective on discrimination differs from that of many. I use the term to refer to situations in which members of a group are at a disadvantage or denied privileges simply because of membership in that group. This perspective on discrimination broadens it far beyond the narrow focus many give discrimination, only addressing it relative to particular racial groups and largely ignoring other discrimination. That approach not only is bad because it ignores discrimination of so many, but also bad because it distorts appropriate ways for the discriminated to behave and effective ways to deal with discrimination.

First, and this will be shocking to some because they fail to comprehend discrimination's vast scope if defined as I do, some discrimination is valid. For example, juveniles are denied the privilege of driver licenses; they are discriminated against in that way. Pre-adults are discriminated against in other ways also: only allowed to marry or conduct business legally with parental or guardian consent, etc. Such age discrimination is considered appropriate by most. Non-seniors are discriminated against when denied discounts or seating preferences offered to seniors when a broad perspective on discrimination is taken. Think of the social chaos from eliminating such age discrimination – as irresponsible agitators suggest sometimes.

Second, many groups have been discriminated against because of race or ethnicity, not just the group given most media attention in recent years. A few examples of such discrimination: government treatment of Native Americans such as restricting where they could live or travel; prohibition of immigration by Chinese for decades; and internment of people of Japanese descent during WWII.

Third, government efforts to compensate for past discrimination against some have discriminated against others. Consider discrimination resulting from Affirmative Action (AA): a bright student denied education at an elite university because the equivalent of 200-300 extra SAT points for AA status gave the slot at the university to an AA applicant, or the janitor unable to find a job because all job openings were filed by AA applicants. Such is as much discrimination (even though dictated by the courts) as past discrimination that AA was instituted to redress. There's another nasty consequence of such an approach: it provides a rational basis to question competence of everyone from an AA favored group because a less capable AA applicant may have gotten the job or education opportunity instead of a more qualified person.

"Politically correct" discussion of discrimination is selective about which discrimination can be considered and fails to address discrimination fully or with balanced perspective. Such retards real progress in improving relationships among groups within the US.

Fourth, a broad perspective on discrimination provides opportunity to discover better ways of overcoming discrimination than when a narrow view of discrimination is taken. The narrow approach to discrimination by government and media, with their emphasis on discrimination against blacks racially and women sexually, legalized reverse discriminations (as noted above) and brought the US to a point where relationships among groups in our diverse society are worse now than they used to be.

A broader perspective on discrimination can show ways some behaved when discriminated against which led to positive outcomes for the group. For example, consider discrimination against Asians and their response. It's easy to tell a person is Asian visually, making discrimination based upon appearance as easy against Asians as for any racial or ethnic group.

Extensive discrimination against Asians has been practiced for a century and a half; the 1882 Chinese Exclusion Act is the only US law to prevent immigration and naturalization on the basis of race. "Chinatowns" show Chinese were prevented from general distribution geographically. In the first half of the 20th century, people of Japanese descent experienced governmental and social restrictions similar to those experienced by Chinese. These government actions and discrimination socially by non-Asians were as prevalent as discrimination experienced by Afro-Americans.

How did Asians respond to such discrimination? In general, they focused on family and hard work, emphasizing education. Since many who originally came to the US from Asia were lower class economically and socially, it is unlikely that average IQ or other indications of mental and personal capabilities was greater for Asians coming to this country than for those of other races. Hence, the approach employed by Asians (focus on family, hard work, and education) may be the main reason for their success. Today Asians on the average have higher IQ scores, greater income, and less criminality than other racial group (blacks come in worse than whites or Asians in those categories). This is so even in the presence of continuing discrimination against Asians.

Other groups that experience significant discrimination might ask if the approach of the Asians might work for them. To do so would require those groups to deal with criminality if excessive within their group and an abundance of families without two parents in the home. Dealing with such would improve educational and income levels for the group more than protests or more laws discriminating against others to help overcome the group's limitations.

Of course that approach would not appeal to some; it removes financial rewards for professional agitators and leaders of protests. It also requires a group to change from blaming others or the system to looking within at things members of the group do that sabotages their future. Both of those factors make it unlikely for a group to take the Asian approach even though that approach has a proven track record of success. A narrow perspective on discrimination makes it far easier for the group to stay in a downhill rut, to continue to be considered as disadvantaged victims, than to make real progress.

Musing 40: Fame
(initially posted August 22, 2016)

Are you famous? It's a question that might be asked to one thought to be a TV celebrity, a sports champ, or otherwise well-known. It's most unlikely anyone will ever ask me that question. In an idle moment I pondered how I would respond if someone did ask if I were famous. In this musing I describe how I hope I would respond and then I explain why.

If asked, "Are you famous?" I would reply this way. "Perhaps; I'm a member of royalty, related to the king, and also I'm a priest. Does that make me famous? I'm on my way home where I will spend eternity; that's in heaven. You could join me there: I can tell you how."

My first comment about royalty might spark the person's interest, but comments about being a priest and heaven might send the person running, fleeing from a religious fanatic. Most people are afraid to have serious discussions about spiritual things. Perhaps they realize they might learn unpleasant things about themselves.

Why might I respond to the famous question this way? Everything I said is true. The Bible tells us every Christian, a person who's experienced the new birth, is a child of God, and He is King. The Bible also tells us Christians are a royal priesthood; every one of us is a priest expected to offer his or her life as a living sacrifice to God. Heaven is the destiny of every Christian; it will be our eternal home. The Apostle Peter urges Christians to be ready to explain to others the hope we have. That's why I would offer to tell the person asking the famous question how to become a Christian.

Fame is a danger we face. You may be shocked to hear that. Many seek fame and most do not discourage it. It feels good to be known by others; but it also encourages pride. The Bible warns of dangers associated with pride; God's does not like it when a person exalts him or herself. Desire for fame often is pride driven. That makes it dangerous. James warns not to presume a place of honor at a banquet, but to head for the low end of the table.

Behavior of many celebrities shows the dangers of fame, personally as well as spiritually. Do not seek fame; but if it comes your way, respond to it with as much humility as you can. Never let fame become your master.

This musing has turned preachy. I had not intended it to be so. Usually my musings present perspectives on the topic that may be helpful; sometimes the perspectives are not widely held and may be unfamiliar to the reader. That can help a person broaden his or her understanding of a topic. My presumption is that being realistic is important; so I try to be realistic in my musings. Realism allows life to be approached more successfully. Unfortunately, realism and ideology do not always coincide. Someone noted that history is not politically correct, and that makes it hard for those whose ideology emphasizes political correctness to honestly cope with the reality of history. Many political leaders engage in extensive revision of history so that it accommodates them, as Communists are well known for doing. Unfortunately that approach has also been done in this country.

One does not have to be famous for pride to be a problem. One of my musings mentioned my verbal snobbery. That's a place pride runs the risk of being excessive. Pride in speaking coherently and meaning what one says is not wrong, just as striving for a beautiful home or dressing attractively is not wrong in itself; but if such becomes too important so it distorts our relationship with God and others, then it is wrong.

I know a lot about pride. I have to deal with it in myself, and I have seen its deleterious impact on people at both ends of society, those within the church as well as outside it. I was involved with a major university (Johns Hopkins) for decades; that exposed me to people among the educated elite. Over the same decades I was involved extensively in ministry to prisoners; that exposed me to many on the lower end of the socio-economic scale. Some were proud of their accomplishments, whether notable in society's eyes, such as earning a PhD, or not admired by society, such as exalting in one's skill at shop lifting. In either case, pride can twist one's thinking; pride can cause a person to miss connection with God and to think of others in ways the Bible says God hates. Most people fail to appreciate how serious God is about anger toward a sibling or so looking down on another person by calling that person a fool; Jesus noted those things specifically in the Sermon on the Mount (Matthew 5:21-22).

Some claim not to care what God says. Time will change that attitude. When judgment day comes, everyone will know the importance of what God says. It's much better for a person to be concerned now about God's attitude about things than to come to appreciate the importance of God's attitude about thing at the Day of Judgment. I hope you are wise enough to be concerned about God's attitude now. The Bible is a good place to discover what God's attitude is about things.

God is very much a part of reality, having created all that is and continuing to sustain it. A realistic approach to life considers God and His attitudes about things; it is foolish to ignore Him.

Musing 41: Playing God
(initially posted August 23, 2016)

When asked what was the greatest commandment, Jesus quoted Deuteronomy 6:4-5 (to love God with all you are); He said the second greatest commandment is to love your neighbor as yourself (quoting from the end of Leviticus 19:18). As I read the passage in the Gospels where Jesus said that I realized I had not examined the context from which those Old Testament quotations come. So I read Deuteronomy 6 and Leviticus 19. You might want to do the same.

Leviticus 19 has a variety of instructions about how people should behave as well as how they should treat others. It is disturbing to see how many of those instructions are ignored and violated today in America. I believe that has dire consequences. What do you think?

Deuteronomy 6:4-5 begins the Shema (a prayer that many Jews recite morning and evening). Deuteronomy 6 not only says to love God totally, but also says to fear Him and warns of the dangers of ignoring Him or disobeying Him. Unfortunately most Americans, including many in our churches, mainly ignore God, treating Him and what He has said as optional curiosities. That behavior reminds me of a joke I heard long ago about a man who fell off a tall building; he said "Okay thus far" as he passed windows on his way to the ground.

The phrase, *playing God*, is used to describe a person doing something normally reserved to God, such as determining when to pull the plug for a person on life support or deciding who lives or dies in a dire situation where everyone cannot survive; the phrase is also used more loosely to defame an action the speaker does not like (as I hear some journalists do). I use the phrase *playing God* in a somewhat different way.

In my parlance, *playing God* applies when you decide you are the ultimate authority for what is right and wrong, for deciding what is truly important in your life. That perspective puts a very different flavor on *playing God*. No longer is it just something other people might do; it is now something you realize you have been doing, and consequences of doing that are serious!

The Bible is clear. God does not like for humans to assume His prerogatives. The first of the Ten Commandments demands He be the only one worshipped, the only ultimate authority. Nothing made by man or conceived by human imagination deserves recognition as divine; God is the only true God. Modern Americans recognize the foolishness of considering an idol created by a person as divine, but many people are not so clear headed about the folly of elevating humans in the same way when they make pleasing themselves the most important thing in their lives.

God is the proper One to identify what is right and good, and what is evil. When people elevate their own thoughts above God's revelation about such things they are *playing God* because they put themselves in the place of God as the authority about what is right and good, and what is evil. It is hard to imagine a more stupid way for a person to behave. Yet it is evident that many Americans choose to do that foolish thing, and even our government is guilty of doing it.

Some people are so foolish as to deny the Bible is revelation from God. Parents know how hard it can be to teach a child some things are dangerous and should never be done. Even after repeated warning, some children are foolish enough to stick their hands in fire, grab a hot pan, or poke a wire into an electrical outlet. The way many think about the Bible is as foolish as such behavior of children.

If someone reading this musing does not believe the Bible is revelation from God, I hope that person took the trouble to check the Bible out before coming to that conclusion because consequences of that belief can be dire. Many who have such wrong belief about the Bible have not read it with an open mind. There are many who initially approached the Bible, or a critical teaching from it such as the resurrection of Jesus, that came to believe in Jesus and recognize the Bible as revelation from God.

Some are impressed by glib comments about the Bible and dismiss it as religious myth without giving it serious consideration. Usually such a person has not read the Bible personally. Others in their adoration of humanity basically make ideas of the brightest people and those with academic acclaim their authority for right, wrong, and truth. Some of them are familiar with Biblical content, but approached the Bible presupposing it cannot be true because miracles don't happen; science not God explains how things are. They too are in a dire condition. I would not want to be in their shoes on judgment day.

My suggestion: each of us should read Deuteronomy 6 and ask ourselves if we see God as He says we should. If not, I hope wisdom will cause us to change so we seek to see God as He says we should. Then I would recommend we read Leviticus 19 and ask ourselves if we understand how it says we should behave. If our beliefs or actions are not consistent with what God says is the right way; I hope we will change.

Following these suggestions will help us to obey what Jesus says are the two greatest commandments. I hope that is a goal of everyone who reads this musing.

Musing 42: Apostles
(initially posted August 25, 2016)

Apostle has several connotations. It is applied to the Twelve disciples whom Jesus chose to be with Him during His public ministry on earth. Later a thirteenth replaced Judas, the one betraying Jesus to Jewish authorities. The Twelve had a special function; they were witnesses of what Jesus said and did, especially His resurrection. Two of the Twelve wrote Gospels (Matthew and John); a third Gospel (Mark) is thought to reflect the preaching and teaching of Peter (another of the Twelve).

However, these men are not the only people identified as *apostles* in the New Testament. About twenty are identified as apostles; the most well know of those not among the Twelve is Paul (Saul of Tarsus). There is no indication the ones outside the Twelve had been with Jesus extensively during His public ministry, therefore they were not direct witnesses to the life and teachings of Jesus. Why then were these identified as *apostles*?

Their function made them apostles. When I was a youngster, my pastor said an apostle was a penny, making a pun on the meaning of the word. A penny is "one cent" and the meaning of the Greek word (apostolos) translated as *apostle* in the New Testament is "one sent." An apostle is a delegate, a messenger.

In that sense, every Christian missionary is an apostle; and in a very real way every Christian should be an apostle representing Christ to others. Unfortunately many do not take that responsibility very seriously.

This musing is about the Twelve. Luke 6 says Jesus went to the mountainside and spent the night in prayer; then in the morning called His disciples to Himself. From that group He picked twelve and named them *apostles*. Some of that larger group apparently was with Him like the Twelve. After the risen Christ ascended into heaven, Peter spoke to a group of 120 followers of Jesus and said that in fulfillment of Scripture it was necessary to replace Judas. "[21] Therefore it is necessary to choose one of the men who have been with us the whole time the Lord Jesus was living among us, [22] beginning from John's baptism to the time when Jesus was taken up from us. For one of these must become a witness with us of his resurrection." [23] So they nominated two men: Joseph called Barsabbas (also known as Justus) and Matthias." (Acts 1:21-23)

I've been trying to image what it was like for the Twelve. Apparently they (and perhaps a number of others) basically were with Jesus most of the time for several years. Even casual reading of the Gospels shows Jesus often was away from Nazareth (where His parents and siblings lived) and from Capernaum (which seems to be the place He called home as an adult). He went to Jerusalem at least once a year (about 85 miles from Capernaum). He went to places a day's walk (15-30 miles) from Capernaum: Caesarea Philippi, Cana, Nain, and Nazareth. He also went farther (about 50 miles) to Sidon and to the Decapolis. The Twelve went with Him.

At least one of the Twelve (Peter) had a wife. It is likely others of the Twelve also were married. What happened to their families when the Twelve traveled with Jesus? Where did money for food come from? Where did the Twelve sleep when they were with Jesus? A dozen plus guys take up a lot of room, even if they sleep on the floor, in the barn, or outside. The New Testament is silent about such things. Use your imagination and try to think it through. You may be surprised at insights you get when you do.

An insight came as I thought about these things; it was appreciation for the commitment of the Apostles to Jesus. Several times Jesus scolds the Twelve for their lack of faith and understanding. The Gospels give unfavorable impressions of their faith by contrasting it with faith that amazes Jesus (a centurion seeking healing for a servant, a woman healed by touching Jesus' robe, a Gentile woman begging for her daughter to be healed, friends of a lame man that tore open a roof). I wondered why Jesus bothered with the Twelve, given their lack of faith and understanding. Then it hit me as I pondered the way things were as the Twelve went about with Jesus. They were committed to Him. They let the normal claims of life on them go so they could be with Jesus. They tried to do what He told them to do, even though their faith and understanding were limited. They sought to please Him, even when they fell down on the job as they did sleeping when told to pray. Their commitment to Him was why He chose them.

Perhaps you will get insights that are helpful to you as you ponder how things were when the disciples traveled with Jesus. I hope so. I hope you will try to think about other things in the Bible too, to fill in the gaps with your imagination and do it in ways consistent with what the Bible says, what is known about the historical circumstances, and your understanding of people. As you do that, I think God will give you insights that increase your understanding of God's truth and of His direction for your life.

I hope that both you and I follow the example of the Twelve and are totally committed to Jesus, even when our faith is not as great as we want and our understanding is limited. Those deficiencies should not limit our commitment to Him.

Musing 43: Consequences
(initially posted August 28, 2016)

Actions have consequences; intentions don't. An indulgent parent may intend to make the child happy, but produce a brat. An old adage warns the road to hell is paved with good intentions. Some think that adage began with Bernard of Clairvaux (about 1150 A.D.), and others find similar ideas as far back as Virgil's *Aeneid* (about 20 B.C.). That adage has provided valuable insight for a long time.

After the First World War there was an effort to separate ethnic groups previously mixed in the Ottoman Empire for centuries; unmixing the populations was viewed as a road to peace in the Near East (an area we now call the Middle East). Leaders of that effort included Fridtof Nansen, a Norwegian artic explorer, Nobel Peace Prize winner, and first League of Nations Commissioner for Refugees; that effort led to the 1923 Lausanne Convention. They had good intentions: they wanted to make the area more peaceful. Brilliant and good people led the effort. Their good intentions forced relocation of a million and a half people and laid the groundwork for sectarian violence that has plagued that region for the past century. It should be noted that previously although the area was troubled frequently by turbulence, there had been peace generally among the different ethnic groups in that region for centuries; there were no genocides or sectarian crusades such as have occurred since the Lausanne Convention. I see this effort of great people as a classic failure of good intentions.

It is not enough to have good intentions. One must ensure actions to implement the good intentions do not produce untoward consequences. Many fail to do that. It takes hard work to make sure the issue has been addressed honestly and comprehensively so that unexpected and untoward consequences are avoided. Many have trouble looking at things honestly and objectively because of ideological biases; this is one of the reasons political correctness has trouble with the reality of history. History is not PC.

The indulgent parent should have thought about potential consequences from catering to the child. The adage based upon Proverbs 13:24 warns: "spare the rod and spoil the child." Currently it is not politically correct to use the rod because of overreaction to abusive misuse of the rod; time will show consequences of that change in attitude about corporal punishment of children and to other changes in disciplining children.

American has changed a great deal during my lifetime. Some of the changes have been good. They corrected things that long needed to be corrected, but some of the changes, though motivated by good intentions, are likely to cause great harm to our nation as those changes are currently implemented. Many are passionate about the changes, rejoicing that they have occurred; but few seem to have given the changes the kind of careful and comprehensive consideration necessary to ensure the change does not have undesirable consequences. Promotors of the Lausanne Convention were passionate about their endeavor, and loudly proclaimed its expected benefits. However, its consequences have been horrendous.

The indulgent parent can point to many benefits for the child and perhaps for the parents from such indulgence, but that is an incomplete presentation of the situation. They fail to apply sound principles, such as espoused in the Bible; consequences of that can be bad.

The situation with some of the changes in America during the past half-century is similar. You may want to give them careful consideration and see which you think may fail to apply sound principles which have long proven themselves, such as insights from the Bible. If you find changes which have that characteristic, you might want to talk with others about them. Those with strong feelings about something, such as being a proponent for a change or an opponent to a change, often have attitudes similar to the mental disorder psychologists call "denial" (the refusal to acknowledge the existence or severity of unpleasant external realities or internal thoughts and feelings). Their attitude may make it difficult for them to honestly deal with the reality of the situation and consequences related to it. Their intentions can skew their thinking.

I choose not to identify changes in America during the last half century which I think have potential to harm our nation. I do that in the hope it will encourage all to think carefully and comprehensively about our nation, where it used to be heading and where it is now heading. If I indicate changes I think are good or bad, those who see things similarly may applaud but neither they nor those with different perspectives are likely to give serious consideration to things. Perhaps my silence here will cause some to look at things carefully to see if they think any of the directions America is going could be bad for us. That is my hope.

Nations have roller coaster histories. They go through good periods and bad. They have wise and effective leaders at times, and at other times no one would call their leaders wise or effective. Some are conquered by others, and some just fall apart from internal problems. Forms of government change. Populations get mixed. However people seem to be pretty much the same as they have been for a long time. Their technology, clothing, and behaviors may change, but the essence of their personalities (mental characteristics such as motivations) seems relatively constant as far as literature and information indicates.

My belief: some directions in which America is heading will be bad for it. I hope you will check that out for yourself, and decide what you think.

Musing 44: Audacious Proposals (initially posted August 31, 2016)

These two proposals touch sensitive points: taxes and race. Whether or not you agree with what I say, I hope you will give the proposals careful consideration; both are important.

A Tax-related Proposal. I do not enter the fray about tax rates and how much of taxes different segments of the population pay. I address shift of tax burden by tax privilege for some. Inappropriateness of such tax privilege is what I address.

Special tax privilege should be related to importance to the nation. If one assumes no job in the US is more important to the nation than that of the American President, then it is inappropriate to grant tax privileges to anyone being paid more than the President. Two tax privileges are addressed. One is compensation in organizations granted non-profit status by the IRS. Some non-profits compensate personnel more than compensation for the US President (which currently is 8 times median household income in the US). Non-profit status allows an organization to avoid taxes it otherwise would pay; others have to pay more taxes than they would if the non-profit organization did not have tax privilege.

I propose limiting compensation in a non-profit to no more than compensation for the US President. That amount puts one in the top 1% of tax payers with 8 times average household income, not an unreasonable limit on personnel compensation for a non-profit. If an organization needs to pay more to personnel, it can do so BUT not as a non-profit. The organization gets to choose: higher pay for personnel or non-profit status.

Another part of my tax-related proposal concerns businesses. Many pay top personnel more than the US President. That compensation is considered a business expense and reduces business profit, which is the basis of taxes paid. Excessive compensation (i.e., the amount greater than compensation of the US President) should come from business profit, and not be a business expense because it makes others bear additional taxation; excessive compensation removes profit from tax consideration because such compensation is considered a business expense.

I do not know how much (or how little) the tax burden on the rest of us would change if excessive compensation (i.e., the amount above what the US President gets) were considered profit for businesses and forbidden to organizations with non-profit status, but it would correct an injustice that increases the tax burden on the rest of us. Let your legislator know what you think about this proposal.

I do not suggest restricting compensation an organization or business may offer its personnel; I merely require they accept tax consequences of what they do and not impose additional tax burdens on others. This attitude is reasonable unless you claim the huge salary given a college football coach or the outrageous compensation of a media celebrity is more important to the nation than the job of US President. You would have to claim the one getting such excessive compensation (i.e., more that the US President gets) was merited because the job of the person is more important to America than that of the US President.

A Race-related Proposal. Racial issues have become so polarized in recent years that meaningful communication seldom occurs between people with different racial or ethnic backgrounds. My proposal is simple: leaders of the black community need to clean up the way the black community behaves.

It is unlikely those outside the black community can do that; it's possible even leaders of the black community cannot clean up that behavior, which is excessive serious criminality: murder, rape, assault, etc. Over 90% of black people murdered are killed by blacks. The rate of criminality by blacks is several times higher than for any other racial group in the US. Some within the black community want to shift blame from the black community to society, to poverty, to discrimination, to bias by police and courts, etc. However, facts don't support such blame sifting. For example, in the 1940s and 1950s, black poverty was far greater than today and discrimination was also greater; yet rates of murder, rape, etc. by blacks then were significantly lower than now. That makes it clear poverty and discrimination are not dominant causes of black criminality.

If leaders of the black community are to clean up the black community, they have to give that primary attention instead of focusing their efforts in less significant areas. For example, family stability is thought to be an important factor in criminality of the black community. Births to unwed mothers have soared in the black community in the past 60-70 years. The vast majority of black births now are to unwed mothers; this coincides with an increase in black criminality. Leaders of the black community have potential to change attitudes of the black community. They could make it socially unacceptable for black males to impregnate and later abandon the woman and child; they could make unwed motherhood unacceptable socially in the black community. Leaders of the black community can determine what might reduce excessive black criminality and work on that instead of looking for scapegoats elsewhere to blame.

It will take courage for a leader of the black community to do what I suggest; too many in the black community have vested interest in exploiting current racial tensions financially, politically, and socially. Exploiters will not welcome leaders of the black community who get serious about addressing excessive black criminality.

I did not specify causes or solutions. My audacious proposals will be ignored by most. One proposal hits pocketbooks of elites; the other has politically incorrect racial implications. Some may respond with hostility because of greed or racism. I hope others will think carefully about the proposals; then act as they think appropriate.

Musing 45: Mental Balance
(initially posted September 2, 2016)

This musing is about mental balance, not physical skill. Mental balance avoids the hysterical or mistaken belief that disaster is imminent. For 25 centuries folk tales warned of the folly of lacking mental balance. I first encountered one as a child when I heard the story of Chicken Little. In the version I heard Chicken Little claimed "The sky is falling!" because an acorn hit her on the head. Mid-19th century versions of the story had Chicken Little startled by a leaf falling on her tail.

Chicken Little rushes off to warn the king of impending catastrophe, collecting others as she goes. The story ends in a variety of ways. In some, Chicken Little and those with her are lured to the den of a fox and eaten. In other versions of the story, they survive. The folly of making a mountain out of a molehill is clear in all versions. Unfortunately, folly from lack of mental balance is not restricted to silly fowls; it appears in people, some of whom are brilliant, educated, and accomplished.

Lack of mental balance shows in failure to prepare for the future. Aesop, an ancient Greek famous for fables, tells of a grasshopper and an ant, warning of consequences from failure to prepare for what's coming. The grasshopper just enjoys the abundance of summer while the ant works hard collecting food to prepare for winter when food is less available. Consequently the grasshopper does not survive the winter because of failure to prepare for it.

Grasshopper behavior abounds in America. People build homes in areas prone to flood, earthquake, fire, and storms. Many expect others to foot the bill for their losses when the calamity occurs, just as the grasshopper turned to the ant asking for food during the winter. Others indulge in addictive behaviors that keep them from being able to provide for themselves. Whether the addiction is to alcohol and drugs, to adrenaline from life threatening sport, or to unaffordable indulgence in luxury, it shows a lack of mental balance. They too, like the grasshopper, expect others to provide for them.

How can you avoid being a grasshopper or a Chicken Little? How do you get and keep mental balance? A very important question. I hope you ask it.

Lack of balance is not a new problem. It did not first appear in modern times; it's been with us for thousands of years, as illustrate by folk tales I mention above. Those folk tales are part of the way society tried to prevent lack of balance by showing its folly. Effective guidance for its prevention (or correction) is not as easy as demonstrating the stupidity of a lack of mental balance.

First, one has to be realistic. Reasonable appreciation of the situation is essential. That includes consequences from actions, what the future might bring, and consideration of other reasons for things. Chicken Little concluded the sky was falling from the acorn or leaf that hit her and did not consider other possible explanations. Those building in a location which has major floods several times a century ignore reality. Adrenaline addicts seem like teenagers, believing they are invincible and never imagine themselves confined to a wheelchair and dependent upon others for life because of injuries from their activities.

Second, one has to be honest. It's not fair to impose on others to do for you what you should do for yourself. Don't expect or demand others support you or pay for consequences of your folly. Stand on your own feet. Use sense and provide for yourself, preparing for the future. Unfortunately that perspective conflicts with aspects of current political correctness.

Most Americans fail to put aside enough to live comfortably during retirement. After indulging in entertainment such as cruises and shows, expensive hobbies, more expensive housing and cars, they have too little left to put aside for the future. Such shows lack of mental balance.

Third, be diligent. Use a realistic appraisal of your situation and your interests to determine what you need to do to achieve your goals with due regard to dangers and opportunities. Be honest in what you think others should do that would help you (or hinder you). Then act wisely.

During my lifetime America has changed in many ways. Some good; and some that concern me because I think they lead America in bad ways. A musing is too short (a thousand words or less) to address such in detail. Let me simply say I am concerned about diminished emphasis on self-reliance and increased emphasis on self-indulgence. I will illustrate this with one example from the federal government.

Our government irresponsibly put cost of benefits for us on the backs of coming generations. That's what the national debt does. We're unwilling to pay the cost of government, services and protection it provides us. By spending more than we have, we impose payment for benefits to us on others. How shameful we are.

In dire emergencies, borrowing from the future is reasonable; otherwise it is a reprehensible burdening of others for our benefit. Four times the federal deficit (i.e., more spent than came in) reached 10% of GNP: during the Civil War, WWI, WWII, and the Obama years. The deficit did not reach that high during the nation's first seven decades, in the Great Depression, or in other hard times. Changing attitudes in America magnify our present situation so we act like it's a dire situation like WWI or WWII, and have a federal deficit of 10%. Shame on us and especially our leaders, for our self-indulgence, making others support our benefits.

Musing 46: Jews
(initially posted September 6, 2016)

As I read Isaiah 40 one morning I thought about my attitude toward the Jews. Its words are very familiar since the first two vocal segments of Handel's Messiah (*Comfort ye, comfort ye, my people"* and *Ev'ry valley shall be exalted*) come from Isaiah 40. The music also came to mind as I read Isaiah 40 that morning, and I realized I had never examined my attitude about Jews in light of the passage.

In general, I think of Jews I know as people and treat them with the same respect and consideration I show to non-Jews. I don't believe I treat Jews differently than I do non-Jews. One of my son's best friends during middle school was Jewish; they stayed overnight at one another's homes and we attended his Bar Mitzvah.

I considered the Jewish nation chosen by God to be the people the Messiah would come from, but that they were set aside as God's people on earth after rejecting Jesus the Messiah (Christ) until He returns, when they again will have a special place in God's plan. Those who follow Jesus are God's people on earth now, the period between the first and second coming of the Messiah to earth.

My attitude toward the modern nation of Israel is mixed. I think that nation often deserves the criticism it receives from the U.N. and cannot be proud of its abusive treatment of Palestinians. Jewish responses to bad actions toward it are far harsher and more abusive than what Palestinians do to Israelis. U.S. policy toward Israel does not always coincide with the best interest of our country; whether this occurs because of Jewish influence within the U.S., skewed and unrealistic political attitudes by some Christians about the nation Israel, or for other reasons I do not know.

As I read Isaiah 40 that morning, I came to appreciate God's love for the Jews more than I had previously. They are precious to Him. The sermon I heard the previous Sunday emphasized God loves us, not just when we're being good but also in other times too. He loves us *all the time*. In reading Isaiah 40 that morning, I realized that is also true of the Jews; He loves them now, even while most of them reject His Messiah. That caused me to rethink my attitude and behavior toward Jews.

I do not know all that will result from my change in attitude, but I expect there will be some changes. Already I've begun to include Jews specifically in my prayers for those who do not know Jesus the Christ as their Savior; I ask that they begin to see the truth about Him and turn to Him for salvation. Previously I had not included Jews as a distinct group in that kind of prayer. From time to time I include specific groups in my prayers: people in areas of particular trouble, such as those flooded in Louisiana, those in earthquake areas in Italy, those in Syria, etc.

My relationship at this time in my life with most whom I know to be Jewish is that of acquaintance. None are people I interact with frequently or spend much time with. Most of my social activities involve family members or Christian friends. Time will tell if that changes.

Thinking about my attitude toward Jews caused me to expand my perspective and think about my attitude toward all. As I did, I put it in the context of loving God. Jesus said to love Him by obeying His commandments. That obedience shows our love for God and failure to obey His commands shows lack of love for God. Hard words from John 14.

Leviticus 19 has a collection of laws God gave the Jewish people. Jesus identified the later part of verse 18 as the second greatest commandment (to love your neighbor as yourself). Later in that chapter, it says to treat the foreigner among you the same way as you treat your neighbor. The chapter also says to be honest and truthful, and show mercy to the poor and needy. That kind of behavior is essential if one loves God, which Jesus said is the greatest commandment.

That kind of living challenges most of us; we seldom are that way *all the time*. It gets even more demanding for Christians, the people who believe Jesus is God's Messiah and turn to Him for salvation. Jesus says they are to love one another even more than they are to love their neighbors. For the neighbor, the requirement is to love them as you love yourself. For fellow Christians, the requirement is to love the other believer as Jesus loves you! WOW!

Isaiah 40 set me on a trek that is life changing. My attitudes require adjusting. I suspect yours may too if you are a person who loves God and understands what Jesus said about the way our love for God shows itself. The trek for me started with review of my attitude about Jews. It moved from there to what Jesus said about obedience showing our love for God. Then it went to my treatment of others (neighbors and foreigners) and finally to my treatment of fellow Christians.

I don't know what kind of trek you may take if you begin to think about these things. You might want to read Isaiah 40, John 14, and Leviticus 19. They are where you find ideas presented in the Bible that I note in this musing. *Obedience to God is always best.* Honest interaction with God's truth is always challenging, but rewarding (and often depressing in how far I fall short).

Musing 47: The World Is Wrong
(initially posted September 9, 2016)

In John 16:8 Jesus tells His disciples that when the Advocate (the Holy Spirit) comes to them as He promised, that the Holy Spirit "will prove the world to be in the wrong about sin and righteousness and judgment" (NIV). This musing is about the world being wrong.

What is "the world" in this context? Obviously it is not the third rock from the sun, as some refer to our planet. Jesus meant something different than the dirt beneath our feet. A hint at what He meant comes from the most famous verse in the Bible, John 3:16. "For God so loved the world that He gave His one and only Son, that whoever believes in Him shall not perish but have eternal life." (NIV)

The *Oxford English Dictionary* (*OED*) has 27 definitions related to *world*, many of which had several distinctive nuances (6 or 7 nuances for some). There are probably 75-100 connotations for *world* in the *OED* (I did not count them) with the first instance of its written use with that connotation for each. The Greek word (*kosmos*) translated as *world* in John 3:16 has a lot of connotations also with largely the same spectrum of meanings as for the English word *world*.

The Apostle John uses the word *world* (*kosmos*) far more than any other New Testament author; about half of the occurrences of the word in the New Testament come from him. The two primary connotations for *world* (*kosmos*) by John are people (as in John 3:16) and the mundane way of looking at life apart from God that is commonly done (as in the John 16:8 reference I started the musing with). That second connotation (the mundane way of looking at things without concern about God) is the one the Bible says the Holy Spirit will prove to be wrong.

I consider realism to be the essence of sound thinking. Many consider a person insane who cannot comprehend normal reality. For example, that is how most would consider a man who was convinced he was a historical character (such as Napolean or Julius Caesar) or someone made famous by literature (such as Romeo or Sherlock Holmes).

Likewise people unable to comprehend or accept reality are likely to hurt themselves and others. Most would consider a person nuts who thought he could fly and wanted to jump from a tall building to prove he could fly. Likewise a person who thought poisons were simply a reflection of bad thoughts and had no real harm would be considered a crazy menace who might serve something poisonous at a meal.

The same kind of faulty thinking can occur in other areas as well. Some think if you cannot observe it, then it can't be real. Not so. Scientists, especially those concerned with astronomy and the nature and history of the universe realize the majority of what exists in our universe cannot be seen by us or observed by current technology. "Dark matter" and "dark energy" are labels given to what is believed to comprise the majority of our universe. Recognition of dark matter and energy's existence is recent, within the past century. Behavior of things we can see cannot be explained without postulating existence of such stuff; all we know about dark matter and dark energy is its gravitational impact on things that are observable.

The world, that "mundane way of looking at life apart from God," is as unrealistic as a person who says if it can't be seen then it ain't real when talking about the nature and history of the universe. The world is wrong when it ignores God in human affairs. As such, Jesus said it was wrong about sin, righteousness, and judgment in the John 16:8 passage. Jesus explains what He meant in the next three verses: "[9] about sin, because people do not believe in me; [10] about righteousness, because I am going to the Father, where you can see me no longer; [11] and about judgment, because the prince of this world now stands condemned." (NIV)

Sin brings death; God's way to life is through Jesus. The world by ignoring God and Jesus miss the only way to life; hence, the world is wrong about sin. Righteousness is possible for people because of Christ's victory over sin and death, demonstrated by His return to the Father. Hence the world by ignoring Him misses the only way to righteousness; showing the world wrong in that regard. Finally by ignoring God and essentially denying His right to judge His creation, the world is wrong about judgment as those in the world will discover on the Day of Judgment. God is God, and He will judge His creation.

Those in the world, i.e., people who approach life in a mundane way and look at it apart from God are as unrealistic as any noted above. Consequences of disregarding God are as serious as the mistaken self-identification of an insane person, or as the serving of poisonous substances to others while thinking the substances are okay. The person who ignores God and His revelation is as likely to make good life decisions as a scientist is likely make correct calculations who ignores relativistic effects or as an astronomer trying to correctly compute galaxy rotation while ignoring gravitational effects of dark matter and dark energy.

Human egotism promotes the idea of people as the ultimate species and stimulates a world view that fails to accept, acknowledge, and appreciate God presence in our universe, His impact on things, and His perspective on right and wrong. The world is wrong. Beware.

Musing 48: Blasphemy
(initially posted September 16, 2016)

Blasphemy is "profane speaking of God or sacred things; impious irreverence." In the past, it also was used to mean "slander, evil speaking, defamation," but that connotation for the word is now considered obsolete.

In America today, blasphemy is not taken seriously. Even a brief exposure to a standup comic's routine, whether in person, broadcast on TV, or seen on the internet is likely to include blasphemy. Sadly audiences not only tolerate such irreverence; they enjoy it. That shows an unpleasant aspect of the character of our people: lack of respect for holiness.

What would you think of a person who teased a blind person by asking what he was pointing to, or the rascal tormenting a paralyzed person by holding what they requested out of reach deliberately? Most would condemn such despicable behavior. Why then do people tolerate blasphemy? It is similar behavior to the despicable actions just described.

Sometimes things considered holy do not deserve that status. The Bible says critical things about idols, at times making fun of them and of those who made them or give an idol reverence. Of course, a person's recognition of what is truly holy is not always correct. This is illustrated both by the mistaken reverence some give to idols (believing wrongly that thing was holy) and by the rejection of Jesus by Jewish leadership of His day (failing to recognize that He was and is the Holy One).

Blasphemy implies one of two conditions. First, the person may be unconcerned about the danger of blasphemy; or second, the person may have decided that what he comments on is not holy and therefore what he says is not really blasphemy even if some consider it such. I say a few words about each of these.

Many Americans are unconcerned about the danger of blasphemy. Our society no longer has the reverence it once showed the Bible and what it says; nor is there as much general knowledge about what the Bible says as there once was. This change in Americans allows more expression of evil in our hearts in blasphemy. It's frightening to realize how callous that makes our society.

More serious are those who decide the God of the Bible and His Son Jesus are not divine and therefore however irrelevant they may speak and act, it is not blasphemy in their eyes. Of course, only a small portion of the population formally admits that attitude, but many act is if that is what they believe. I include both sets of people in those who face serious danger from God because of blasphemy.

In the multi-cultural society that characterizes modern America, there are many beliefs about God and many things considered sacred. Political correctness says all such beliefs should receive equal respect and be given equal dignity, implying truth is unimportant since it is politically incorrect to say a particular religious belief or practice is wrong or does not deserve respect.

That politically correct attitude does not deal with reality. There are phonies around in religious realms as well as elsewhere. From involvement with jail and prison inmates for four decades, I realize there are bogus religious ideas as well as religious con men and women. A classic example of such is Harry W. Theriault's Church of the New Song. As an inmate, Theriault in 1970 initiated a law suit seeking recognition by the court of the religion he started. During the 1970s Threiault and the Church of the New Song received attention in the press and in court, but it had nothing real to do with God and is generally recognized as an inmate's way of agitating the prison system for notoriety and additional privileges within the prison. Religious silliness can be found in society, not just in jails and prisons. Movies of the 1930s abound with séances, Ouija boards, and other aspects of divination (such as palm reading). A realistic attitude calls these silly, as they are.

These sillinesses show the dual dangers of blasphemy. One danger is to elevate something wrongly to a place of reverence; and the other danger is to dismiss truly holy things, such as Christ and the Bible, as if they had no more spiritual substance than such silly things. It takes wisdom and courage to stand firmly for truth about God.

Unfortunately there is danger some will distort true religion, as was done centuries ago with extreme claims about benefits from indulgences (criticized by both Protestants and Catholics) and today by those who fake miraculous faith healings.

How a person, such as I, who recognizes Jesus as the divine Son of God and the only way to a living relationship with the one true God should deal with other religions such as Judaism, Islam, and Eastern beliefs is a touchy subject because it involves both truth and respect for others. I cannot be faithful to the Bible and to my belief in Jesus if I say anyone might have a good relationship with God except through Jesus Christ. At the same time I respect all people and understand they have a right to believe and behave as they choose except when such poses explicit harm for others. That kind of tolerance has problems, Some think it is disrespectful if I say non-Christians are wrong; and I compromise important beliefs if I do not challenge legal and currently accepted practices which I think pose explicit harm to others (such as abortion which takes the life of a fetus, or homosexuality which the Bible says is a perversion). Dealing with such makes one think seriously about blasphemy.

Musing 49: Democracy
(initially posted September 19, 2016)

Democracy, the idea of government for the people controlled by the people reaches back to ancient Greece, but expressed in many different ways. Historically democracy was feared and lambasted by leading thinkers as well as praised and encouraged. Scholars say the ancient Athenian concept of democracy was more like Lenin's dictatorship of the proletariat than what is promoted as democracy by Western nations.

I add my connotation of democracy as a form of government to the plethora of connotations that exist. At least ten modern countries have *Democratic* in their country's name; more than half of them (such as North Korea) are authoritarian regimes. This illustrates how varied connotations of democracy can be. My connotation for democracy (from a portmanteau word in Greek that combines words for *people* and *power*) is *"a government that treats its entire population fairly and with respect, whose leaders are selected by a significant portion of the population."*

Most modern concepts of democracy are "representative democracy" where those with political power represent the people; in ancient Greece, the people themselves were the ones with political power. Those people, the ones with political power, were a subset of adult male citizens and excluded many residents; for example, a famous and respected resident of Athens, Aristotle, was not considered a citizen and never had political power in Athenian democracy.

Some wrongly equate democracy with permitting everyone to vote (i.e., universal franchise or suffrage). Every government restricts who has a say in selecting government leaders. Sometimes a small, select group determines who the leaders will be. In some governments, that group directly chooses the leaders; in others, that group chooses ones the population can select from. In other countries, selection of leaders involves a large portion of the population.

Even when a large portion of the population selects leaders, franchise is limited. Usually only citizens of the country are allowed to vote or participate in selection of leaders (non-citizens residing in a country normally are not allowed to vote). Every country has age restrictions for voting; this prohibits youngsters from voting or having a say in leader selection. Some also restrict franchise based upon gender, ethnicity, religious affiliation, property ownership, intellectual competence, criminal history (e.g., most felons in the U.S. can't vote), or other factors. I'm not aware of studies that correlate quality of government treatment of its citizens with franchise extent. Many assume (without evidence) that broad franchise (i.e., one granting most people the privilege of voting) is better than narrow franchise (i.e., one restricting who can vote); this assumption may come from careless and haphazard thinking or emotional response.

In every government, some of the population receive preferential treatment and others are denied fair treatment. Segments of the society oppose one another and antagonize one another. Leaders tend to implement policies reflecting ideas of those who put them into power, which in a democracy can lead to tyranny of the majority. A diverse society may not have coherent ideas about what is right or good for the nation; for example, it may legitimize things some consider immoral or criminal. This is illustrated in America: things once considered criminal are now legal and things previously considered legal are now considered to have been atrocious. Abortion, and homosexuality are examples of the first, and slavery is an example of the second. Data show as franchise increases, the portion of a nation's wealth spent by the government increases, leaving less to discretion of the individual and thereby reducing individual freedom regarding how his or her resources are used.

This musing does not suggest solutions; I hope to stimulate people to think carefully about issues related to democracy. This includes how fair and respectful treatment of all in the county is ensured, both for minorities and for the majority. This requires far more than mouthing a party line; it requires grappling with different perspectives to determine what should be given to all, what opportunities should be available to all, and what responsibilities fall upon all (for example is it right for government to take money by force [taxes are such] from hard working responsible citizens to provide free medical care for scumbags who though healthy choose not to work and expect government to provide life's necessities). Such fundamental issues are seldom addressed clearly and explicitly. Likewise the extent of franchise needs careful consideration. Allowing people with no knowledge of issues or candidate qualifications to participate in selecting leaders is stupid; that selects leaders on the basis of promised benefits (regardless of who has to pay for them), non-functional factors such as how handsome or cute a candidate may be, influence of others on the voter, etc. I believe this is a primary reason there is little correlation between quality of government and extent of franchise. Things were different in the early days of our nation; franchise was severely limited. Our first president was selected by only 5-6% of the population.

Many think the government then dealt with challenging issues it faced after a war on our soil better than our governments of the past century would have done; this suggests it might be useful to rethink our attitude about extent of franchise – more may not be better.

As people think carefully about issues related to democracy, many previously assumed truisms will begin to show their warts. That should cause each to look at the issue more carefully and begin to have a more realistic attitude about what would be good for our nation. If enough people begin to think carefully that way, it will be good for the nation and for each of us.

Musing 50: Government
(initially posted October 2, 2016)

I never took a fresh look at government. I just assumed the American government was basically sound, at least in theory; I recognized it often did not live up to its ideals. In college and by my own reading, I was exposed to a variety of approaches to government (such as Plato's republic, God's instruction for the Jewish nation in the Bible, communism, fascism, various forms of monarchy, etc.), but I never tried to formulate my ideas on the subject in a comprehensive way. This musing has a few ideas on the subject. Be warned, this musing will be no help relative to how you should vote in the presidential election. So don't waste your time if that's what you want; you will not find it here.

From my perspective, government has three proper functions: 1) to protect its people from others who would harm them physically, economically, or socially; 2) to ensure its endeavors treat people fairly and with respect for their rights as individuals (this is basically done through laws and their enforcement); and 3) to ensure its people are equipped to function well (by education and provision of life necessities for those unable to provide them for themselves). Of course, government at times also has done other things, such as enriching its rulers and pursuing nationalistic aggression to expand its influence and perhaps enrich itself. Sometimes the other things governments do is given fine sounding labels, such as the way European colonization in Africa was touted as bringing the benefits of modern society in medicine, education, etc. to backward peoples instead of describing what they did as exploiting mineral and agricultural resources of the land taken by the colonizing power. Sometimes historians are candid about what really happened and the motivations for such, but often historians just whitewash the reality of what was done.

Most people, regardless of political affiliation and philosophy, would agree that the three functions I mention are proper ones for government; however, some might not think those three functions are the only proper ones for government and there would be many different ideas about ways to accomplish those functions. In this musing, I will not address other proper functions of government (should such exist), but I will share a few thoughts about the three I identified.

Relative to the first function mentioned, protection of the nation and its people from those outside it, an obvious issue is how far a nation should go in defending itself. Without question the government should protect the nation from military invasion; but other things are not quite so clear. For example, should a nation close its borders to immigration so that potential harm from letting in those who are willing to break its laws or those who merely are people who need extensive assistance with basic necessities of life? Some citizens will be harmed by immigrants who break the law, such as demonstrated by the well-publicized skyrocketing level of sexual assaults in Germany by immigrants. Likewise in the real-world with limited resources, some citizens may not get assistance they need because of resources being spent on immigrants. It is important to remember that resources used to help the immigrants are then no longer available to help residents of the country. When a country, even a well-to-do country cannot (or does not) provide all the help required for its needy, it does not seem right to let strangers in who need such help because that will in essence take from the native needy ones. This issue has no easy or clear resolution that is correct from every perspective. Sometimes those arguing that we should help needy immigrants seem to have little compassion for helping our native needy; such selective compassion is found in many activists – they only seemed concerned about some, not equally concerned about all. Often discussions of such an issue are too emotional for calm and comprehensive consideration of all relevant aspects of the issue so that truly wise conclusions can be reached.

The second function mentioned is concerned with the nation's rules for how its people should behave. At one point in our nation's history, ideals about crime, social behavior, individual rights and privileges, etc. were largely those held by many developed nations, especially those of Europe and English-speaking nations. During the past half century there have been many changes in our country and that past tradition may no longer be as true as it was before. In the past half century, a lot of emphasis has been placed on individual rights; at times this leads to ridiculous extremes, as at present when according to current government decisions the physical genitalia of a person do not necessarily determine the person's gender. A better basis for determining proper behavior is needed than popular fads and government edicts. Thinking about such things was one of the stimuli for this musing.

The third government function mentioned concerns equipping people to function effectively in society. The primary way the US government has addressed this function has been by compulsory education. Recently there have been suggestions about extension of free education for all, and efforts to ensure that all citizens have access to extensive medical care. I was too wordy in my comments about the two government functions discussed above to say anything about this third function. My comments about this function will have to be found elsewhere.

People need to think carefully about proper functions of government because the natural tendency of every bureaucracy is to seek more and more control of those within its sphere. Our own government poses a great tyrannical threat to each of us.

Musing 51: Plain Talk
(initially posted October 3, 2016)

Shortly before the American Declaration of Independence, Thomas Payne published a pamphlet that in relation to the population had the largest sales and circulation of any book in America's history. That pamphlet, *Common Sense*, is still in print today. It helped to convince the public America should break from Great Britain. Something similar is needed today to counter the abundance of foolishness about racism.

There's an old adage about misplaced emphasis; it's "penny wise and pound foolish," a saying that's been around for at least four centuries dealing with great attention to less important aspects of an issue while largely ignoring the more significant aspects of the issue.

Such misplaced emphasis is evident in comments about racism. Massive attention is given to instances where it appears police used lethal force inappropriately, especially when the one killed is black. Black Lives Matter is a mantra used to emphasize this problem. But is inappropriate use of lethal force by police the major problem? Or is it a lesser problem relative to black lives taken by violence? What are the facts?

A thousand people a year (all races) are killed by police, usually appropriately (as when a violent person points a gun at a person and is shot by police to protect the person the gun points at). Estimates by criminal justice experts is only 4-5% of lethal uses of force by police may be inappropriate; that's 40-50 deaths a year (half are black). These deaths get a lot of attention in the media and stimulate massive protests.

However there are 2,500 black murder victims a year; more than 80% (perhaps more than 90%) of whom were killed by black offenders. The media largely ignores these victims, and there are no protests about excessive criminality of the black community. Leaders protesting inappropriate police killings invest little time and effort in trying to change behavior of the black community (rates of violent crime by blacks are several times greater than rates of crime for any other racial group). Of course, protest leaders are less likely to profit from working to solve the bigger problem of murders of black people by blacks than from drawing attention to killings by police (even though 50-100 times as many blacks are killed by black murderers as by inappropriate use of lethal force by police). This is an example of misplaced emphasis. Indeed black lives matter; hence it would be wise to work most on the biggest contributor to black deaths.

Why do leaders of protest against inappropriate killing by police and leaders of the black community give so little attention to excessive criminality of blacks? The black community suffers from that more than anyone else? It's the main reason rates of victimization from serious crime are greater for blacks than for any other racial group. Though blacks are less than 15% of the population, a much higher percentage of perpetrators in violent crimes are black.

Could those protest leaders and black community leaders think it's impossible to reduce black criminality? Could they think such is an inherent characteristic of the race? Might that be the reason they do not expend much effort trying to reduce black criminality? Reducing black criminality would save the greatest number of black lives.

Some seem to think excessive black criminality is inherent, noting three genocides in Africa during the 20th century and the first genocide of the 21st century was also in Africa. They also note correlation between violent crime rates and racial distribution in U.S. cities. I have not heard explanation from those concerned about black lives regarding such or why so little attention is given to reducing criminal activities by blacks.

It is likely some law enforcement and judicial personnel are biased, and their judgments may be skewed some about black criminality, but such is not the major reason so many blacks are in jails and prisons. That's primarily caused by excessive criminality by blacks (excessive in the sense that a much higher percentage of blacks commit crimes than is done by members of other races).

I do not excuse inappropriate action by police, and believe all who do such things should be punished appropriately. My purpose is to encourage everyone, especially those with significant influence in the black community, to emphasize dealing with a major problem of racism: black criminality. If as much effort and attention were given to that problem as given in recent years to inappropriate action by police, I think there could have been noticeable progress in reducing black criminality. The goal should be to make predominantly black neighborhoods as safe and desirable as predominantly Asian or white neighborhoods.

An Emergency Room doctor worrying about a patient's broken eye glasses while ignoring blood gushing from a knife wound would be severely reprimanded and probably fired; misplaced emphasis in dealing with problems hurts people.

Most churches in predominantly white communities are more heterogeneous racially than black churches. Black churches can look at what white churches did decades ago to be more welcoming to non-whites and do similar things to become more heterogeneous. Changing black criminality must be done mainly by the black community. Those elsewhere can encourage but have little potential to reduce excessive black criminality. Thus far, leaders of the black community have not given reducing black criminality a great deal of attention. They do not criticize the black community for its behavior; instead they seek scape goats elsewhere. They do not make massive efforts to deal with the problem, and instead do things like protests against the police. I hope black leaders will change and focus on the far more serious problem of black criminality.

Musing 52: Hard Thoughts (initially posted October 4, 2016)

Jesus said things that are hard to think about. This thought impressed itself upon me as I read Jesus' words in the Gospel of John to His closest followers, the Twelve, in the upper room a short time before He was arrested, tried by the Sanhedrin, Pilate, and Herod, and ultimately crucified. John's Gospel and that of Matthew have more detail about what Jesus said, especially to His disciples, than do the Gospels of Mark and Luke. It's what you expect since both Matthew and John were among the Twelve and were with Jesus in person for most of what their Gospels say. Mark and Luke mainly got their information from others. We think Mark largely got his information from Peter, and Luke carefully researched all the information (written materials that no longer exist, and people who had known Jesus or known those who had been with Jesus) that he could find three decades after the public ministry of Jesus, using the two years he spent in Judea and the surrounding area while Paul was in custody awaiting till he was sent to Rome for trial. Of course, Luke had also gotten information about Jesus and His life from Paul and other Christians he met while traveling with Paul.

In John 16 Jesus says things that those with Him do not understand and they turn to one another, asking for clarification instead of asking Jesus to explain what He said. It hit me that I do the same silly thing, and so do many of the Christians I know. When I come across something Jesus says, or something elsewhere in God's Word, that I am perplexed about, often I turn to what another Christian thinks about it (in a commentary or in discussion with another believer) instead of first turning to God (or Jesus) for clarification about that point.

How can I let God or Jesus explain something to me? First, I can read the passage carefully, making sure I pay attention to the context (who's talking, to whom is it said, what circumstances exist) and making sure I know what words in the passage mean. Then I can pray, asking God to reveal the meaning of the passage and think about it as I give the Holy Spirit time to work in my mind and heart about the passage. I might feel a need to see how that part of the Word of God relates to other things that the Bible says about the subject. Also, I find at times that the Holy Spirit will draw attention to a problem in my life that is preventing me from understanding the passage as God wants me to understand it. It may be a grudge against someone; or it may be a failure to do something

I said I would do (or know I should do). I may become aware that the problem must be dealt with before God will reveal the meaning of the passage to me.

I am amazed at how much clarity God gives to His Word when I approach Him in this way, and deal with things in my life that need attention. Of course, then I can ask others for their insights about the passage. Often I will discover things, whether from a commentary or from a person, that provide insight about the context of the passage or about some of the ways others have understood it, which deepen and broaden my appreciation of the passage; also I find that letting God guide me first about the meaning of a passage protects me from those who might put spin on the passage distorting its meaning (as happens too often).

Everyone knows how people take things out of context, or put undue emphasis on one passage while ignoring other things in the Scripture about the subject. The Gospels give us multiple examples of such from the way Jesus criticizes the Pharisees and others that put their tradition (based upon the Scripture, but not balanced because of over-emphasizing parts while ignoring other parts) above all else so that they were blind to the Messiahship of Jesus, the very Son of God.

It is a hard thought to realize that I should first seek God's explanation of His Word to me, and then let others help me to understand it. Letting God explain His Word takes time; it also takes a heart that wants to know what God says and is willing to deal with problems within one so that God can reveal His truth to you fully. I find that there often are barriers to my understanding that God wants to deal with before He reveals His truth to me; and at times I hold tight to those things because they mean a lot to me and may comfort me. I think of Peter's reluctance to go to a Gentile with the gospel of salvation in Christ (as described in Acts 10). His racial prejudice and the comfort he felt in his Judaism made that hard; but when he let go of that barrier God revealed to him great truths about God's plan of salvation.

I have experienced God's marvelous teaching capabilities when I respond to the things He shows me that need to change in me before He will open my mind to understand His truth more fully. He will not give us knowledge until the heart is receptive to Him. The Scripture suggests that is part of the way God deals with all of us. There is no harder thought than realization that the hardness of my heart limits what God can show me.

Musing 53: Christian Agnostic (initially posted October 5, 2016)

Christian Agnostic is an oxymoron; the word "oxymoron" is a rhetorical term, joining contradictory and incongruous terms to make a point. Some say, since I classify myself as a Christian agnostic, that moron is appropriate for me; the oxy-prefix is unnecessary.

What do I mean when I describe myself as a Christian agnostic?

By Christian, I mean that I believe in the Triune God of the Bible and salvation made possible by the death and resurrection of Jesus, the Son of God; second Person of the Trinity. By agnostic, I mean that I recognize reality consists of both the known and the unknown, some of which is unknowable. I do not claim to know the unknown. Known are things explicitly stated by the Bible, demonstrated as fact by science or firmly evidenced by history. Unknown is everything else; although there may be theories and speculations about parts of the "everything else", such are not knowledge. I accept that some of the unknown is unknowable, because what people can know is limited by their finite reasoning, and aspects of the infinite are beyond the capabilities of finite reasoning.

What is distinctive about being a Christian agnostic? Commitment to Jesus the Christ for salvation distinguishes me from all who are not committed to Him for salvation, whether that comes from adherence to non-Christian religious beliefs or from other factors. My commitment to recognizing only the known as knowledge distinguishes me from many, because they call various theories and speculations knowledge; even some Christians do that.

People have a tendency to go beyond the evidence to produce a coherent and complete description or explanation of something; sometimes journalists call that a narrative. It is not restricted to news or description of historical events, but occurs in science: as theories try to provide a more complete description of processes, causes, and effects. It even occurs in religion. It is the primary cause for the multitude of Christian sects: their theological distinctiveness come from expanding what the Bible says into a more complete doctrinal description; and that expansion for one group may be different than the expansion by another group.

It is hard for us to restrict ourselves to what is known. Conan Doyle's master detective Sherlock Holmes was prone to describing a plausible explanation for the facts and then declaring it as truth, without demonstrating that no other explanation of the facts was plausible. That portrayed Holmes as brilliant, but unfortunately reality is not as accommodating to such practices as Conon Doyle was to Holmes in his stories.

As a Christian agnostic, I try hard to clearly distinguish between the known and my theories or speculation about the unknown. I confess that I do such imperfectly because it is very hard to restrict what one recognizes as known to only what is actually known. Let me illustrate this in the religious area; but note that I am aware that this is also a major problem in both science and history, although few explicitly acknowledge such.

The Bible says God created mankind in His image and gave mankind dominion over the earth and life on it (Genesis 1-4). The Bible does not explicitly describe what being in God's image means, and there are many different ideas about such. Likewise the Bible does not say man is the only species among God's creation that might have special and personal relationships with God. Some people *assume* mankind is unique in that. The Bible does not say God cannot or does not have personal interaction with animals or vegetation; yet many assume such is not possible. Such attitudes *assume* something not stated; they would move that point from unknown to known. This is done either in ignorance of or in spite of the fact the Bible talks about vegetation singing (1 Chronicles 16:33), rejoicing (Psalm 96:12), and exalting (Isaiah 14:8).

I carefully picked these examples that show how people go beyond what is known without clearly indicating their idea is theory or speculation so that I could illustrate the problem without touching on behavioral, social, political, or religious sensitivities. The problem exists in all of those areas as well as with the examples above.

Why is it important to distinguish between the known and theories or speculation about the unknown? The reason is simple. The known is reliable; it will not change. That is not so with theories and speculation about the unknown. Hence, it is important to distinguish between the two.

Even casual students know how often well-established history has to be revised, for example, the city of Troy in the *Iliad* was assumed to be merely legend for a long time and then it was discovered by Schliemann in the late 19th century. For many centuries, everything in the material universe was assumed to be observable. In recent decades, scientists have come to believe that the majority of the material universe is not observable and label such as Dark Matter and Dark Energy.

I hope you will join me in Christian Agnosticism. Committing to Jesus for salvation is the most important thing a person can do since one's relationship with Jesus determines his eternal destination of heaven or hell. Clearly distinguishing between the known and the unknown, even if the unknown is a well-attested theory or convincing speculation, is far better than assuming things unknown are actually known. Restricting what one says is known is neither easy nor popular, but I consider it wise and I hope you will also. If a lot of people were to do this, it would be very good for our nation as well as for each of us personally.

Musing 54: Unasked Questions
(initially posted October 6, 2016)

There are times when America's pundits disappoint me, and this is one of them. A simple version of the Merriam-Webster dictionary says a pundit is "a person who knows a lot about a particular subject and who expresses ideas and opinions about that subject publicly." Pundit should provide wise and helpful insights.

Of course, some who claim to be knowledgeable and express their opinions, and some who are treated as pundits by the media, are nothing more than blowhards with no real expertise in the area they comment upon. My disappointment here is not from the phonies who pass themselves off as true pundits, although the media which use and accommodate such deserve nothing but utter disgust for doing so. My disappointment is with the way true pundits have failed us in the current racial turmoil from inappropriate use of force by police on black people, especially lethal force that results in death.

Pundits have addressed police behavior extensively and have talked about need for improvement in training and in the way police departments handle possible inappropriate behavior of law enforcement personnel, but I have not heard any pundit give serious discussion to the question of "Why are police inclined to react more vigorously toward black people than toward those of other races?" Some attribute such to presumed racial prejudice by police without giving substantial evidence for such an opinion; it seems to reflect more bias and assumption by the "pundit" than careful consideration of the facts. Such an attitude is consistent with contemporary political correctness, but PC is well-known for failing to deal honestly and fairly with reality.

What factors are pertinent to the question? First, consider the frequency of inappropriate use of force by police by race of the victim. Only half of inappropriate uses of lethal force by police is against blacks. That's a very different impression than presented by the media with their pundits. If you doubt my statistic, check data on the Department of Justice website for yourself.

Second, it is appropriate to ask if police have valid and rationale reasons to be more anxious about possible action from a black person than from one of another race in a confrontation. Those who simply assume police act more violently against blacks because of racism are not facing reality. People who know the facts understand that certain characteristics go with various behaviors. For example, football coaches know that size, strength, and speed characterize good players and give more attention to tryouts for the team with those characteristics than to others.

Police are well aware that rates of serious criminal behavior (murder, rape, assault, etc.) are significantly higher for blacks than for any other racial or ethnic group. That means they expect that it is several times more likely the black person the police officer is confronting will behave in a violent, criminal way than a non-black person would. No one accuses a football coach of prejudice because more attention is given to a big, strong, and fast person than to others because there is a solid evidential basis supporting such decisions. Why do we think differently when a police officer acts the same way based upon facts about criminal behavior of people with certain characteristics? Behavior of people protesting inappropriate police behavior confirms the attitude that black people are likely to be violent and disregard normal rules of behavior since many of those protests involve rioting, looting, fires, and vandalism (you can check the racial distribution of those behaving in such criminal ways).

While pundits sometimes criticize police departments for training and supervision failure when officers behavior inappropriately, I have not heard those pundits criticize protest leaders for failing to screen and exclude people from the protest who would damage property of others (cars, buildings, etc.) and do harmful things (such as throwing objects at police and others) from the demonstration. Protest leaders have as much responsibility for controlling the behavior of their participants as the police departments do for controlling behavior of officers. Media and their pundits apply double standards in what I hear from them.

My disappointment comes from the failure of real pundits, not the phony blowhards, to address this serious problem of racial tension in a balanced and comprehensive way so that perhaps they can provide insights that might help Americans to deal with this problem constructively. Their partial and unfair approach has not been helpful, and perhaps even aggravates the problem instead of being helpful.

My attitude about the media prevents any disappointment in its selection of pundits that do such an inadequate job and its toleration and promotion of a number of blowhards as "pundits" since I am so disgusted with contemporary media that I expect nothing of value from it. I would love to be given reason to believe I have misjudged the media, but my exposure to it keeps reconfirming my impression of it as deplorable and sadly failing the American people.

I think the real solution to the racial problem in regard to police treatment of blacks lies within the black community. When the black community cleans house so that rates of criminal behavior by blacks are as low as they are for other races, I believe their treatment by police will become like the police treat members of other races. I don't think those outside the black community can change the black community; blacks themselves will have to change. I believe if leaders of the black community give as much attention to reducing crime by blacks as they do to protesting police behavior, much more real progress would be made in dealing with racial issues.

Musing 55: Juvenile Media
(initially posted October 8, 2016)

America's media is juvenile. It's vocabulary is oriented toward juveniles, and its content and quality of discussion are also juvenile.

That's a sweeping accusation for a nation that prides itself on a free press and strives to have an educated population. Can I support this claim of a juvenile media?

Half a century ago, when I was a young adult, a number of literary sources complained about the low intellectual level of the general print media. It was said that popular publications such as *Time* magazine used a vocabulary tailored to 12-year-olds. That appears true now for most popular magazines and the popular shows on TV and talk radio. It is certainly a marked contrast with the level of vocabulary from a century or two previously. If you want to check that out for yourself to see if I speak the truth, compare political discussion in any daily newspaper or popular news magazines such as *Time* with the vocabulary of Thomas Paine's pamphlet *Common Sense* (I pick that for comparison because in terms of the portion of the public who read it originally it is the most widely sold/read publication, except for the Bible or Shakespeare, in America's history).

It will be obvious in just a few pages that Paine assumes a bigger vocabulary and uses more careful reasoning than is found in most popular media discussions, whether in print, on the air, or on the net. That simple comparison alone should indicate the validity of my accusation that America's media uses juvenile vocabulary and discusses things at a juvenile level. Perhaps a major part of the blame for this behavior by the media can be attributed to advertisers who want their message, in whatever aspect of the media they use, to be as widespread as possible; so they encourage use of juvenile vocabulary and discussion in the media to expand its audience.

Of course, the ultimate blame lies on the public; yes, I refer to you and me because we tolerate this deplorable condition. It contributes to the deplorable state of literary capability by many who progress through America's educational system.

Let me illustrate the adverse consequences of a juvenile media by a recent event. We are in the middle of a presidential election campaign. There are significant issues in areas of policy that should have a major impact on how people vote. Those issues include how America should deal with terrorists and adverse actions by foreign governments; what should be done in regard to immigration, legal and illegal; how to address America's deteriorating infrastructure; America's approach to health care and individual rights; etc.

It is hard to find extensive discussion of such issues in the media except at juvenile levels. Juvenile levels of discussions simplify issues by ignoring significant aspects of the issues and critical factors. Think about economic articles you see or hear in the news. The unemployment rate (as measured by the number of unemployed people seeking work) is used by the media as a significant indicator of the nation's economic health. How often do you hear about a much more significant indicator of the nation's economic health: the total number of people working (or the percent of prime age workers who are working)? I have not seen that mentioned in the more popular media, in print or on the air.

The media have not reported that several percent fewer adults over age 16 are employed now than when Obama became president. To me, that says a lot about the wisdom (or its lack) of economic policies used by his administration. It is no doubt part of the reason that the national debt doubled during his administration; and the federal deficit reached levels (10% of GNP) only previously experienced during major times of war (the Civil War, World Wars 1 & 2) as the Obama administration eased the pain of its economic policies by burdening future generations with additional debt. Have you heard or seen discussion of such aspects of economic issues in the media? Mainly you find blather about the unemployment rate; not discussion of more significant economic issues. I attribute that to the juvenile behavior of the media.

What are the kinds of things America's juvenile media gives attention to? Recently the media, from *The New York Times* to talk-show blowhards, have been giving lots of time and attention to some lewd remarks Trump made more than a decade ago in a private environment. It is not news that Trump is a vulgar man, but what he said was in regard to consensual sexual interactions. Distasteful comments, but not deserving of such media attention. Of course, it caters to juvenile interests and provides an excuse for the media to continue to avoid discussion of serious policy issues (such as noted above in the economic arena).

There is certainly a lot of juvenile silliness in making much about this incident. Particularly since the husband of Trump's opponent was found guilty of both indulging in sexual activities with a person under his supervision while president and not having the candor of Trump in commenting about it before the public and authorities. The press largely ignored such sexual interactions by the Kennedy clan, including while in political office. And the press has been very gentle with a black celebrity who has been accused of drugging them for sexual purposes by dozens of women. Given such background, it shows media's current attention and focus on Trump's words spoken in private a decade-plus ago as just another indication of the juvenile behavior of the media.

Because we live in serious times America needs an adult, not a juvenile media.

Musing 56: American Stupidity (initially posted October 12, 2016)

American Stupidity is a ridiculous title for a musing; there is no way to do justice to such a vast topic in a mere thousand words. So I confess: the title is an example of American stupidity since I am an American and selecting such a title was stupid. My purpose is to address one particular aspect of stupidity that has become prominent in America during my lifetime. If curious about what I have in mind and will say about it, please read on; otherwise just go your way with my blessings and my wish for you to have a wonderful day (I also hope those who choose to read this musing also have a wonderful day).

The stupidity I comment upon in this musing is the emphasis and importance given to diversity. During recent decades, ideals about diversity have changed radically. Previously importance was given to toleration of others, those of a different race, cultural background, political perspective, educational level, social or economic background, etc. Now that ideal seems to have morphed into a requirement for diversity; i.e., it is wrong if your group or associates does not include such others. Freedom to associate only with those of your own kind is no longer considered acceptable. Some cite this as an example of liberal tyranny, a trait noted for reducing individual freedom by requiring all to act in accord with its prevailing ideology.

There are sound reasons for tolerance. Christians and Jews find such taught in their Scriptures. Jesus summarized the Mosaic Law in two commandments: first to love God totally, and second to love your neighbor as yourself. His parable of the Good Samaritan was told to answer the question from an expert in Jewish law about who qualifies as a neighbor. That parable showed racial differences did not deny one neighborship. It is interesting to note that the same chapter in the Old Testament book (Leviticus 19) with the commandment to love your neighbor as yourself also says to treat the alien among you as your neighbor. Moral guidance from the Jewish and Christian Scriptures have shaped ideals in Western societies for centuries.

Coerced inclusion of others in one's circumstances is beyond tolerance and I think is bad (i.e., wrong and has adverse consequences). In the middle of last century, America began to deal with a variety of wrongful intolerances such as racial discrimination. Unfortunately some of the things done to correct previous wrongs created new wrongs. As compensation for past discrimination, the courts required new discrimination in a different direction (as in Affirmative Action). Unfortunately the old adage has proven true: *two wrongs do not make a right.*

The kind of unbalanced attitude reflected in the willingness of the courts to do wrong to correct previous wrongs seems to be the foundation for requiring diversity. Now it is no longer required to show some one discriminated (i.e., lacked tolerance) to be considered guilty of having done wrong; all that's required is demonstration of a lack of diversity (such as shown by distribution of racial backgrounds of students in a school). I consider that approach stupid.

It is very interesting to observe the double standards practiced by the courts, media, and parts of academia in regard to diversity. Caucasians have often been criticized for the lack of diversity in their churches, social groups, and business organizations; but you seldom hear similar criticisms of black churches and other organizations that mainly have black participants for their lack of diversity even though many of them have few non-blacks in them. If diversity is such an important characteristic why is criticism of those without acceptable levels of diversity not directed at all non-diverse activities?

From my perspective this kind of double standard deserves as harsh condemnation as given to the false "separate but equal" claims of education in the South decades ago along with separate toilet and water fountains for blacks as well as required seating in the rear of the bus. Many who have been quite vocal in their criticisms of such discrimination are strangely quiet in their failure to criticize all equally for lack of diversity; their hypocrisy in their double standards removes any legitimate claim to ethical high grounds by them.

Instead of requiring diversity, encourage those considered disadvantaged by discrimination to achieve such greatness that a neighborhood or organization predominately populated by members of the group would be considered as desirable as a predominately white or Asian neighborhood or organization is today. Of course that might require cultural and behavioral changes by the disadvantaged group, since at present it may be characterized by behaviors that make it undesirable (behavior such as greater rates of criminal behavior, a high percentage of pregnancies by unwed mothers, etc., traits associated with significant social problems).

In education, homogenous grouping by ability tends to improve educational performance of better students; and heterogeneous grouping of students with different levels of ability may improve educational performance of less capable students, but at a cost of learning by better students. Those who promote diversity often take a limited look at the benefits of diversity and at times do not acknowledge its costs.

This musing might be considered a rant against diversity; and it is. However it is a rant that emphasizes the importance of tolerance; do not discriminate against those who are different. Ban liberal tyranny which compels heterogeneous involvement. Leave freedom of choice to the individual. However, if our society is so perverse that its liberal tyranny denies people such choice, at least require all segments of society to be criticized if not diverse, not just Caucasians. Expect squawks from those previously uncriticized.

Musing 57: Realism
(initially posted October 14, 2016)

My musings are undergirded by a commitment to realism. I believe that truth is correspondence with reality, and that truth is important.

Truth in the material realm is what enables scientific and technical progress. I am glad the growth of knowledge made possible modern transportation, communication, and conveniences. I much prefer throwing clothes into a washing machine to toting things to the nearest creek and spending hours washing clothes by hand.

I dislike most labels because they tend to describe something complex by a gross simplification or by a term that has many possible meanings. There are a few labels that I do not mind being applied to me. One is Christian, when the term is applied in its historic meaning as a person who believes that Jesus of Nazareth is the Christ (Messiah) Who died and rose from the grave to make salvation possible for people and who also trusts Jesus as Savior. I dislike abuse of the term Christian to merely mean someone is a nice person or that someone lives in a nation with a majority of the population claiming to be Christians.

Another label I do not mind being applied to me is realist when it means a person committed to truth as correspondence with reality. Unfortunately sometimes people abuse the term realist by making it simply mean a person with a cynical or pessimistic perspective.

I fault many perspectives because they are unrealistic. They ignore significant factors in issues, or they distort the issues by presuppositions of their perspective. If my perspective is unrealistic or distorts things, I hope those who perceive such will let me know. I have no wish to perpetuate unrealistic views.

For me, reality consists of both the known and the unknown. Unfortunately most of us have limited appreciation for the known. We may not be aware of much that is known, even in limited topic domains. In addition some of what is known may be distorted by our understanding of it. A primary kind of reality distortion is confusing fact and theory. Many fail to understand that most of what modern science considers as established is not fact, but merely theory that has not yet been falsified, as noted by the distinguished philosopher of science, Karl Popper. Practically I am willing to consider both fact and widely accepted well-supported theory as known, but try to make clear distinctions between fact and theory.

The unknown has two aspects: 1) unknown because of information limitations, and 2) unknown because something is unknowable. Information limitation may be local (i.e., the unknown is known by some, but not by me or those needing the information) or the information limitation may be universal (the unknown is basically not known by any one); for example until the age of space flight man had no knowledge about the back side of the moon (a 1959 Soviet lunar probe provided the first images of it).

The unknowable in reality mainly come from infinite aspects of reality. Christianity (as well as other religions) posits a divine being with infinite characteristics; thus reality which includes both material aspects and supernatural aspects has infinite characteristics. The unpleasant simple truth is that finite reasoning, which we humans are restricted to, cannot correctly express aspects of infinite reality. This is illustrated by mathematics. In infinite set theory actions are permitted which are not possible in finite mathematics. For example, as illustrated by the Cantor Point Set, a line segment can basically be thrown away while at the same time all of it remains. In dealing with infinite reality, sometimes A and Not-A are equal. Likewise, in infinite reality, apparently contradictory aspects of something can all be true at the same time.

In addition to its limited capability for correctly expressing aspects of infinity, finite reasoning has many limitations. For example, one cannot draw valid conclusions when information is inadequate. For example, in mathematics, to get the unique solution to a problem (if such exists), one needs as many equations as there are variables in the problem. In addition, one cannot always determine the truth or falseness of a statement even for a relative simple system (such as that of real numbers) even when one has perfect knowledge of the situation. This was demonstrated in 1931 by Kurt Gödel. Unfortunately much of reality that we grapple with is more complex than the real numbers and not so well understood; hence, we cannot know the truth or falseness of many things we believe.

The expansion of information from modern science is a two-sided sword. It helps us to understand many things, and it also has shown that there is much about the material universe that may be unknowable. The terms Dark Matter and Dark Energy are given for what many now believe constitutes the vast majority of stuff in our universe (or multiverse). All we know about that stuff is its presumed gravitational impact on the parts of the universe we can observe.

As a Christian, I have substantial reliable information about supernatural aspects of the universe. That information comes from the Bible. It tells us about God and other spiritual beings, and some of their interactions with people. That information is as much a part of the known aspects of my perception of reality as the most widely established scientific theory. What the Bible says about the infinite God gives me information when defies explanation in consistent terms of finite reasoning; I simply accept such as true, even though I cannot explain it. The Triune nature of the Godhead is an example of such truth beyond full explanation in finite terms.

Musing 58: Unborn Souls
(initially posted October 15, 2016)

"Unborn Souls" is a challenging subject. Some considered the topic an oxymoron because they do not think the soul exists before birth; others have a different view. I am in that second group.

In a subject like this, it helps to make sure everyone understands the discussion by clearly defining the terms used. The primary definition for the noun "soul" in the *Oxford English Dictionary (OED)*, an authoritative source for meanings of English words, is "the principle of thought and action in man, commonly regard as an entity distinct from the body, the spiritual part of man in contrast to the purely physical," with citations for that use of the word going back to about 1300 A.D. As noted in the *OED* and as used in contemporary English in America, the word "spirit" is often a synonym for "soul" when referring to the non-material aspect of a person.

Generally the words "soul" and spirit" refer to the personality of the individual and reflect the person's intelligence, emotional character, and will. In the Bible at times people are described as "body and soul" with the warning to fear the one with the power to send the soul to hell, and at other times people are described as tripartite: "body, soul, and spirit." When the tripartite description of the person is involved, the spirit refers to the person's relationship with God and the soul has the general meaning of the non-material part of the person (intelligence, emotions, and will).

Some materialists contend that the soul (intelligence, emotional character, and will) is nothing more than the peculiar combination of chemistry and nerve connections in the person's body. That has not yet been proven, and is just a speculation of materialists. We all know that both a person's genetics and environment have major influence on what the person is and becomes.

However this musing is not about development of the soul after birth; rather this musing is concerned about when the soul comes into existence. That has major importance legally as well as otherwise. Both murder and manslaughter are crimes that involve taking life, i.e., killing a "human being;" the difference between the two crimes and the variety in each of the two crimes is determined by intent.

Many legal references use the term "person" to refer to a "human being;" that introduces an uncertainty since American law allows corporations to be considered as "fictitious persons" in legal documentation. It is unclear when the organic material in a pregnant woman becomes a person; when the organic material, i.e., a "fetus," can live outside the mother's womb is considered a person by some legal authorities. Studies a decade ago showed 20-35% of babies born with 23 weeks of gestation survive (laws permitting abortion up to the 24th week of gestation appear to care little for such babies).

When the fetus becomes a person is quite significant. It can change a medical procedure that terminates the fetus from a simple medical procedure legally to murder or manslaughter. Most people would consider killing of a new born infant murder; legally that might even be how some terminations of pregnancies should be considered.

Neither the courts nor medical authorities have defined explicitly when the material in the mother's womb changes from a lump of organic material into a person. Hence the question of whether there are unborn souls becomes important. If the soul began before the mass of material emerged from the mother's womb and took its first breath, then at some point the fetus transforms from a lump of organic matter (like an appendix or an arm) into a person prior to birth. Since neither medicine nor the courts have specified when the fetus is a person, perhaps we can examine that issue from a religious perspective. What insights are available from the Bible on this point?

First, this subject is not one that has been considered simply because of modern controversy over abortion. Discussion of the origin of the non-material aspect of a human was discussed by ancient Greeks such as Socrates, Plato, and Aristotle. Biblical comments come from two millennia and more ago; prominent Christian writers and thinkers, such as Origen in the third century and Thomas Aquinas in the thirteenth century, gave significant attention to the soul, its origin and its destiny.

Second, the Bible has more to say about the soul's eternal destiny than its origins. When a person's material life ends by death, the soul continues to exist and goes from association with that lifeless body to its eternal destination (heaven or hell) based upon the person's relationship to Jesus, the Savior.

The Bible only hints at the soul's origin. The Apostle Paul in the early part of his letter to the Ephesians says that God chose those who would be saved in Christ Jesus before creation of the world. Hence God had knowledge of those souls before our world came into existence. That knowledge might come from existence of those souls at that time (before creation of the world) or from awareness of when those souls would come into existence. An omniscient God knows both. The Bible does not specify which is the case. Over the years, prominent theologians have been in favor of each alternative.

Christians today have different opinions about when the person begins. Some believe that happens at conception; others think it occurs at birth; and others believe it occurs between conception and birth. My conclusion is that it is possible that there are unborn souls, and that should make us very cautious about how we treat the organic material in a pregnant woman we call a fetus.

Musing 59: Presidential Election (initially posted October 18, 2016)

In a few weeks we will elect the person to become President in January; some have already cast their ballots in early voting. Many of our citizens are disturbed by the way this election's campaigns have been conducted.

I was amazed when I received a voter information package to discover that I have many more candidates to choose from than I expected. Not only can I choose from the four national parties (Democrat, Green, Libertarian, or Republican – listed alphabetically), but there were thirty more candidates listed on the ballot for President (as well as the option for a write-in). I did not expect such a large number of candidates.

I do not know enough about previous presidential campaigns for meaningful comparison of this one with them, but I am disgusted with media coverage of the major candidates and by their behavior. They focus more on personality than serious issues and specific explanation of policies with supporting information. This is such a problem that a major reputable news magazine labeled the campaigns as "post-truth politics" and called them "art of the lie."

It is easy to blame candidates and their campaigns for this disgraceful situation, and to castigate the media for encouraging such behavior by the candidates in the media's greedy pursuit of ad dollars based on ratings, but ultimately the blame is on us, you and me, the American public for tolerating this national atrocity.

What can we do? First, we can confess our guilt in this. Whether based upon guidance from the Bible about the essential role of repentance and confession in dealing with a bad situation or from the wisdom of 12-step programs which help people deal with addictive behaviors by starting with admitting reality of the problem, we need to begin by honestly acknowledging the mess we are in and our responsibility for it.

Next we need to seek God's guidance for ourselves in dealing with the situation and ask His mercy upon our nation in this time of crisis. Then we need to put forth the effort to determine what we believe are the top half-dozen issues (things that will significantly impact the future of our nation); then find out what the candidates have said or done in regard to such issues. After that, we should vote for the candidate we believe to be most likely to do the best job in dealing with those issues.

This means that we do not vote simply by party affiliation, personal like or dislike of a candidate, disgust or appreciation for a candidate, or the sound-byte level description of policies that the media seems content with. Sensible people know sound-byte descriptions seldom provide reasonable understanding of issues. Also we will ignore things that only appear in the media in the final month of a campaign (as often happens) though candidates have been public persona for decades. If we do those things, perhaps what is best for the nation (given present choices) will come from this election.

I've described a wise process for American voters. Now I identify some of the issues you may want to consider in your evaluation process. You may feel other issues are as important as or even more important than ones I mention. Just pick the half-dozen you think are most important, whether they all come from ones I suggest or only some or even none of them come from ones I mention. I suggest you limited yourself to half-dozen for your decision process because with more than that you might not be able to choose among the candidates because one candidate would appear better for one issue and another candidate would appear better of a different issue.

Issues I consider likely to have major impact on America's future include abortion, foreign involvements, government size, immigration, judicial selection, national debt, terrorism, and trade (issues listed alphabetically). A recent major news magazine identified four topics that at least a quarter of voters surveyed said were a top-3 concern: economy and jobs, terrorism and national security, health care, and immigration.

A few words about issues I suggested: Abortion laws emphasize a woman's rights without due consideration for other factors (e.g., most permit abortion through 24 weeks of gestation, yet 20-35% of babies born with just 23 weeks of gestation survive – what rights do those with 23 weeks gestation have?). Foreign involvement puts American lives at risk and unwise involvements do not make our world safer. Excessive government is an economic burden for the country, and expands the number many consider parasites on society. Immigration poses both potential benefits and dangers, especially dangers from illegal immigrants. Judicial appointments tend to have long term impact, and there is likely to be a choice between future judges who emphasize adherence to the Constitution and those who are more inclined to be activists depending upon who becomes President. The growing national debt (doubled during the current administration) puts America's economic future at risk. Effective dealing with terrorists has many aspects including use of military and police resources as well as policy and social attitudes. Trade policies impact American jobs and there seem to be major differences in how the main candidates would deal with trade issues.

It is not my intention to tell you who you should vote for, but I hope you will follow my suggestions for how to decide whom you will vote for. I suspect most voters will not use the kind of processes I suggest for deciding whom they will vote for; instead they will make their selections based upon other factors and that may not be good for our nation.

Musing 60: Election Choice
(initially posted October 19)

In my musings related to politics, I have not encouraged readers to vote for a particular party or candidate. Instead I discuss factors that I considered significant and I suggest processes which I think will help people make good choices about what is good for our nation and our society. In my decades as an analyst dealing with matters of national defense I became acutely aware of the importance of getting the facts straight. So often information was incomplete, and what was available often was distorted. Thus properly understanding the evidence, its scope and reliability, was critical. Equally important with getting the facts straight is proper process. Too many like Sherlock Holmes are ready to declare a possible explanation as what really happened before all other possible explanations are eliminated. That can lead to wrong conclusions. So my approach in the musings which touch on politics in some way, such as this one about election choices, is to focus on significant factors and helpful processes.

For this election, the basic choice is 1) to continue on the path the federal government has been following by electing a person long inside the political establishment, Hillary Clinton, or 2) to possibly turn the federal government from that path to a different direction by electing one who is at odds with leaders in his own party as well as with those in other parties, Donald Trump. Unfortunately a clear indication of where things might go under a Trump presidency does not seem to be available; at least such is not something I have access to. Therefore, this musing boils down to the following: looking at how things are likely to be if the nation continues on the path it has been going on in recent years and asking if any other approach would be as bad for the nation as doing that. The horror of that being the choice we face in this election is what this musing addresses.

Like many Americans I feel sad that our next president is likely to be a person who is far from the kind of person I wish were President, but I am reminded that the Apostles Paul and Peter instructed Christians to be obedient to the laws of the land in which they live (Romans 13:1-7 and 1 Peter 2:13-17). It helps to remember that it is most likely that those words were written during the reign of Nero, a man known for his debaucheries, political murders, and persecution of Christians. He wrecked economic havoc on the Roman Empire and even had his wife and mother murdered. That both Peter and Paul instructed Christians to obey the law even under such atrocious leadership provides perspective on our present situation; no one likely to become the U.S. President is as evil personally as Nero.

There are many things in the current direction the federal government is going that I feel are bad for the nation, and I believe that Clinton would continue to lead the federal government in going that way. I list some of the things that concern me. Anyone else in the White House would be less likely to lead the government in those directions.

Wrong directions America is going:

Disregard for the unborn. Emphasis on the woman's choice in abortion allows termination of fetuses in the 23rd week of gestation; studies a decade ago indicate 20-35% of such fetuses can survive outside the mother's womb.

Expansion of personal liberties (such as gender identification and "marriage" between people of the same sex) has extended into licentiousness with disregard for rights of others (such as women who do not want anyone with a penis in their restrooms or locker rooms) and disregard for historic connotations (such as marriage being union of a man and a woman).

Burdening the future with the cost of contemporary benefits, as illustrated by the doubling of the national debt during the Obama administration with federal deficits reaching levels (10% of GNP) only previously experienced by wartime necessity (specifically the Civil War and World Wars 1 & 2).

Unwise trade arrangements that have cost many American jobs.

Failure to control our borders so that millions of illegal immigrants now exploit American education and social benefits at great cost to our nation.

Increased involvement of the federal government in all aspects of American life, a danger that our nation's founders feared greatly.

Appointment of activist judges who fail to abide by the Constitution.

The reader may not agree that all of these are bad things, but I hope every reader will think at least some of them are bad for our nation. If even one of them strikes you as a serious danger, it could be better to avoid that danger by not electing a person likely to continue the federal government on its present course. If most of these things strike you as harmful to the nation, then you have good reason to vote for anyone other than a person that will keep the government on its current path.

The reader may have a different list of things the government is currently pursuing that pose grave hazards for our nation. This election gives you the choice of voting for someone who will continue to take the government in that direction, or voting for someone else.

Thank you for your attention to this musing. I hope its comments will encourage you to think seriously about our nation's future and that you will vote in the way that you honestly think is best for the nation, and not indulge in voting for any other reason.

Musing 61: More On Miracles
(initially posted October 20, 2016)

On June 28th, I posted a musing about miracles (#19). That musing focused on the possibility of miracles (given the common meaning of the word as something not explicable by natural or scientific laws). This musing focuses on the nature of miracles and puts that in the context of natural occurrences (i.e., things people understand and can explain).

Since any discussion of miracles is largely determined by presuppositions, it is good to be candid and explicit about the presuppositions of the speaker or writer. For example, a materialist presupposes that everything that happens can be explained by the laws of natural processes (whether currently known and understood or not); hence for such a person miracles as a demonstration of supernatural activity is impossible. On the other hand, I believe Jesus was correct when He said "with God all things are possible" (Matthew 19:26 & Mark 10:27). Luke 1:37 reports the same perspective from the mouth of the angel Gabriel in his announcement to Mary that she would have a child: Gabriel said "nothing (the Greek word can mean either word or thing) is impossible for God." Thus my presupposition is that God can do anything, whether compliant with the way He causes the material world to normally behave (which we call natural laws) or in a different way.

That changes my perception of what a miracle is. Now a miracle merely becomes something people cannot explain with their current knowledge. It is not a violation of processes God chooses to use in dealing with the situation, but it may involve processes that people do not understand. Sometimes those processes will be added to what we call natural law as human knowledge increases, and sometimes those processes may be outside the realm of natural law.

Natural law can be violated in one sense easily. If I let go of a stone, the law of gravity would predict that the stone will fall to the ground. However that expectation would not occur if the stone is lying on a surface, such as a table top, or if some upward force is exerted on the stone (like a blast of air, similar to what keeps people airborne in some amusement park rides). If the object were a piece of metal instead of a stone, a magnetic field could prevent the object from falling to earth. Hence what is expected by simple application of a natural law (such as the law of gravitational attraction) may be violated (overcome) by application of other processes.

All processes of the material world, including those related to the human body, as well as processes of the supernatural world (by which I mean everything that exists outside the material world), function in accordance with God's dictates and actions. He created and sustains all that is, both that within perceptive capabilities of people (i.e., the material world) and that normally outside human perceptive capabilities (i.e., such things as heaven, hell, and the realms of spiritual beings such as angels and demons).

Modern science has admitted its comprehension of what exists is limited. It currently thinks most of our universe consists of stuff we cannot observe but whose existence we posit because we think it makes objects we can observe behave in unexpected ways (i.e., they do not obey the law of gravity if only what we can observe exists); Dark Matter and Dark Energy are terms used to describe the unobservable stuff. In addition modern science speculates that our universe is just one of a multitude of universes; and we do not even know the number of dimensions in our present reality but it is greater than the traditional four of x, y, z, and time.

One would expect those so open about their knowledge limitations to also be open about the possibility of a spiritual realm whose interactions with our universe might not be restricted to our laws of nature, but surprisingly many with a scientific bent are as pig-headedly closed-minded as 19th century Luddites.

In general, our bodies heal themselves. Modern medicine helps by providing environments that promote such bodily healing (by killing or removing bad cells, restoring chemical balances in the body, etc.). The processes involved, whether or not aided by medical activities, are directed by God, as is the timing of their result. We normally tend to call an unusually rapid healing a miracle and forget that the slow healings are as much from God as a rapid one. You can find this view expressed eloquently and far more completely in works such as that of C. S. Lewis' *Miracles*.

This musing has one major point: nothing is impossible for God. When Jesus fed a multitude (5,000 men plus women and children) using a handful of bread and fish, when He made a man born blind to see, or when He brought a man four days dead who had already begun to stink from decomposition back to life, God's power to do what is impossible for people and natural processes happened. Whether those miracles happened though natural processes yet to be discovered or from supernatural interactions with our material universe, I cannot say. They just illustrate the truth: God can do anything. Sometimes He uses natural processes we know and understand; sometimes He uses processes we may yet come to know and understand; and sometimes He may use processes beyond human comprehension.

My presupposition that God is indeed God (He can do anything) makes this possible. Hence miracles are not an obstacle in my perspective. Some have presuppositions that make miracles hard for them; I think they would be wise to reconsider their presuppositions.

Musing 62: Poor Mary
(initially posted October 21)

Although Mary, the mother of Jesus, is a person that many respect and honor, actually we know relatively little about her. The only sure facts about her come from the Scripture; everything else is tradition that originated in later generations (some of these traditions have become official teachings of various religious organizations). This musing concerns what the Scripture says about Mary and will not address ideas that originated later than the Scripture (by Scripture I mean the 27 books that compose the New Testament).

We know nothing about Mary's parents; the idea that the genealogy of Jesus in the Gospel of Luke is actually His human heritage through Mary seems to have originated in the 16th century in the 1502 A.D. writing of Annius of Viterbo (the earliest mention of that idea in known Christian materials, the late date of which gives me sufficient reason to dismiss it, although many Christian leaders in our day have taught it – it is also noteworthy that Annius, an Italian Dominican friar, is now remembered mainly for his fabrications: he lied about many things).

The Scripture (Matthew 13:55-56 & Mark 6:3) tell us that Jesus had siblings, names four brothers [Joses (Joseph), James, Judas, and Simon] and mentions sisters. John 19:25 mentions Mary's sister (she has been identified variously from comments in the New Testament – the one I think is probably correct is Salome, mother of the sons of Zebedee, James and John, part of Jesus' inner circle of three). Identification of Salome as the sister of Mary gives added reason for John to be at the crucifixion: to care for his mother and her sister as well as because of his relationship to Jesus; it also makes it reasonable for Jesus to tell John to care for Mary, who was his aunt.

The first chapter of Luke tells us that the parents of John the Baptist (Zechariah and Elizabeth) were relatives of Mary and that she visited them shortly after Gabriel told her she would have a son miraculously. Even though they lived in the hill country of Judea, about a week's journey on foot from Nazareth Mary went to see them and spent three months with them.

As an unmarried but espoused first century Jewish girl, Mary was probably a teenager when Gabriel visited her. She had to be a remarkable person for God to choose her to be the one through whom His Son would become a human. Certainly her response to what Gabriel told her shows she knew that having a child without a human husband would be a miracle and probably that it would involve numerous problems; but she said she was willing for whatever God had for her to do. That's a remarkable commitment for anyone.

Luke 1 suggests that Mary and her relatives talked about what God was doing in the amazing births of John the Baptist and Jesus, but we know nothing about what they may have told others (including their own children) about these things. We know nothing about what John the Baptist may have been told about the conditions of his birth or about Jesus; we do not know if John had ever met Jesus before the day he baptized him. Anything you hear or read about such is simply someone's speculations (a fancy word for guesses) from later generations, often many generations later.

We do not know when Mary told Joseph, the man she was engaged to, that she was going to have a baby; it may have been before she went to see Elizabeth or perhaps it was after she returned three months later (possibly even showing signs of being pregnant). His initial response to whatever she told him was a plan to end the engagement, but to do so in a way that would cause the least public scandal. God intervened and told Joseph to marry Mary because the child would be the Messiah (the Christ).

The story of Jesus' birth in Bethlehem is well-known, but why Joseph had to travel a week to register for the census is not clear (with another week of travel required to return to his home). It is hard to believe Rome would require that kind of economic disruption (with the attendant potential for encouraging rioting and rebellion) simply for taxation identification. They collected taxes where people lived and worked; not from their birth places or locations of their tribal and family origins. Explanations I have seen for why Joseph went to Bethlehem (other than to fulfill prophecy about Christ's birth) are not satisfying.

The offering given by Mary for her cleansing from the ritual uncleanness of childbirth (made more than a month after Jesus was born) shows that Joseph and Mary were not wealthy; her offering was that of a poor person, one with limited means. This happened before the magi (the wise men) visited them. We do not know how long after the birth of Jesus the visit by the magi occurred, but it was at least a month and Jesus' family was residing in a house (not a barn or stable). The gifts from the magi enabled the family to travel to Egypt and spend time there so that Jesus would not be killed by Herod. It is possible that the gifts from the magi moved the family from a poor status to a well-to-do one when they returned from Egypt to Nazareth. We do not know the economic class of Jesus' family during His childhood.

I will end this musing here, but expect to say a bit more about Mary in a future musing.

Musing 63: More About Mary
(initially posted October 22, 2016)

In a previous musing about Poor Mary, I noted that she and Joseph were poor when Jesus was born, basing that assessment upon the choice of offering Mary gave for her cleansing from the ritual uncleanness of childbirth. We know the magi after that gave them valuable gifts. We have no idea of how much those gifts were worth. It is generally believed that those gifts enabled the flight into Egypt by Jesus and His parents, and probably supported them while they stayed in Egypt. The gifts may have had enough value for Joseph, Mary, and Jesus to return from Egypt in a richer condition than when Joseph and Mary left Nazareth before Jesus was born. We do not know. Joseph's occupation (and that of Jesus), usually translated as carpenter but actually involves both masonry and metal working as well as working with wood (we get the word "technology" from the Greek word describing their trade), does not imply an impoverished economic status. It is quite possible that the family had a business with hired men working for them; the magi gifts might have enable establishment of such (even after the cost of fleeing to Egypt and returning after staying there for some time, possible several years).

Nazareth was just an hour's walk from Sepphoris (Autocratoris), the provincial capital of Galilee. It would be a place with lots of work for builders. About a decade before Jesus began His public ministry, Sepphoris was built/modified to be a model Greco-Roman city. If Joseph had established a building business as well as performing the humble carpentry tasks of a village, he could have gotten work on projects in Sepphoris.

As the eldest male in the family, Jesus would have been expected to take over the family business when Joseph died. Perhaps the building business was such a going concern that Jesus could put it in the care of one of His brothers, confident that His mother and the rest of the family would be well cared for, when He went away as an itinerant preacher and teacher. The few things His family says about Him during His public ministry do not include criticism for stepping out of the lead role in the family business.

We have no indication in the Scripture about what Mary may have told Jesus or her other children about the unusual circumstances of His birth and the things the angel told her and Zechariah about Jesus and His forerunner (John the Baptist). When Jesus' claim to Messiahship was challenged because He was from Galilee, not Bethlehem as predicted by prophecy, Jesus did not correct those saying such things. Was that just silence in the presence of controversy? Or had Mary not told Him about His birth?

Some presume Mary was from the tribe of Judah, basing that mainly upon the assumption that Luke's genealogy of Jesus is hers, not Joseph's as it says in the text itself; but her relative (Elizabeth) was from the priestly tribe and most often ones relatives were from the same tribe. If Mary was from the priestly tribe, it would make Jesus more like Melchizedek (as argued in the book of Hebrews) since He would have both regal ancestry (through Joseph) and priestly ancestry (through Mary); He would be King and Priest.

Mary was at the crucifixion, but the Scripture does not mention her as one to go to the empty tomb. She is mentioned as present with other believers in Jesus in Acts 1; and then she is not mentioned again in the New Testament other than Paul's statement in Galatians 4:4 "God sent his Son, made of a woman, made under the law." I do not think the "elect lady" in 2 John 1:1 or the passage in Revelation 12:1 refers to Mary, although some interpret them that way: "A great sign appeared in heaven: a woman clothed with the sun, with the moon under her feet and a crown of twelve stars on her head." Lack of significant mention of Mary in the New Testament epistles or the book of Acts, although the ministry and leadership of a number of women are noted, suggests that Mary did not have a prominent role in the ministry of the church after the Day of Pentecost.

The first comment about Mary in post-Biblical material that I am aware of comes from the apocryphal *Gospel of James* (also known as the *Infancy Gospel of James* or the *Protoevangelium of James*) that was written about 145 A.D., more than a century after the last Biblical mention of Mary. That document makes comments about the birth and upbringing of Mary.

The earliest Christian creeds, usually thought to be the Apostles Creed and the Nicene Creed, date from the fourth century, although elements of them are thought to have been used previously, such as in recitations at baptisms. The earliest recorded prayer to Mary (*sub tuum praesidium* as *Theotokos*) is from the third century. All non-Biblical references during the second century to Jesus being born of the virgin Mary are essentially in the context of quotations from Bible passages about the birth of Jesus. The second century *Gospel of James* is the primary item I know before the fourth century that has other information about Mary. The dogmas about Mary by the Roman Catholic Church, the various Orthodox

Churches, and others originate after the fourth century creeds. I do not give such dogmas the truth-status that I give to the Scripture.

It is interesting to speculate about what Mary said to her family (parents, siblings, children) about the miraculous birth of Jesus and related events.

Musing 64: Judicial Activism
(initially posted October 23, 2016)

Judicial activism is a term with varied meanings. The term appears to have been coined by Arthur Schlesinger (noted liberal Harvard professor of history associated with the Kennedys) in a 1947 article in *Fortune*. The term (judicial activism) is sometimes used when a court rejects laws and regulations on Constitutional grounds, but more often the term currently is used when courts do not confine themselves to reasonable interpretations of the law and instead essentially create new law by the ways in which existing law is interpreted. Judicial activism is justified by some as creative (re)interpretation of the Constitution and the laws to serve what the court considers vital needs of contemporary society when the legislative and executive branches of government appear to be failing to meet society's needs.

Laws can be ignored as illustrated repeatedly by the many who fail to comply with posted speed limits for vehicles. This unreliability tendency is also evident in the frequent failure of people to keep the solemn promise of fidelity to a spouse made in the marriage ceremony. Judicial activism has nothing to do with such violations of the law or failures to keep solemn promises unless those laws conflict with the court's social perspectives; then judicial activism may essentially nullify laws by failing to apply them as intended.

Laws can be misapplied. This is illustrated by the way Jewish leaders of Jesus' day misapplied the Mosaic Law about the Sabbath; Jesus had to remind them that "the Sabbath was made for man, not man for the Sabbath" in response to criticism for doing good on the Sabbath. They even criticized His giving sight to a man born blind because it was done on a Sabbath; they treated the man and his family badly. If courts correct such misapplication of laws, it is good. However, history suggests courts are often the ones misapplying laws in that way. In a sense judicial activism is itself such a misapplication of law since the creative (re)interpretation of law in essence creates new law and that is not the court's proper function.

Laws may need to change. As time passes, needs of society change and if laws are not modified and updated to accommodate changes in society the law itself becomes harmful instead of helpful. Sometimes changes come from technology advances. Some of the traffic laws passed in the late1800s or early 1900s (such as a state law requiring a car to stop every mile, send up a rocket, and wait a few minutes for animals and livestock to clear the road ahead before continuing) may still be on the books. Most governments are lax about removing or updating obsolete laws. Sometimes laws need to change because society has changed. Certainly most Americans would not approve of laws about the divine rights of kings, laws which provided the legal authority for absolute power by kings and queens.

The question is, what is the proper way for laws to be modified, updated, or created? The Constitution has provision for it to be modified. As it was realized that important things were omitted from the Constitution, it was modified with the Bill of Rights (the first ten amendments to the Constitution). Today twenty-seven amendments have been made to the Constitution; six other amendments adopted by Congress and sent to the States were not ratified and are not part of the updated Constitution (although four of the proposed amendments are still open and pending – if ratified by other States could become modifications to the Constitution).

The proper way to change the law is to play by the rules; let those responsible for creating and modifying the law do so in the proper way. To change the law otherwise is basically to destroy the law; that is the curse of judicial activism. While desire to do good for society by changing the law so it better serves society (by correcting past wrongs, recognizing ignored rights, etc.), the process ultimately destroys the law and that is bad for everyone. It means that only one rule counts: the rule that power makes right. A primary function of the law is to control and curb the abuses of that rule.

Think for a moment, if the meaning of the law is only whatever the court declares it to be, without regard to its original intent, then what is to prevent a later court from changing that law simply by applying its own interpretation to it. That is how judicial activism destroys the law and facilitates return to the simple rule: power makes right. Unfortunately some proponents of judicial activism are so blinded by their desire to implement their political ideology that they cannot see the ultimate consequences of what they are doing. Liberals desiring to see various rights recognized and extended applaud judicial activism which moves in their desired direction, ignoring the consequences of that approach. What is held dear today can be dismissed tomorrow if all it takes is a creative (re)interpretation of the law by the court.

Insisting that the law's original intent is constant is essential for a society which wants the rule of law to protect it from the "power makes right" approach (an approach often employed when military juntas take leadership of a country). Those accepting that a law's original intent is constant understand the need for the law to be modified and updated, but believe that should be done in a proper way. Such modification of law should not be left to court creativity because such judicial activism will ultimately destroy the law.

Musing 65: Prayer
(initial posted October 25, 2016)

Prayer is important, perhaps the most important aspect in a Christian's life; yet it is something we often neglect and few seem to do well. Certainly it is an aspect of my life that shames me because I do so poorly in it. This musing shares a few of my thoughts on prayer.

The Bible has a lot to say about prayer. It is said there are about 650 prayers contained in the Bible. Some have listed prayers by where they occur in the Bible; amazingly no prayers are contained in Leviticus, the book addressing many aspects of Jewish ritual. Others provide an alphabetized list of those who prayed (along with where in the Bible the prayer is found). In addition there are specific instructions about prayer.

Jesus gave us a model prayer (Matthew 6:9-13), the Lord's Prayer. He also gave instructions about prayer: pray privately (Matthew 6:5-8), with persistence (Matthew 7:7-12), in faith (belief) and from a forgiving heart (Mark 11:22-26). Jesus used parables to show the earnestness that should characterize our prayers: the shameless persistence of the man badgering his neighbor (Luke 11:5-13) and the importunate widow compelling an unjust judge to grant her request (Luke 18:1-8). What an audacious way to approach the all-powerful creator and sustainer of all things. Only a person confident he or she is a child of God with a loving heavenly Father would not dare to approach God in that way. Jesus' third parable about prayer, that of the publican and the Pharisee (Luke 18:9-14), shows that humility must accompany the bold persistence of the other two parables.

The New Testament epistles indicate the importance of prayer in the lives of the apostles and in the lives of those to whom these letters were sent. All believers are encouraged to pray without ceasing and to bring all things to God in prayer; they are to have an attitude of thanksgiving. The Apostle Paul notes that the Holy Spirit helps our prayers (Romans 8:26-27).

With such abundant guidance from the Scripture on the subject of prayer and full recognition of prayer's importance in the life of a Christian, one might expect that most Christians would be well-experienced in prayer. Unfortunately in our prayer lives many of us are like the duffer who shows up on the golf course occasionally with no clue about which golf club is best for a shot other than to use a wood from the tee and a putter on the green; instead of being like any serious golfer or the club's golf pro in our prayer life.

I confess that I seldom approach God in my prayers with the shameless persistence of the man badgering his neighbor for bread in the middle of the night, or with repetitive annoying requests like the importunate widow presented to the unjust judge. Perhaps that reveals an important aspect of prayer: the behavior of those in these parables was driven by their conviction of the importance of their requests. Perhaps my lack of such fervency in my prayers shows that what I pray is really not that important to me.

Ouch! That's an embarrassing reality – I am not that serious about things I bring to God in prayer. Yes, what I bring to God in prayer is important, but . . . . You may have similar problems with your prayers.

What can I fix this? Do I expect God to do what I ask? Or do I expect something else?

My prayers as communication with God help me understand His will for me. If I come with a heart seeking to know Him better and seeking to understand better what He wants of me, I begin to know what I can pray for with shameless persistence and importunity; I can have the faith/belief about such that Jesus says ensures it will happen. As I seek God in this way, I realize some of the things I pray are inappropriate, and I remove them from my prayers. Such communication with God includes spending time in the Scripture which gives God opportunity to guide my thinking by His Word and by His Spirit using things in the Scripture that stimulate my thoughts as well as the Spirit working directly in my mind and heart.

Let me give a simple illustration. The Lord's Prayer teaches that we should ask God to provide for our immediate needs (daily bread); it does not say to ask for economic security for the next decade. A child expects parents to provide food for the next meal and is not concerned with food for a month or two later. We need that kind of dependent relationship on God. We're to pray for our immediate needs and leave the longer term future in his hands.

It's hard for me to approach God with an audacious attitude most of the time, but when my communications with Him through the Word, His Spirit's work in my mind and heart, and my prayers have led me to the place of conviction that something is indeed His will in the situation then I badger Him shamelessly with my petitions; His responses have been amazing in some situations.

Sometimes I rush things; that usually does not work. It takes time to get me in tune with what God wants; I have to get lined up with that before I can pray with the fervency illustrated in the two parables. You may be more pliable than I, and it will not take God as long to get you in line as it does in my case.

Musing 66: Offensive Language
(initially posted November 23, 2016)

Offensive language is a difficult topic to corral; it has so many aspects and they keep changing. At one time, it was considered offensive to curse in the presence of a lady. That was a different era from the current one in which we live; one is as likely to hear as foul language from a female as from a man in the gutter. At one time, some topics were considered offensive and not suitable for polite public discussion; and today, such topics are the main discussion items in many radio and TV talk shows and the theme of movies, plays, and TV series.

Some have been super sensitive to terms considered racial slurs or derogatory expressions; organizations exist which strive to address such. The Anti-Defamation League (ADL) was established a century ago (1913) to counter anti-Semitism expressions which they felt defamed Jewish people. Most black men bristle if called "boy," especially by a white person. There are many terms used in derogatory ways to refer to someone of a particular ethnic group. Some even consider such racial slurs to be hate crimes.

Instead of considering the complex issues in this arena of how offensive language and reaction to it relates to freedom of thought and speech or other such complexities, this musing addresses a different aspect of offensive language. That aspect is the selected sensitivity of many to offensive language. For example, the ADL reacts vigorously to what it considers anti-Semitism, as do others at present to what they perceive as racial slurs (or to abusive terms about LGBT people), but those same sensitive people often seem oblivious and totally unconcerned to similar kinds of offensive language in widespread use when it does not address their pet topics. I consider such selectivity in sensitivity to be a grave character and ethical deficiency; to me it is a form of gross hypocrisy. It seems that all they really care about is promotion of their selected interest groups and not decent behavior toward others of all varieties.

Let me illustrate this selective sensitivity by referring to the terms CE and BCE in dating years, which I consider offensive in their connotations for the last several centuries. The current Gregorian calendar used widely throughout the world identifying when things occurred numbers the years relative to the assumed year of the birth of Jesus of Nazareth, the Christ. That numbering system has been in use for centuries and has been designated for many years as AD and BC (for *Anno Domini*, which means *the year of the Lord* in Latin, and *Before Christ*) relative to the time assumed for Christ's birth. A few hundred years ago CE began to be used meaning

Christian Era, but then its connotation was changed to Common Era or Current Era.

This emphasis on CE with its contemporary connotations instead of its original meaning as Christian Era or of the older way for referencing the year (AD) seems to stem from an unwillingness to acknowledge that this numbering system is specifically related to Jesus the Christ and that is a slur as nasty as use of the notorious N word (which for several centuries only meant a Negro or a member of a dark skinned race, but now is presumed to be a derogatory reference, particularly to a person of color).

When have you seen or heard any of those supersensitive to slurs against the LGBT community or prone to agitate against what they perceive as racial slurs show any concern about such religious slurs as CE? Their selective sensitivity to offensive language reflects badly on both their lack of character and lack of ethics as well as their willingness to debase language by changing connotations of words and phrases to suit their personal preferences. They are as callous about the meaning of words as Petruchio's calling the bright sun the moon when talking to Katherina in Shakespeare's *The Taming of the Shrew*.

Likewise think of the widespread acceptance of profanity in speech and the media. Many people would be horribly offended if someone important to them, such as a spouse, relative, or colleague is described in derogatory ways. Would you be offended by someone calling your spouse or another person important to you a cheat, liar, crook, or some sexually derogatory term? Most people would be offended; however, I think few are offended when God's name is abused in such a way in the many profane expressions one often hears most days.

We should be offended by offensive language of all varieties, not just offensive to pet topics of some; and we should be careful not to use such if we believe in treating *ALL* people with respect and consideration. Those who show selective attention to offensive language should be ashamed of themselves. I urge them to conduct a rigorous and thorough self-evaluation to discover why they have such character and ethical deficiencies. Then perhaps they can work to correct it.

Unfortunately I suspect many will simply ignore criticism of their selective sensitivity and continue to exhibit such in thought and action; that seems to be the way many behave, but then they bristle when the word which describes behaving similar to what one criticizes in others is applied to them. That word is hypocrite, and it is most appropriate in this situation.

Musing 67: Ethical Perspective (initially posted November 25, 2016)

When ethics, identification of right and wrong, are ignored, only one approach to determining right and wrong for a society remains: "might makes right." History shows this rude fact repeatedly, as demonstrated by the Holocaust, slaughter of a million Armenians early in the 20th century, and genocide in Rwanda two decades ago. America seems to be moving in the direction of ignoring ethics; that can lead to very bad circumstances for our nation.

This musing is not about where one turns for guidance about right and wrong. For a long time, Western society generally accepted the Christian Bible and its teachings expressed by churches as a basic source for guidance about right and wrong; however many now choose other sources as their ultimate source of guidance about right and wrong. For some, guidance about right and wrong comes from rational implications of scientific knowledge. For others, guidance about right and wrong comes from a different religion than Christianity. For yet others, they turn to some kind of philosophy or political approach for guidance about right and wrong. This musing does not enter the heated arguments about which one is best.

Instead I focus on a factor that is crucial to avoid falling into the pit of "might makes right." That factor is *repeatedly rewarding bad behavior*. Whenever bad behavior is rewarded repeatedly, it destroys the crucial role that ethics (regardless of what source the ethical system is based upon) play in protecting society from "might makes right." If this premise is rejected, then the reader will not benefit from continuing to read this musing.

How has bad behavior been rewarded in America? The thousand words I permit for a musing are too few in number to allow me to even start to list comprehensively the ways bad behavior is rewarded; I simply use a few examples to illustrate the problem. Providing care at public expense for those who engage in unprotected sex with people who might have AIDS, providing medical care for sick infants caused by bad behavior during pregnancy by alcohol and substance abuse on the part of the pregnant woman with no sanctions on the woman, and providing funds for infants from repeated pregnancies by those without adequate resources to rear the children are rewards for the bad behavior of those involved. Years ago Dr. William Glasser applied something initially called "reality therapy" in treatment of alcoholic vets by making them fully face implications and consequences of their choices; their behavior began to change. Rewarding bad behaviors such as mentioned here by having society pay the tab instead of making folks comprehend fully the impact of what they did and letting them suffer the consequences of their choices and actions encourages others to behave in similar fashions. There are proposals from some to reward the bad behavior of those who enter the U.S. illegally by permitting them to stay and enjoy the benefits of our society, benefits which have been earned by the blood of Americans paying for our freedoms and the sweat of our people in making our society prosperous. The more bad behavior is rewarded, the less commitment there will be the ethics accepted by our society; the slope to "might makes right" becomes very slippery — then it is far easier to slide into the pit of "might makes right."

At present, there's a lot of fuzzy thinking about what should be done with people in difficulty, whether the difficulty is caused by choices the person makes or circumstances. Many seem to think that society has an obligation to take care of all in need within it. Usually such ideas only consider part of the situation: the part about what it takes to deal with the need of the person or group. Seldom have I seen or heard much discussion of where society gets its resources, and what rights or concerns should be considered in that arena. Society is not magic. Depending upon the society's political structure, the society may or may not produce things (wealth, items, etc.); or the society may merely take what it needs or wants from its citizens who produce things (that is basically what taxation and other methods of government appropriation do). Those who talk about society responsibility to meet the needs of those within it seldom have mentioned or discussed the propriety (or impropriety) of exploiting the endeavors of some for the benefit of others, at least not so far as I have seen or heard.

Valid ethics take a comprehensive approach in dealing with issues, not the partial kind of approaches most people employ. Such partial approaches to ethics are a subtle aspect of rewarding bad behavior; that too is pushing America toward the pit of "might makes right."

Anyone who has not been in a Rip Van Winkle slumber for decades can easily understand why I am concerned about the way America is rushing toward to the slippery slope to the pit of "might makes right."

Is there hope for a change? If each of us determines to express our objection to rewarding bad behavior of every sort, that will be a big help. If each of us determines to behave ethically, that too will be a big help. The

Christian Bible is the best place to go for guidance about ethics (right and wrong), as well as for sound spiritual guidance; but in this situation whatever ethical source one uses will be helpful, especially if those ethics are employed in a valid way, as together we seek to pull the U.S. back from the slippery slope to the pit of "might makes right."

Musing 68: Stupid People
(initially posted November 26, 2016)

The media and their advertisers think people are stupid, and the way the public behaves justifies that assumption about people. Harsh words, but unfortunately they are true.

Consider the way the media broadcasts weather and news. They make a big deal of having the commentator shown with the wind blowing on his or her face, with raindrops or snowflakes falling around the person, and expect the viewing audience to feel the information is better than what might be provided by the same person in a studio. Often the information is less and certainly no more reliable than it would be from a commentator in the studio, and obviously it costs the media more to provide such *"in situ"* coverage than a broadcast of the same information from someone in the studio.

In the case of weather information, temperature, wind speed and direction, and amount of precipitation come from measurements elsewhere (such as the weather station at the local airport), not from measurements made by the commentator or performed at the broadcast location. The media thinks such glimpses of the location gives the information more impact because the media think people are stupid and easily impressed by such silliness.

An ad I saw recently on TV illustrates the attitude of advertisers. The ad explicitly states that statistics show people pay more attention to an ad if it is exciting. So the ad showed the speaker in a fast car speeding down an airport runway with explosions nearby to tell about goods from a pawn shop. That ad shows how stupid the advertisers think people are. No information was presented about the pawn shop giving better value on hocked goods or on items it sells, the kinds of things that would be of interest to non-stupid people.

Here is the most unfortunate thing I will say in this musing. I think the media and their advertisers may be correct in their assessment that people are stupid. The public certainly behaves that way.

Why do I say that? Many people in the media and advertising are hard headed business men and women. They would not persist in the approach based upon public stupidity if it did not work. They would do something different, something that seemed to work and make money. The evidence seems to support the idea that people are stupid.

I don't like the idea that I am stupid or that I permit people to exploit me because of my stupidity. That runs counter to my self-image. I try to approach life with adult sanity. Consequently I now seldom watch TV. News broadcasts are a couple of minutes of information with some modest level of usefulness and 20-25 minutes of ads and fluff. A great amount of information important for the public to know never is mentioned. So I avoid the time-wasting process of watching news on TV. Likewise, I consider any product or service advertised on TV as probably not worthwhile in value. Retailers advertising on TV appear to invest more in promotion than in product value; so I avoid their products and services. Usually I mute their ads because I do not need to be agitated by their pitching to the viewers as if they are stupid.

As long as the public behaves as stupidly as it currently does, it is unlikely the media or advertisers will change how they act. Only when significant numbers of the public begin to act like sensible adults is it likely for the hard headed business men and women who run the media and advertising firms to change their approach.

What do I consider sensible adult behavior? A sensible adult wants meaningful information in news; not pictures of the environment or the gut-wrenching images of someone hearing bad news. The fact someone is upset because of a tragedy may have an emotional impact, but that image seldom provides a balanced or comprehensive perspective on things. For example, the relative's reaction to violence against a loved one is the kind of thing the media has given a great deal of attention to in the recent past, especially when police were involved in the violent incident. At the same time as that one person was hurt, the media blithely ignores the dozens killed the same day by drunk drivers and never show their grieving loved ones. Of course, the media is very careful about presenting adverse news about those who advertise heavily because the media seldom bites hands that feed them advertising dollars.

Public tolerance of such behavior by the media is one reason the media and their advertisers know people are stupid.

A sensible adult wants meaningful information about products and services so proper assessment of their capabilities and value can be determined. Advertisers try to sell products and services by leaving impressions that the product or service will improve one's sex appeal, enhance one's status and reputation, or other such appeals; the ads seldom provide meaningful and reliable information about product or service capability and value. It is common for ads to be totally stupid, such as leaving the impression they are willing to give you something for nothing. Apparently there are a sufficient number of very gullible people about so that such advertisers do not become bankrupt by the costs of their ads.

So at this point in our history I have to confess, the media and advertisers are correct in their assessment of the public: people are stupid, and least a large enough number of people behave stupidly so that the media and advertisers can get rich acting as if people are stupid. What a deplorable situation we live in!

Musing 69: What Is Wrong With The World? (initially posted November 29, 2016)

Recently I started reading a book. It's title is *What Is Wrong With The World*. Its author is reported to have answered an enquiry that *The Times* (a London newspaper) sent to a number of people asking them "What's wrong with the world today?"

The author of the book I've started is reported to have responded to the enquiry simply by saying:

"Dear Sir,
I am.
Yours, G. K. Chesterton"

Whether it actually happened or not is unknown. The story has been told so often of Chesterton, and I think acknowledged by him, that it is probably true. It's certainly the kind of thing he might have said. It has been noted that this reply captures the essence of New Testament theology.

A Wikipedia article says Chesterton (who died in 1936) was "an English writer, poet, philosopher, dramatist, journalist, orator, lay theologian, biographer, and literary and art critic." Chesterton is often referred to as the "prince of paradox". *Time* magazine noted that his writing style: "Whenever possible Chesterton made his points with popular sayings, proverbs, allegories — first carefully turning them inside out."

I have not read much yet of Chesterton's book, which was first published in 1910. Actually I have only read the first section in Part 1 of the book; but the closing words of that section made an exceedingly important point. After talking about a variety of social ills, Chesterton says, "The only way to discuss the social evil is to get at once to the social ideal. We can all see the national madness; but what is national sanity? I have called this book 'What Is Wrong with the World?' and the upshot of the title can be easily and clearly stated. What is wrong is that we do not ask what is right."

How perceptive that is. At present in our country, we are polarized. In part that comes from focus on dealing with a variety of social ills for which different groups propose different approaches. The different sides to such controversies have a hard time communicating constructively; they mainly throw slogans at one another with little effort to understand the other or desire to identify common ground that might be built upon in developing constructive and effective solutions for dealing with the various social ills. Chesterton suggests that such loggerheads come from focusing upon the ills and proposed solutions without first establishing a commonly accepted description of what is right.

Let me illustrate this with discussion of abortion. One side has emphasized the woman's right to do with her body as she wishes. Obviously such an emphasis has to have bounds, but sometimes those emphasizing female rights here seem to reject the idea of any bounds on the woman's right to choose what is done with her body. Assuming people, both women and men, have rights to control what is done with their bodies is never asserted as absolute. For example, most accept that a person has no right to put a lot of alcohol in their body and then drive an automobile. It is generally accepted that it is appropriate for government to restrict individual rights when a person's behavior poses a hazard to others. Likewise the government is generally assumed to be able to properly limit where most people can go on the basis of national security (casual visitors are not permitted in defense laboratories, for example). Such restrictions of individual rights are exercised in many ways. A person without certain technical qualifications is not permitted to pilot an aircraft or perform heart surgery.

Such restrictions on what a person can do are widely accepted. However, advocates for abortion rights at times seem unwilling to acknowledge government's right to restrict abortions for similar kinds of reason. Partially that occurs because there is not a commonly agreed upon source for determining where such rights can properly be restricted, controlled, limited.

Those opposing abortion face similar problems since many approach the issue drawing their perception of what is permitted from a particular source, and others addressing the issue turn to a different source. As Chesterton noted in the part of his book that I have yet read, discussion about the issue without coming to common agreement about what is right is a futile way to develop a constructive and effective way of dealing with the problem.

Unfortunately I find little willingness in contemporary America for serious discussion of how one determines what is right. Some want to make the Constitution the basic source of right and wrong, but its changes over time suggest it is not always a reliable guide to what is right. Our legal system is recognized as having many unjust aspects, and the highest court in the land has shown its unrighteousness by dictating that two wrongs make a right when it says it does. A better source for right and wrong is needed than the Constitution and the law.

There is not much serious public discussion of where we should turn. Promoters of particular religious teachings, various philosophical approaches, or insights from modern science pontificate at times, but serious constructive discussion among people from various communities seems to be lacking, or at least not given much attention by the media, politicians, or the public.

As I expect Chesterton would say if he were still alive today, failure to discuss and agree about what is right is the fundamental cause for what is wrong today in any area of social ills one might want to consider. Unfortunately I have little hope of Americans beginning to be serious about this problem and starting to deal with it as mature, thinking people.

Musing 70: Sensible Economics (initially posted December 9, 2016)

I am disgusted by the stupidity of comments on TV about the economic situation in America. The newscasters and their pundits talk about a number of things which provide indications of the economic situation of the nation, but they do not give much attention to what is perhaps the most significant indication of the nation's economic well-being. It is not because the information is not readily available. The Bureau of Labor Statistics (BLS) publishes it and keeps information about it up to date as well as historical information about it.

What in the world am I talking about? Good question.

Hundreds of times I have heard or saw discussions of the unemployment rate, the number of new jobs created in the past month or so (although they seldom indicate the number of jobs lost during that period – jobs do go away when business go under, plants move abroad, or technology eliminates jobs; there are very few elevator operators any more as everyone knows; what is important is the net change in number of jobs and that is not reported or discussed), and the percent of the population living in poverty. It is true that such things do provide indications of the economic situation.

But only once do I remember any mention on the air or in a print newspaper of what I consider to be the most significant indicator of the nation's economic situation. That indicator is the portion of the adult population ("adult" is defined by BLS as 16 and older) that is employed. This indicator shows whether new job creation is keeping up with population growth AND it indicates what portion of the adult population is contributing to the nation's economy. Anyone with sense knows that some people are willing to freeload on the efforts of others. Some well-intentioned policies encourage those inclined to freeload to do so by making it easier for them to be parasites on the efforts of others.

For more than two decades before election of President Obama, through good times and not-so-good times, from 60% to nearly 65% of adults (16 and older) in the U.S. were employed. Since Obama took office, only 58-60% of adults have been employed. His policies have both prevented enough new jobs development to keep up with population growth (largely due, in my opinion, to excessive regulation and trade deals that made it easier for products made elsewhere to replace those made in America) and facilitated freeloading by the scum inclined to do that.

I have not seen any explanation for why the media are so inclined to ignore such a significant indicator of the nation's economic situation. Whether it is a matter of ignorance and stupidity of popular economic pundits, bias by the media in its promotion of Obama and his agenda, or for other reasons, I cannot say. I am always suspicious of conspiracy theories, regardless of their direction or source, and I am well aware of how much incompetence abounds in nearly every area of human endeavor; but I cannot put my finger of the reason(s) for the media's disregard of this important economic indicator.

I do not contend that I properly understand the impact of the noticeable change in the employment proportion since Obama took office (compared with what it had been for the previous six presidential terms which included two by a democratic president); others may provide fuller and more insightful explanation than my brief comment above. The purpose of this musing is not what conclusions should be drawn from BLS data about the portion of adults employed, but a criticism of the media and their pundits for ignoring such as significant indicator of the nation's economic situation in their comments about economics.

The stupidity of broadcast economic commentary was illustrated by a few comments I heard on December 7th which suggested that the attack on Pearl Harbor caused a switch to be flipped and the U.S. suddenly got started in World War II. Actually as knowledgeable people realize, the U.S. had been engaged in full-scale industrial mobilization for two years before the attack on Pearl Harbor. This is illustrated by the fact that when Pearl Harbor was attacked, the U.S. Navy had more major warships under construction than were in commission. Some of the warships under construction on December 7, 1941, were not finished and commissioned before World War II ended. Although President Roosevelt had declared in 1939 that the U.S. would remain neutral legally in regard to the war in Europe, the U.S. had already begun to provide significant military supplies and other assistance to the allies, such as providing the British with 50 destroyers in the Land-Lease deal. Typical of broadcast failure to provide reasonable, comprehensive, and balanced views on things were the kind of comments made about the attack on Pearl Harbor suddenly waking the U.S. up to war dangers. Actually the U.S. had been preparing as fast as it could to get ready to enter the war for two years before Pearl Harbor. No comment I heard from broadcast news on December 7th commemorating the attack made any reference to such. Instead broadcast news deals with things at the kindergarten level, and we the American public tolerate such because as a whole we must be as stupid as broadcast news seems to think we are. Otherwise we would protest so much that those supporting the broadcasters with their advertising would abandon them.

My rant is over. Perhaps what I said may cause you to reflect on how much credence you should give to "information" and comments from various sources. I hope that happens.

Musing 71: Big Problems
(initially posted December 17, 2016)

Recently I came across a series on Bloomberg.TV called Big Problems. Big Thinkers. I believe this series started airing in September 2016. Episode 3 concerns Values. It is the only episode of the series that I have seen. I stumbled across it as I was killing time while Andrea was baking cookies to be part of the batch that the church would provide for inmates at our local jail as part of a Christmas concert and worship service. I think the church planned to provide the jail ministry with 500 dozen cookies for this purpose. Many women from the church had taken cookie dough the young people at the church had prepared and cooked the cookies, returning them to the church for delivery to the jail ministry.

The episode I watched was hosted by a noted journalist (Terre Blair). She set the stage for brief comments by a variety of people recognized as leaders in financial realms, political positions, and philosophical expression. I was struck by the fact that though the subject of the episode was Values there was no explicit mention of God. The pundits expressing their views set forth a variety of indications of life success, and mentioned doing right or living a principled life as important; but none said anything about God being a reliable source of information about right and wrong, or of values (ethics) in the terminology of the episode.

For centuries people have turned to God for insight about right and wrong, about how they should live. The pundits of the episode did not acknowledge that past approach. They neither said they rejected it; nor did they indicate such might have provided a foundation for their ideas. Certainly that failure to address the subject of God diminished the value of the episode.

For centuries, and still today, many acknowledge God as the Creator. As such God is the ultimate authority on right and wrong, and on how people should live. Likewise God is the ultimate authority that all will have to give an account to of their lives. For all of the "big thinkers" who commented on the big problem of values in the episode to totally ignore God in their discussions shows how unreliable guidance can be when promoted as from the best human minds as indicated by their success in business, politics, and society.

I am not such a big thinker. I'm a little guy, a bit brighter than some but not in the big leagues intellectually in any way. BUT even a little guy can grasp some fundamental truths that the brilliant may overlook. This is not a new problem; it has been recognized from centuries. Two millennia ago, the Apostle Paul observed:

"For what can be known about God is plain to them (people), because God has shown it to them. For His invisible attributes, namely, His eternal power and divine nature, have been clearly perceived, ever since the creation of the world, in the things that have been made. So they are without excuse. For although they knew God, they did not honor Him as God or give thanks to Him, but they became futile in their thinking, and their foolish hearts were darkened. Claiming to be wise, they became fools." Romans 1:19-22 (English Standard Version).

There are many big problems, and it is good to see a serious effort to discuss them by people to whom many will listen. I cannot comment on how the Big Problems. Big Thinkers series is addressing these problems in any of its episodes other than Episode 3 about Values. The discussion of that episode noted that money, success, etc. does not guarantee happiness; and suggested that helping others and living a principled life was more likely to produce happiness and life satisfaction. Certainly I agree with those insights. The pundits of the episode made many valid points in their comments; BUT they failed to identify a source for values. They were like the ones that the Apostle Paul talked about in my quote from the first chapter of his epistle to the Romans.

The important question for each of us is this, Am I like the ones Paul mentioned? Or am I wise enough to turn to God for information about true values? I hope the latter is true of you.

It may be that some of the pundits in Episode 3 took their values from God, but just failed to acknowledge that explicitly in the episode. I hope that is the case; that at least some of them know that God is the ultimate source for proper values. AND I hope also they have the wisdom to accept what God says is the only way for a person to live the kind of life that pleases God. That way involves a commitment by the individual to Jesus the Christ in faith for the salvation He offers.

I also hope the same for each person who reads this musing.

Musing 72: Caution Needed
(initially posted December 24, 2016)

Christmas reminds us that caution is needed when we approach the Scripture. Even a casual comparison of what the Bible actually says about the birth of Christ with much of what is said during the Christmas season shows that caution is needed because people are inclined to distort what the Bible actually says by additions, modifications, and carelessness.

Unfortunately, caution is needed in general when we approach the Bible. It is God's Word, and what it actually says should guide the thinking and lives of thoughtful men and women. Fluff lovers beware; this musing is for serious thinkers.

Wise men and women believe and act according to things the Bible clearly and explicitly says in a number of places; but those wise men and women are very cautious about things that are mentioned only once or in passages that are unclear or ambiguous. Unfortunately many preachers and Bible teachers are not so cautious and promote ideas they claim are Biblical which in fact may not be such.

This problem occurs in many areas; not just in the few mentioned in this musing. Eschatology (the study of the end times) is an area where a lot of ideas are promoted as Biblical, but which may not be so. Today many have beliefs about the end times that go far beyond what the Bible clearly says; popularity of fictional works (such as the *Left Behind* series) shape many people's ideas more than what the Bible actually says. The Bible is clear that Christ will return and that His return could occur at any time; much of what is presented beyond that is not actually Biblical.

Going beyond what the Bible says about the return of Christ is not a new problem. A Wikipedia website (*Predictions and Claims for the Second Coming of Christ*) lists about 40 predictions for when Christ would come (from 500 A.D. to the present) and a few that are yet future; these predictions were made by significant religious leaders (e.g., Pope Sylvester II relative to a prediction that Christ would return about 1000 A.D.). In the 1840s, a farmer turned Baptist preacher named William Miller attracted many with his predictions about when Christ would return; some of his followers founded the Seventh Day Adventists.

Let me illustrate why caution is needed when we interpret the Bible. As I noted earlier, if something is clearly taught by the Bible in multiple places then one can confidently take that as guidance from God. However, caution is needed for everything else. Check this out for yourself. Look at a number of passages in the New Testament which note fulfillment of an Old Testament prophecy. Then look at the Old Testament passages which are cited by the New Testament. Ask yourself if the original recipients of the Old Testament passage could have understood it as the Holy Spirit guided the New Testament writer to interpret it. Some are clearly so. Jewish leaders knew the Messiah was to be born in Bethlehem (as they explained to King Herod in response to his question in Matthew 2). However, in many situations, you may not feel that those who originally received the Old Testament passage could have understood its fulfillment as noted in the New Testament. This is why great caution is needed when one goes beyond clear teachings of the Bible in multiple passages.

Let me illustrate this by showing how focus on a single verse that is somewhat unclear can lead to erroneous ideas. In Ecclesiastes 7:28, Solomon, a man noted for his wisdom, says that he could only find one man in a thousand who was upright/truthful (how translated, or implied by context). How horrible life would be if one takes the implication of comment. Who would dare enter any kind of business arrangement with another person; or even who would be foolish enough to get on the road when none of the drivers could be trusted? In addition, as few reliable men as Solomon could find, he said he found no upright/truthful/reliable women.

This illustrates how easy it is to draw ideas that might be something other than the whole truth from a single somewhat unclear verse. This is why we need to be very cautious in the way we approach the Bible. We need to understand how some of the things we believe, even things taught by respected Christian leaders, may miss the mark when they go beyond what the Scripture clearly teaches explicitly in multiple passages.

This is a different problem from the problems caused by rejection of what the Bible says; that is a problem that many have to wrestle with because they want to give priority to their own thoughts or those of their peers (or society) over clear Scriptural teaching. That is a major issue in America right now as many, even some of our laws, choose to reject what the Bible says about a variety of sexual activities. But that is not the issue addressed in this musing.

This musing addresses a different problem. It is the danger of corrupting Biblical truth by adding to it ideas that are not clearly taught explicitly in a number of places in the Bible. This is particularly a problem in eschatological ideas, but it is not restricted to that topic. This musing has one objective: to bring this danger to your attention and to urge you to be cautious in the way that you interpret the Bible. Remember that adding to God's Word displeases God as much as taking away from it.

Musing 73: Limited Perspective (initially posted January 21, 2017)

Obamacare has aroused strong emotions in many Americans. Some have been agitated by its existence and others are angry at efforts to modify or end it. Personally I am astounded and disappointed by the limited perspectives that I see from those on every side of this issue.

First from the Need for Healthcare Perspective. It is true that some, perhaps many, do not get the healthcare they feel they need; and sometimes that is because of their limited financial means. Much of what I have seen only talks about this "need." That kind of limited perspective fails to address what level of healthcare is reasonable for everyone. That kind of limited perspective also fails to address individual responsibility to live a reasonably healthy lifestyle and not to expect others to pay cost of addressing unhealthy behaviors (behaviors such as smoking with its cancer impact, abuse of alcohol or drugs with their impact on the body, unsafe sex with strangers with its potential for STD, etc.). There should be explicit and comprehensive discussion of such considerations and the other aspects of this issue so that the real need for healthcare can be established in a balanced and comprehensive way, not distorted by a limited perspective. When such a balanced and comprehensive approach to healthcare is available and it has stood the test of scrutiny from all perspectives, then it would be possible to develop a national consensus about the need – and that is a prerequisite for developing a program to address that need which the vast majority of Americans can accept.

It would benefit the nation greatly if leaders from various perspectives on how to deal with healthcare needs would cooperate to produce such a balanced and comprehensive assessment of the healthcare need. I suspect one of the major foundations in the U.S. would underwrite the cost for doing so if leaders from various perspectives approached it with a proposal to produce that kind of comprehensive assessment.

Next from the Cost of Healthcare Perspective. Resources are finite. That is true for governments as well as for individuals. It is also true for the nation. There are not enough medical personnel or medical facilities to provide everyone in the country with every possible medical care to address their needs (and wants – since many optional medical procedures, such as plastic surgery, are for wants, not for medical necessity). Extreme amounts of medical resources can be expended to extend life a few weeks or months (often in unpleasant circumstances for the patient) for the seriously ill. Is such a reasonable expenditure of resources since such expenditures restrict resources available for use with others? I seldom see even the smallest consideration of such issues, but that kind of consideration is fundamental in a limited resource environment.

When the Titanic sank, recognition of such resource limitations guided the choice of who went into the life boats and who went down with the ship. Unless explicit and comprehensive consideration of resource limitations is done, limited perspective decisions about healthcare will lead to gross misuse of our limited healthcare resources.

Already the level of U.S. healthcare expenditures is impacting availability of resources for other socially important areas. For example, our infrastructure is in poor shape, in part because government resources have been spent elsewhere.

As with healthcare needs, I believe a major U.S. foundation would underwrite costs of developing a comprehensive assessment of healthcare costs if approached cooperatively by leaders from various perspectives on healthcare. Of course, such cooperation by some might imperil their support from the partisans upon they depend; some benefit from current divisions.

Finally from the Government Approach Perspective. I am not aware of clear and widely accepted comprehensive statements of what government (federal, state, or local) is responsible for in the healthcare arena. There are laws about requirements for those practicing medicine and medical facilities; various regulations to ensure appropriateness of medications and their descriptions (advertisements) also exist. However, I am not aware of general guidelines from the government (other than requiring some vaccinations and prohibitions/restrictions on use of specific substances) for individual healthcare activities. No laws say a person cannot overeat, has to exercise so often, must see a doctor every so often, etc.

Unfortunately the government at times takes a covert approach to healthcare. For example, when the government decided to provide healthcare for some who could not afford it themselves, instead of overtly establishing that as something the government would do and budget for that in the way it budgets for welfare or other needs, the government enacted law (Obamacare) that covertly forced the public to pay for such. By requiring medical insurers to do things that increase the cost of their business (such as not allowing exclusion of coverage for pre-existent conditions), those businesses have to pass the additional cost onto their customers in higher premiums. Thus the government hides the costs of what it is doing instead of dealing with that cost overtly. Such an approach from my perspective is distastefully deceptive. I make no suggestion for how to improve government behavior; such seems beyond hope.

My Bottom Line.

Healthcare issues currently are divisive in America. Divisiveness and antagonisms among various groups could be significantly reduced by development of facts with balance and broad perspective. I think that when reality becomes clear to most people, they act reasonably and responsibly. At present, most people don't trust what others say about healthcare because they think their comments are driven by limited perspectives. My goal is to encourage development of reliable information based upon comprehensive treatment of healthcare issues. Such could help our nation a great deal.

Musing 74: Scumbags
(initially posted January 23, 2017)

"Scumbags" is the title I have given to this musing. I thought it would be wise to check to make sure that my connotation of a scumbag was the same as others might have. So I went to an authoritative source for the meaning of English words, the *Oxford English Dictionary (OED)* – which has several times more word definitions than most other authoritative sources such as *Webster's*. The *OED* also indicates the first published use of a word. The *OED* has two definitions for scumbag: 1) a condom (which it says is current slang, first noted in the late-1960s) and 2) a base, despicable person; also as a term of vulgar abuse (first noted in 1971).

My connotation for scumbag is the second one: a despicable person. I also checked the internet to see if contemporary usage of the term is consistent with that found in the *OED* and it is. The definition of scumbag from yourdictionary was particularly interesting. It said "The definition of a scumbag is a person who is dishonest, contemptible, undesirable or sleazy." Such people are what this musing is about.

Unfortunately most of us encounter many scumbags. Some we meet in person; others we may only know about from the media, on-line, or by what others tell us. Scumbags are in all levels of society, both high and low. By my decades in jails and prisons, I have met many scumbags from the lower end of the social scale; but because of my involvement in technical, academic, and religious activities, I have been exposed to scumbags in higher levels of society also. Occasionally I touch different levels of society in a short period of time, as on the day when I was at the White House for a meeting with the President's Chief of Staff in the morning and at my county's jail in the evening to meet with inmates. Scumbags can be found nearly everywhere.

This musing is a rant against a particular kind of scumbag, not against a specific individual or group. You probably have observed the kind of scumbag I will describe; perhaps some of you even approve of them (or of some of their actions). It is possible that some who will read this musing even qualify as that kind of scumbag. I would not be surprised. I have met many people who have approved of others doing despicable things. Some condone adulterous breaking of marriage vows by people they know. Others applaud misrepresentations of things that enable ordinary people to sock it to a large insurance firm or the preferential hiring of someone of their favored group. There are many examples of despicable actions being approved by others, but I will not go into them here. Instead I will address the scumbags that are the focus of this musing.

The scumbags this musing focuses upon are the people who deliberately do things that interfere with the smooth and effective functioning of our government while enjoying the benefits of living in our great nation. That qualifies a lot of people for the scumbag label. Criminal behavior, whether street crime like muggings or non-violent crimes like tax evasion or fraud (as well as other forms of crime), qualify one as a scumbag. So does vandalism, whether it is defacing public property or destroying things in violent protests. It does not matter if it is rioting, looting, and burning vehicles and buildings, as has been done in protests against police misbehavior and in protests against the new President; such also qualifies one as a scumbag. Most of us know people who qualify for the scumbag label. Perhaps if we start calling them what they are (scumbags), some will be too embarrassed to continue to act like a scumbag; that would benefit both the individual involved and the rest of us too.

As residents in the U.S., each of us has a responsibility to be a good citizen. That means obeying the law, even laws which we think are unwise and perhaps even wrong. At present, the U.S. has laws which I believe are both unwise and wrong. For example, abortion is permitted at points in pregnancy where the fetus can survive as a baby outside the womb even when conditions do not require abortion to preserve the mother's life (current information indicates that by the 22nd week of pregnancy between a quarter and a third of the fetuses could survive as babies outside the womb). There are proper ways to deal with such laws; one of which is persuading the public and government that the law should be changed.

Recently there have protests against the new President. Those protesting should ask themselves if what they are doing contributes to improved functioning of our government or do their protests contribute to governmental malfunctionality and growing divisiveness within the country that is bad for us all. If their behavior interferes with the smooth and effective functioning of our government, then those protestors should admit that they have been scumbags and deserve that negative label,

Some may be offended by what this musing says. Reality is often embarrassing. Those working with addicts (of all kinds, especially in 12-step programs) know that coming to grips with reality and admitting the problem is essential to dealing effectively with addictive behavior. Instead of simply resorting to partisan slogans and self-justification, it would be useful to think carefully about what is said in this musing.

Certainly we as citizens have a responsibility to help the country change things it does that are unwise or wrong; but doing so should be done in a proper way, not by behaving as scumbags.

Musing 75: Does It Matter
(initially posted January 31, 2017)

Recently a friend from Oxford, England, visited us for the weekend. I had gotten a book from the library a few days before and discovered that the author was working on a doctorate at Oxford. The book was *No God But One: Allah or Jesus?* I mentioned it to her since in a way they were neighbors geographically. I noted that the author was a former Muslim and seemed to be addressing views on both sides of the issues in an informed and respectful way. Her response to that comment was, "Does it matter what his conclusion is?"

I was struck by that response. I said to her at the time that if the Bible is correct, as I think it is, the answer to that question matters a great deal for the individual because it could determine one's eternal destiny. Unfortunately I think many people are like my friend; they do not give serious attention to some very important issues.

My friend is an intelligent woman. As part of her graduate studies, she was a research assistant for a man who was one of the three people awarded the Nobel Prize for chemistry in 2016 (his work in nanotechnology was the basis for his award). Nor is she ignorant of Christianity since she was educated in Catholic schools as a child and young person. Yet she rather cavalierly dismisses the importance of the question, Who is God? I hope you are not so foolish as she in that regard.

Unfortunately, it is not just the question of one's eternal destiny that many fail to address with the seriousness that the question merits. There are many things in our society that many fail to give appropriate attention to.

For example, America's legal system currently permits one to take another's life simply because one chooses to do so; that choice can be made on the basis of personal convenience. That comment may surprise you. The legal definition of a person or human being is one who can survive outside the mother's womb. At 24 weeks of pregnancy, the likelihood of infant survival is 39% and at 23 weeks it is 17% (statistics from https://www.verywell.com/premature-birth-and-viability-2371529 – other studies report even higher survival likelihoods). Some infants have survived with even less than 23 weeks of pregnancy. Our legal system and medical institutions permit termination of infants that could survive outside the womb. It is amazing how few people give much attention to this. Many consider callous taking of life murder.

At present there have been a great many protests over decisions by President Trump about immigration and the executive order restricting people from certain areas coming to the U.S. at this time. Certainly that has inconvenienced a number of people, but it has not taken the lives of many persons as abortion does. Somehow it seems like misplaced emphasis to create uproar over something like immigration policies while totally ignoring activities that are terminating many lives. It seems to me to come from the "does it matter" approach to serious issues that I mention above.

I think it is important to give serious attention to important issues that one can do something about; I do not think it is so important to give serious attention to issues that one is unlikely to be able to do something about. Sometimes it is clear one can do something about an important issue, such as what is likely to be one's eternal destiny. Other times, it is not clear that one (such as an ordinary citizen like me) can do anything meaningful about the issue. Letters, calls, and visits to government representatives might have an impact, but usually not a lot. The same applies to participation in demonstrations. They often just create trouble for the authorities and other people, but do little to impact policies. Other factors usually dominate policy decisions.

I find giving a lot of attention to issues that I cannot impact significantly can disturb me unnecessarily (and then I create unpleasantness for others); so I do not give such issues a great deal of attention. That approach has been criticized by some who are inclined to give serious attention to many kinds of issues.

Let me close this musing by returning to the issue of one's eternal destiny. It is something that each of us can impact significantly. Many think that their eternal destiny will be determined by human type evaluation – were they good enough as people to merit entrance into heaven? The Bible presents a very different view. It says no one will make it to heaven based upon a human perspective. Entrance into heaven is determined very differently.

To check that out for yourself, read four books of the New Testament (Luke, John, Acts, and Romans); they come in that order. Luke tells what Jesus said and did; John explains what the life of Jesus meant. Acts presents a bit of history of the church, covering the first few decades of the church; and Romans explains why God has acted as He has relative to human salvation.

The key to one's eternal destiny is one's relationship to Jesus; and is based upon what Jesus has done for us. There is no place for human merit in God's plan; it all depends upon what Jesus did and acceptance of God's gracious offer of salvation for people because of what Jesus did. It is so easy even a child can do it, and yet so hard for some to understand and accept. I hope you are one of the wise ones who act on God's gracious offer of salvation by accepting it.

Musing 76: Surprising Facts
(initially posted February 5, 2017)

Based upon information about National Vital Statistics from the U.S. Center for Disease Control (CDC), since 1973 more than twice as many black lives have been terminated or prevented by abortion than by the combined total for AIDs, violent crime, accidents, cancer, and heart disease. Economically abortions by black women have saved the nation a massive amount of health care and welfare money if the costs of the 15 million-plus for persons not allowed to be born because of abortion had been typical of such costs for black people. Of course such savings are partially offset by increased medical costs of women who had abortions (e.g., a 1993 Howard University study showed that African American women over age 50 were 4.7 times more likely to get breast cancer if they had had any abortions compared to women who had not had any abortions).

I mention the above to illustrate that issues widely discussed, such as abortion, often only have part of the issue addressed. Many favoring abortion focus on female rights aspects of abortion (i.e., a woman should be allowed to do with her body as she chooses) and those opposed to abortion often emphasis mainly the moral issues involved (such as terminating a life merely for the woman's convenience when no significant medical issue is involved). It is my conviction that significant issues should be addressed comprehensively, not partially. Decisions and actions based only upon discussion about part of a significant issue can be harmful, even disastrous.

One often hears views about significant issues castigated, but sometimes what is castigated is a distortion of views by those opposing the perspective of the one castigating the view. For example, based upon the information presented above, one could castigate those promoting abortion rights as doing so to reduce medical and welfare costs by reducing the size of the black community; or one might claim that those promoting abortion rights were trying to reduce the political influence of the black community by limiting its population growth. Others might say promoters of abortion are merely people working to reduce crime in the U.S. since blacks are several times more likely to commit violent crimes than are members of other racial and ethnic groups.

As another example of failure to address all aspects of a significant issue, let's consider the contentious issue of "equal pay for equal work." Many claim that the "wage gap" is about 30% (that is the gap between what women are paid and what men are paid). It is hard to get reliable information that compares pay for women in the same job at the same skill level and with the same amount of experience as pay for men in that situation, but the little I have seen suggests the size of the gap is nowhere near the widely quoted 30%. In addition, the wage gap usually focuses on the weekly, monthly, or annual wage and does not consider the fact that on the average women work about 10% fewer hours in a day/week/month than men according to information from the U.S. Bureau of Labor Statistics. Nor do those making much of the wage gap usually note that a female is a more expensive employee than a male one. The reasons for this are multiple. Females require more facilities than males (often this is found in building codes about toilet facilities based upon number of occupants by gender) and insurance costs vary with gender. Just as with the abortion issue, most discussion of equal pay for equal work fails to address all significant aspects of the issue.

Many people are surprised by the facts when all significant aspects of issues are addressed. Recognition that such surprising facts exist and may cause one to come to a different conclusion about the issue is the objective of this musing.

I picked two issues that get a lot of attention in the media, and about which many people have very strong feelings. I chose these two issues because they are the kind of issues one would expect to be thoroughly discussed and people's opinions about them would then be grounded in the reality of solid information about them. Unfortunately I suspect that the brief comments above show a number of things about these two issues that many are not aware of. If such is the situation then our nation is in a dire state because important issues such as the two noted above are being addressed with many aspects of the issue unconsidered; and that is a sure way to create disaster.

I hope you will join me in helping our nation by demanding that our leaders, the media, and the experts and pundits providing information about issues produce comprehensive information about the issues and not just focus on some aspects of the issue while ignoring other significant aspect of the issue. It will require diligence on our part. We will have to think carefully about issues, and not just jump on a bandwagon for or against an issue because one aspect of the issue hits a resonant chord in us. Our nation and all of us will benefit if we show such diligence because then we are likely to have better decisions about significant issues than we would otherwise.

Will you do your part?

Musing 77: Good Of The Country
(initially posted February 8, 2017)

I am concerned about what seems to be the attitude of many activists. I use the term "activist" as a catchall for those promoting or protesting an issue vigorously. They may be doing this by participation in demonstrations and protests, or by their social media postings and communications. They may be financial supporters or active participants. That broad spectrum of people is what I mean by activists. The issue or issues of interest to an activist vary. For some, the issues relate to civil rights and public behavior; for others, the issues may be ecological or environmental; and for others the issues may be in other areas.

This musing is not about any particular issue or kind of issue; instead it is about the attitudes and behaviors of activists. In my opinion, the motivation of the activist is important. Is what he or she does for the good of the country? Or is it for some other reason? Aggrandizement may be the reason some are activists.. Financial motivation certainly is involved for those paid to participate in demonstrations and protests. Some people just enjoy causing trouble and making a ruckus. And some are motivated by desire for improvement or advantage for their group. Most people, and I believe this is also true of most activists, have multiple motivations. The question comes, what happens when motivations conflict? Which one dominates?

This musing is primarily about the conflict among motivations. What happens when an activist's motivation conflicts with the good of the country? It is possible for an activist to believe in something that he or she thinks will be good for the country as well as having other motivations, and then find that what he or she believes in would be bad for the country if carried to extremes or if his or her other motivations were pursued in particular ways.

Let me illustrate this with a couple of examples. For example, most of us believe "freedom of speech" is good for the country, as recognized by the Bill of Rights (a label given to the first set of amendments to the Constitution). However, freedom of speech carried to an extreme (such as permitting someone to yell "fire" in a crowded theater when there is no fire) is not good for the country; it brings unnecessary harm to people.

As another example, consider emphasis on the same rights for a group as are enjoyed by other groups, such as members of a racial or ethnic group. This often is viewed simply as a rejection of previous discrimination. Sometimes the remedies advocated by activists (even those in the judiciary) impose new discrimination as compensation for past discrimination, even though the victims of the new discrimination were not guilty of the past discrimination in any way (because they had not even been born when it occurred). This is exactly what happened with Affirmative Action in the U.S. Contrary to what the American Congress and judiciary seem to believe by what they have done, two wrongs do not make a right (in fact two wrongs never make a right, not even when justified by comments such as "fighting fire with fire").

This is a problem that many activists fail to acknowledge: promotion of the issue they support can impose new problems as well as address old problems. This has been shown repeatedly by what has happened in many demonstrations and protests against misbehavior by police; the protest has resulted in a riot with looting and burning of cars and buildings. Often the activists claim no responsibility for the harm done to others, most of the victims (such as the property owners) had no part in alleged police misbehavior, yet they suffered because of the protest orchestrated by the activist. This is a well-known and very obvious illustration of how what activists do can be at odds with the good of the country.

Some activists are so concerned about their issue(s) of interest that they do not care about the impact on others. This has been shown repeatedly in regard to activists concerned with various forms of animal life or ecological issues; they do not care about the economic impact on people and think preservation of the habitat of an insect or other kind of creature is more important than the livelihood of people in the area. Such lack of balance by activists is not good for the country.

I admire activists who are willing to promote important issues, who are willing to go to substantial personal expense and inconvenience in doing so, and who at the same time maintain a balanced perspective about conflicting rights and interests so that what they do as activists does not conflict with good for the country. At the same time, I despise activists who promote their issue(s) of interest without regard for good of the country.

The question facing each of us is, How important is the good of the country to us? If the good of the country is important, then first we should never become activists who allow our promotion of our issues of interest to conflict with good of the country. Second we should let other activists know we feel they should let good for the country limit or modify the way they promote their issues when such conflicts with good for the country. And third, we should let activists and others know who we despise because they promote things that are not good for the country or promote issues in ways that are not good for the country.

What do you think?

Musing 78: Miss Marple
(initially posted February 10, 2017)

My wife and I often eat lunch or dinner in front of the TV. We usually watch a movie or an episode from a TV series as we eat. What we watch usually comes from Netflix or a DVD; sometimes it even comes from what is now antiquated technology (VHS) or Amazon. Recently we watched the Margaret Rutherford portrayal of Miss Marple in the four films starring her in that role.

Jane Marple is a character created by Agatha Christie. Miss Marple is an elderly spinster who lives in the village of St. Mary Mead and acts as an amateur consulting detective. She appears in 12 of Christie's crime novels and 20 short stories. Probably most Americans know Miss Marple from TV presentations of her. Joan Hickson played Marple in a dozen TV stories from 1984-1992. Geraldine McEwan played Marple in a dozen TV stories from 2004-2008; and Julia McKenzie played her in eleven stories from 2009-2013.

The first Miss Marple novel appeared in 1930 and the last one in the 1970s; the short stories about her were also written during that time. Although the Marple novels and stories were popular from the first, they did not make it to the big screen for more than three decades after the character first appeared in print. The first film was *Murder, She Said* in 1961 starring Margaret Rutherford.

Rutherford (who was 70 at the tine) presented Miss Marple as a bold and eccentric old lady, very different from the prim and birdlike character Christie created in her novels. As penned by Christie, Miss Marple never worked for a living, but the character as portrayed by Margaret Rutherford briefly works as a cook, a stage actress, a sailor and is offered the chance to run a riding establishment-cum-hotel. Her education and genteel background are hinted at when she mentions her awards at marksmanship, fencing and equestrianism (although these hints are played for comedic value).

The first Rutherford Miss Marple film (*Murder, She Said*) was based on Christie's 1957 novel *4:50 from Paddington* (U.S. title, *What Mrs. McGillicuddy Saw!*), but with major changes in the plot. In the film, Mrs. McGillicuddy is cut from the plot; Miss Marple herself sees an apparent murder committed on a train running alongside hers. Likewise, it is Miss

Marple herself who poses as a maid to find out the facts of the case, not a young friend of hers as in Christie's novel.

None of the other three Miss Marple films with Rutherford (1963 *Murder at the Gallop*, 1964 *Murder Most Foul*, and 1964 *Murder Ahoy*) were based upon a Christie Marple story or novel about Miss Marple, although some plot elements are similar to ones in several of Christie's Poirot stories. The films also included a rather meek librarian (Mr. Stringer) friend and cohort of Miss Marple, a character that is never found in any of the Christie Marple stories. The actor (Stringer Davis) who played Mr. Stringer was Rutherford's real-life husband. The two of them often appeared together in theatrical endeavors during the several decades of their marriage.

Actresses Angela Lansbury, Helen Hayes, and Ita Ever (an Estonian) have also played Miss Marple in films (the one with Ever was in Russian, an adaptation of Christie's novel *A Pocket Full of Rye* with the translated title of *The Secret of the Blackbirds* for the film).

In many ways, the character of Rutherford's Miss Marple is far more entertaining than the portrayal of Marple by other actresses (most of whom portray Marple more like the character in Christie's stories than Rutherford did). Both Andrea and I really like the Rutherford Miss Marple films.

Musing 79: Presidental Evaluation
(initially posted February 11, 2017)

Presidents are evaluated many different ways. Their appearance makes a big difference to some, which is why Franklin Roosevelt was seldom portrayed publically in his wheel chair. Some attribute part of Kennedy's victory over Nixon in 1960 to the differences in their appearances in a televised debate. Personally I hope that most Americans evaluate the president by more significant criteria than the president's appearance.

Some evaluate the president by the policies the president announces and supports. That is akin to what I have heard said of European liberals: they are mainly concerned about the intentions of politicians, not about results from them. Others, and I try to be in this group, evaluate a president by the consequences of his time in office. That may not be a fair basis for assessment because so much that happens during and after a president's time in office is outside his control. This is illustrated by the following example. In my opinion, Jimmy Carter was the best person as far as human goodness is concerned of any president we have had, but he was a disaster for the country by his response to the behavior of Iran when it took Americans hostage. The failure of his presidency, in my opinion, was due to something outside his control: the behavior of people in Iran.

Even though looking at what happens to the country during and after a president's time in office may not be fair, it is a valid basis for assessment since it is the best indication of a president's impact on national well-being. Unfortunately, the mouthy pundits paraded before us by the media seldom look at things that way.

Of course, evaluating a president by impact on the nation cannot be done during the early days of a president's administration. Mouthing off about a president in the early days of his administration is as foolish as judging the taste of a cake before it goes into the oven if one is assessing the president by impact on the nation. Unfortunately the media throws a lot of that kind of foolish assessments at us, which is one reason I have such a negative attitude about our contemporary media; its behavior is mainly contemptible.

However, it is not too early to make some preliminary evaluation of the previous president since some impacts of the actions of his administration are evident already. Because of the thousand word limit I impose on my musings, I will only address two impacts: 1) economic burden on future Americans to pay for benefits given to people during his administration (crudely, he bought popularity by things the future must pay for), and 2) discouraging employment. Some are surprised by my picking these two things. Most people do not appreciate the impact of economic factors on what happens. For example, the battle of the Atlantic in World War II was won initially by America's capability to build ships faster than the Nazis could sink them; later in the war the Allies devastated Hitler's U-boats militarily. Likewise, the U.S. had been industrializing at full bore for two years before Pearl Harbor (e.g., we had more warships under construction than in the fleet on December 7, 1941), otherwise the outcome of World War II might have been quite different.

The Obama administration increased the national debt more than any previous president (by some measures doubling it), having federal deficits at a level (10% of GDP) that were not reached before except in the crises imposed by the Civil War, World War I, and World War II. No one could claim that Obama served during a time of crisis comparable to those wars. It looks like he bribed the American people with governmental largess which the future will have to pay for. In my opinion, that was a very bad thing to do if one is concerned about the future of the country. He could have restricted benefits or increased taxes to pay for them or cut government expenditures elsewhere to obtain pay for the benefits. He chose not to do such, and simply dumped the cost for his largess on future taxpayers.

During the Obama administration, the employed portion of the U.S. adult population dropped several percent from levels it had been at for several decades (since women largely entered the workforce outside the home, usually dated from the 1970s). Why did this happen? Part came from the economic policies of the administration that prevented enough new job creation to keep up with population growth (e.g., increasing the minimum wage reduced jobs at the bottom of the pay scale) and part came from increasing available benefits (which may have decreased willingness of some to work if they could get by on the benefits). The portion of the population employed is a valid long term indication of a nation's economic well-being.

So on the basis of these two factors, unnecessary economic burden on the future and reduction in the portion of Americans employed, the Obama presidency gets a negative evaluation. Looking at results in this way says nothing about what one thinks of Obama as a person or about his social policies. It merely says that his presidency was bad for the nation's economic well-being.

Some I know are similar to what I heard about European liberals: they only evaluate on the person's intent, not on the consequences of the person's action. The ones I know with that approach do not seem to care about the facts, even though their children and grandchildren are likely to have a harder time because of the consequences of the Obama presidency.

Musing 80: Toxic Communications (initially posted February 17, 2017)

Polarization has become so pronounced in contemporary America that effective, constructive governmental decisions and actions are nearly impossible. This toxic state of communication is the result of extreme advocacy by all parts of the political and social spectrum. If this horrible situation is not corrected, we will soon discover the unpleasant consequences of a non-functional government coupled with an uncontrollably rowdy population.

Nearly everyone is to blame for this deplorable situation. Obviously those guilty of communicating toxically by demonizing all who do not concur with their view and putting promotion of the position they advocate above facts or the good of the country are clearly guilty; so are those who tolerate or support such communicators, whether for partisan reasons or for expectation of some kind of benefit (financial, social, or otherwise) or just for the fun of watching the resulting chaos.

More important than allocating blame for this mess is identification of what can be done to correct the situation and then helping to bring that correction about. There is an easy to identify <u>first step</u> in correcting the problem: stop toxic communications.

You can choose not to produce any such, and you can turn off any and every one you hear or see who is communicating toxically. Refuse to listen to, acknowledge, or support in any way anyone and everyone engaged in toxic communication, even when they are promoting a topic you consider extremely important. That may cause you to walk out of a meeting for a cause you would like to support and promote because those speaking at and for it are communicating toxically.

The <u>second step</u> in solving the problem is more difficult. It is recognition that effective and constructive governing usually requires compromise among those with vested interests. Promoting one's perspective without regard for the perspectives of others has contributed a great deal to the current bad situation. Of course there are some pig-headed diehards who would rather see everyone starve than subsist off half-a-loaf or to watch everyone drown because the only available life boat was overloaded; but you do not have to be one of them.

Compromise is extremely difficult for advocates of a perspective who come with an attitude of "I'm right and you're an idiot." Courtesy in dealing with those with a different perspective and emphasis upon *ALL pertinent facts* in a calm and thoughtful way is much more likely to lead to a workable conclusion that is beneficial to most of those involved. A person who feels strongly about an issue will have a hard time doing this unless that person accepts the reality that compromise is almost always required for an effective and constructive resolution to a complex and disputed issue (which is the kind of issue that has to be resolved for social programs by government).

The <u>third step</u> in solving the problem is a determination that all pertinent facts about an issue need a fair hearing and wide exposure to all parties in the discussion. Unfortunately most people are satisfied with a conclusion based upon only part of the facts; making sure all pertinent facts are considered takes both diligence and significant effort.

Now the onus is on each of us. Are we willing to take the three steps indicated? Are we willing to do that even for issues we consider extremely important? Are we willing to do that even if criticized by family and friends? Are we willing to do that even if lambasted by people we respect and esteem? Do we care enough about the well-being of our country? About improvement in our society? About avoiding the chaos to which our nation is currently speeding? <u>If we care enough, we will take the steps needed</u>.

Americans have faced hard choices in the past. During the American Revolution, people were forced to choose between loyalty to their king (the ruling power they, their parents, and possibly their grandparents had served their entire lives) and the rebellion leaders. In the Civil War and leading up to it, families were torn apart by the issues of slavery and States' rights. During WWII some were torn by affection for their German, Italian, or Japanese heritage and the need to fight against those nations.

At present, we are faced with hard choices. There are many things that need to be changed in our nation, and some advocating change do so from good motives, but the way advocacy has become toxic has to be changed or we will destroy ourselves as a nation. Join me in taking the steps noted above and encourage others to do so as well. Perhaps we can contribute the beginning a needed change in the way our society behaves.

Thank you for your attention to this musing.

Musing 81: Divine Insights From Nature (initially posted February 21, 2017)

In Romans 1 the Apostle Paul mentions some of the things people can learn from nature and says that takes away their excuse if they do not believe those things about God. I thought it would be interesting to see what I think we can learn about God from nature (a shorthand way of referring to all that God has created).

The point that the Apostle Paul makes is found in Romans 1:18-32. I present verses 19-23 here to make Paul's point explicit for this musing: "For what can be known about God is plain to them, because God has shown it to them. For His invisible attributes, namely, His eternal power and divine nature, have been clearly perceived, ever since the creation of the world, in the things that have been made. So they are without excuse. For although they knew God, they did not honor Him as God or give thanks to Him, but they became futile in their thinking, and their foolish hearts were darkened. Claiming to be wise, they became fools, and exchanged the glory of the immortal God for images resembling mortal man and birds and animals and creeping things." I quoted from the English Standard Version (ESV) because I believe it is in the process of becoming the primary translation in English (although at present, the New International Version, NIV, is currently the most widely sold version). The points that Paul makes in this passage come through clearly in every major English translation; so the version one uses is not critical.

I believe that the things which I think we can know about God and His behavior from His creation are consistent with what the Apostle Paul says. First, God's creation shows God is. He exists. Of course, there are some who deny this. They want to think the creation is eternal (even though the cosmology currently accepted by the vast majority of scientists says the creation we observe had a beginning (which is called *The Big Bang*). None of the ideas of those who deny the existence of a Creator (i.e., God) have wide acceptance, and we know why: there always are people around with foolish ideas.

The creation shows us that God (the Creator) has great power to bring the creation into existence (the created universe is so large that we believe it takes billions of years for light to travel from as far as can be observed from the earth in every direction from the earth; and the mass of the part of the creation that can be observed from earth is so great that it exceeds our ability to estimate, and current estimates about the universe by scientists think there is even more mass than can be seen from the earth, they call it *dark matter*). The universe (or multiverse, as some prefer to call it) is so huge that most scientists think it has more dimensions than the standard four of time, length, width, and height.

God's creation implies the Creator is smart beyond human comprehension since He designed the universe we can observe with order and gave it rules that are followed consistently at all places we have been able to observe. We call those rules the "laws of nature." The consistency of those rules should frighten us. If the consequences of actions within the material universe always occur, then we should expect similar consequences for actions within the moral, ethical, and spiritual realms as well. The Apostle Paul is clear about that in Romans also. All have failed to live up to God's standards, and the consequences of that are devastating (Romans 3:23 & 6:23).

The law of gravity tells us that if we let something fall from our hand it will fall to the ground. This happens every time we simply let something fall from our hands. God's laws work just as consistently in the moral and spiritual arena as they do in the material world. Gravity will take everything to the ground, <u>unless</u> another law also impacts. For example, if I let something fall from my hand that is metal over a strong magnetic field, it may float and not fall to the ground. This also happens in amusement park rides where a person's body is kept from falling by the upward pressure of an airstream.

We can observe how different laws of nature interact and understand how one may over rule another one; but our observations of nature cannot reveal similar interactions among God's spiritual laws. The deadly consequences of sin are clear in nature, but we must turn to God's revelation of His laws in His Word (the Bible) to learn how his laws of love and grace can overcome the deadly consequences of sin.

For a person to grasp the essence of that quickly, I suggest reading the Gospel of John to learn the significance of what Jesus said and did, followed by Paul's letter to Christians in Rome for an explanation of why God acted as He has. Paul explains things more completely in his letter to the Romans because in it he wrote to people he had not been with (in contrast to all his other letters in the New Testament). With people you know, you leave things unsaid which you know they already understand. With those you do not know that way, you explain things more completely. These two books in the New Testament (the Gospel of John and the letter to the Romans) give you an overview of how God's spiritual laws interact. I hope you will read them both.

Musing 82: Diversity and Intolerance (initially posted February 24, 2017)

When I was a young person, discrimination was a major social issue in the US. That issue was largely addressed by civil rights legislation in the 1960s and has been working itself out in the decades since. Some groups have benefitted far more than others in efforts to overcome past discrimination; and America has had to endure both the turmoil of change from past behavior and legislatively endorsed new kinds of discrimination (such as that from Affirmative Action efforts that give some legal advantages over others who in no ways were guilty of the discrimination Affirmative Action was designed to address since those now discriminated against by the law had not even been born when Affirmative Action was introduced). Perhaps at some point America's courts and legislatures will come to realize that one cannot correct past wrongs by doing new and different wrongs (two wrongs never make a right).

In recent decades diversity has become a major social issue, often with allegations of intolerance being used to demonize those who oppose diversity in any way. Diversity is assumed to be beneficial (without much evidence to support such a claim for many situations or to define its appropriate limits). Rationality and realism often have been overridden by partisan proponents of diversity who repeatedly mouth sound-byte slogans. Unfortunately both individuals and the nation suffers when that is done.

Let's simply explore the question of reasonable limits on diversity. At times, groups and organizations have been criticized by proponents of diversity for the homogeneous character of their members or participants. Such criticisms often are very selective: addressing some groups and ignoring others. For example, many white religious congregations were criticized for their lack of involvement by members of racial and ethnic minorities; but those critics never seemed bothered that the religious congregations of those racial and ethnic minorities were far less diverse than the white congregations they criticized. Do the proponents of diversity believe that diversity is only important for some and not for others? If so, they should declare that publicly. If they do not believe that, then they should be concerned about the lack of diversity within the racial and ethnic minorities as well as in organizations and groups that have been mainly white.

If diversity is such a great virtue, then it would be good to be very explicit where it is not such a great idea. Think about housing. Should diversity be demonstrated in the kinds of people who live in the neighborhood? Should the distribution of the neighborhood racially and ethnically reflect the distribution of those groups in the larger community? Or is it ok for pockets of the population with common interests (perhaps racially, ethnically, religiously, economically, socially such as neighborhoods that historically attracted a high percentage of artists, etc.)?

Most proponents of diversity tacitly accept restrictions of various sorts. For example, few would advocate no restriction on sexual perverts convicted of molesting children. At present, such people have to be registered with authorities and often have court mandated restrictions on their activities (such as being required to stay away from places where lots of children are present). Such examples show that diversity legitimately has limits, and that it is appropriate to be explicit about such limits.

I believe that studies about educational diversity sometimes show that poorer students and those with less adequate educational background (as is sometimes alleged for members of certain ethnic and racial groups) benefit from participated in what had been a more exclusive academic setting; but such benefit to the poorer students often comes at the cost of reducing the educational benefit to those fully qualified for the more exclusive educational environment. Often proponents of diversity seem only willing to address one side of such issues.

How often have you heard proponents of diversity lament the wrong of denying an academic (or job) opportunity to a more qualified white applicant in order to accommodate the diversity required by Affirmative Action? It is hard to find such laments. Such selectivity by proponents of diversity is deplorable, and unfortunately is encountered far too often.

It is easy to confuse issues. For example, it is easy to confuse legitimate and proper requirements for a position or activity with discrimination that might deny them to qualified applicants from ethnic or racial minorities or on the basis of gender. At one time, certain physical size and strength requirements for jobs (such as fire fighter) were criticized for restricting females from such a position because statistically most women were not able to satisfy those requirements. The issue was posed as a diversity issue, when more appropriately it should have been an appropriateness of job requirements issue. Posing the issue as a diversity issue made it likely the requirements would be lowered to accommodate more females applicants (even those who might not have adequate physical size or strength to do what needs to be done). Scuttlebutt from fire fighters mentions the way duties of the crew have to be shifted to accommodate the physically weaker members of the crew.

Let me be very clear. I am not against diversity; but I am for being realistic and dealing with all aspects of issues fairly and comprehensively so that significant aspects of an issue are not ignored. The behavior I see by diversity partisans makes it necessary for me to comment on this problem because the selective way they address diversity issues is bad for the country and for individuals. There are differences between the characteristics and behaviors of groups, and those differences need to be considered, not ignored as some diversity partisans seem to do.

Musing 83: Persons
(initially posted February 24, 2017)

What is a person? "Silly question," you say. It's as silly as saying, "Is John dead?" after being told his funeral was that afternoon. However both legal parlance and modern technology would show you to be wrong. It is not a silly question.

An on-line legal site (LAW.COM) defines *person* as "n. 1) a human being. 2) a corporation treated as having the rights and obligations of a person. Counties and cities can be treated as a person in the same manner as a corporation. However, corporations, counties and cities cannot have the emotions of humans such as malice, and therefore are not liable for punitive damages unless there is a statute authorizing the award of punitive damages."

Another site quotes *Duhaime's Law Dictionary*: "**Person Definition:** An entity recognized by the law as separate and independent, with legal rights and existence including the ability to sue and be sued, to sign contracts, to receive gifts, to appear in court either by themselves or by lawyer and, generally, other powers incidental to the full expression of the entity in law." The sites then notes that some individuals (such as minors or those under court findings about mental incapacity) may not be "persons" under law and various organizations, associations, etc. also may be considered persons.

You can see how the question of what a person is legally has complications. Generally a human being is considered a *person* unless that individual is a minor or deemed by the court to have mental incapability. Then the individual may not be able to sue (or be sued), to sign contracts, etc. The question is farther complicated legally by asking when an individual becomes a human being? Think of the possibility. Some Christian theologians (e.g., Origin) thought souls (the essence of human beings) existed before their bodies were conceived and they were born. Others think the soul comes into existence at some point during conception. If the fetus is a person when aborted, then such is legally murder. Legal issues about this are unclear; "born-alive" is a phrase in some legal documents which is taken to mean the fetus is capable of surviving outside the mother's womb. That condition can occur as early as the 21st or 22nd week of conception. That fact could make some of the abortions permitted in the U.S. (those in the 23rd and 24th weeks of conception) technically murder.

Now you can see some of the complexities related to the question, what is a person? It is not a silly question; and now technology is beginning to make the question even more complex.

Advances in computation technology are giving machines the decision making capabilities previously thought as essentially human. For decades computers have been able to answer questions of fact based upon access to digitized data about things. In the past decade or two reasoning capability of computational devices has increased enough so machines can now beat the world's best humans at strategy games such as Chess (1997) or Go (2016). The topic of reasoning by machine computation is generally called Artificial Intelligence (AI), with many applications in logistics, data mining, medical diagnosis, and other fields. Such capabilities are beginning to have potential impact in areas such as vehicle control. Question of responsibility for damages in vehicle accidents have yet to be resolved. Should it be the human operating the system with some level of control over it? The designer of the software guiding the vehicle? The manufacturer of the vehicle? Or someone else?

If the responsibility of such accidents falls on anyone other than a human, then it suggests that legally something other than a human is being considered a person (i.e., the one responsible legally). You can see how this complicates the question of what (or who) is a *person?* Could that computer chip in your car that warns (or fails to warn you) of the danger in changing lanes be responsible for an accident? Would that chip become a person in the eyes of the law?

In the late 1960s I read the Robert Heinlein science fiction story *The Moon Is a Harsh Mistress*. In it, the Lunar Authority's master computer had almost total control of the machinery in the human colony on the moon; that computer develops enough computational power to achieve self-awareness. In the story, the computer (called Mike) by a computer technician becomes the leader of the moon colony's revolt against political control from earth. That was my first exposure to a machine behaving like a person.

Of course, Heinlein was not the first to bring that idea into play in fiction. The famous 1927 Fritz Lang movie *Metropolis* had a mechanical woman become a functional human briefly in the film who created a great deal of chaos and trouble for the city. She was held responsible for the damage and burned at the stake.

I expect the question, "Who or what is a person?" will get increasing attention legally from now on, as we begin to encounter vehicles, processes, and decisions that impact our lives which are controlled or significantly impacted by computational machinery. I doubt that there will be clear and comprehensive settlement of the issues related to that question before it stops having any impact on me (that is, after I am dead and no longer a person living on the earth). Nominal life expectance for me at this point in my life is about a decade; if I should be one who lives longer than most, I might be here for two decades. I am sure that the person-related issues I mentioned will not be resolved fully within the next two decades.

Musing 84: Special Focus
(initially posted February 28, 2017)

I am struck by why we give special focus to something, but fail to provide similar focus for other comparable entities or so dramatically change the meaning of something that it becomes a travesty of the original. Let me illustrate this with a couple of examples.

The Olympic Games are designed to identify by competition the most capable athletes from nations around the world. The modern version of them began in 1894 with the competition being held at four year intervals. The games draw upon the ancient example of such competitions held in Greece from the 8th to 4th century before Christ. A variety of events incorporate the name "Olympic" into their title (such as Teenage Olympics) because they are competitions for a specified category of athletes. Then there is the travesty of the Special Olympics. The *Who We Are* portion of their website says "Special Olympics is a global movement of people creating a new world of inclusion and community, where every single person is accepted and welcomed, regardless of ability or disability. We are helping to make the world a better, healthier and more joyful place — one athlete, one volunteer, one family member at a time." The travesty is not the goal of inclusiveness that the group professes, but their corruption of the term "Olympic" which has long been associated with exclusive athletic achievement. Stealing a term in that way and totally changing its meaning is despicable, even if done for good intentions. Better to choose a different name for the group and its aspirations than to so corrupt the meaning of the word. Of course, it is clear why they behave so despicably. They want the fame associated with the term Olympic, though they cannot have it without destroying the historic and common meaning of the word.

The other example I will mention is likely to agitate many. Since 1976, February has been recognized as Black History Month by the U.S. government (for the fifty years previous the second week of February was recognized as Black History Week). The question I ask, is why is there a special recognition of one racial or ethnic group for a focus on its history and not similar recognition of *ALL* other racial and ethnic groups (such as Native American; Asian or even the varieties Asian groups – Vietnamese, Korean, Chinese, Japanese, etc.; Hispanic; Caucasian; etc.). The Blacks or Afro-Americans are a smaller portion of the population than some noted but larger than others in the list mentioned. Why draw special attention to one group and ignore the others?

Actually not all others are ignored. In 1978 Public Law 95-419 designated a week in the first ten days of May as "Pacific/Asian American Heritage Week" and in 1990 it was expanded to be Asian-Pacific American Heritage Month. In 1988 National Hispanic Heritage Month (mid-September to mid-October) was initiated. And in 1990 November was designated as Native American Indian Heritage Month. However, the media does not give any of the others the level of attention that it gives Black Heritage Month even though some of them represent a larger portion of the national population than Blacks do.

Media bias is well known. That is obvious from the things that do not seem to be presented or discussed in materials about Black History Month. For example, there often are comments about the evils of slavery and its impact on the Black people, but seldom is any kind of slavery mentioned except that of the Atlantic slave trade to North America. Seldom does anyone say anything about the African nations that waged war on their neighbors to capture large numbers of Africans so they could sell them as slaves. Nor is there anything said about the extensive slave trade of Africans to Asia, which had been going on for many centuries before the Atlantic slave trade started around the 15th century. Nor is there much mention that Black Americans are much more likely to commit violent crimes (rape, murder, assault, etc.) than any other racial or ethnic group in America? The violent crime rates for Blacks are several times higher than for any other group. That Black tendency to violent criminality is a major blight on the nation.

Perhaps media bias is the only reason for its greater emphasis on the Black History Month and its selective silence about significant aspects of that history, but could there be other factors too? Perhaps the Special Olympics provide an insight about what could be other factors. The Special Olympics tries to make people feel good about themselves even though they are not able to compete at the levels required of athletes in the regular Olympics. Perhaps the media (for whatever reason) is doing something similar, trying to make a group feel good regardless of their capabilities or behaviors. Of course, the media is the one who can explain why it acts the way it does, but given the way the media sometimes presents things, one may take their explanation with a big dose of salt.

As noted above, many racial and ethnic groups are given special recognition by the government with a month or so designated to the history or heritage of that group (all such recognitions were initiated within the past century), but there are other groups that do not get similar recognition. One can ask the question, Why are the others ignored?

Some suggest that the government is simply being biased and discriminates against them. Others might suggest that such recognition is not needed. American history itself demonstrates the significance of their contributions to the nation. Or there might be some other reason.

Musing 85: Immigration
(initially posted March 2, 2017)

Immigration is a very controversial topic. People on all sides of immigration have very strong feelings about the subject. It can be hard to find calm, rational, and informed discussions of this touchy topic. Yesterday I had an eureka experience relative to immigration.

Eureka as an expression of triumph (joy) upon finding or discovering something stems from what Archimedes said when he discovered how to measure the volume of an irregular solid, which would then allow him to determine the purity of a gold object (*eureka* in Greek means "I found it!").

Yesterday morning I went to the library. As I left the library to go to lunch, I stopped in the entrance to the library where a collection of free papers were. I picked two, each from a separate stack to have something to browse through as I ate a sandwich at Subway on my way home (my wife was out for the day). One item was a paper called Recreation published for 55 area governmental associations. I picked it because of an article about scenic trains and train museums in the Mid-Atlantic region, which is where I live. The other paper was *Epoch Weekend* (Feb 23-Mar 1) by *Epoch Times* because it had an article on Immigration Economics. I was not aware of either publication; I think it was the first time I read anything from either publication. My purpose was merely to have something to browse as I ate lunch.

Reading the article on Immigration Economics provided the eureka experience I mentioned. I became curious about *Epoch Times*; according to the website about *Epoch Times* (http://www.theepochtimes.com/n3/about-us/) it is an independent voice in print and on the web which tries to report news responsibly and truthfully. My impression is that their claim is true from what I found on the web about *Epoch Times* and from the article on Immigration Economics.

That article stimulated this musing, but my comments are not simply a rehash of the article. My comments are my own thoughts. Some of which come from the article, but not all; however I acknowledge that the article clarified my thoughts about differences between immigration now and in the late-19th and early 20th century as well as providing most of the financial data I mention.

In the past, the hundred years from around 1850 to 1950, immigrants came to the U.S. because it was the land of opportunity. They expected nothing but freedom to achieve what they might by their own endeavors. Accomplishments of many of them are the basis for many positive comments and attitudes about immigrants.

However, during the past half-century or so, things have changed a lot. Previously the majority of those immigrants from over a century ago quickly integrated into American society, adopting attitudes and behaviors of those born here and generally respecting and complying with American law because that was the way to success and accomplishment. Now many immigrants come to the U.S. expecting a handout and support from our welfare system; also many do not try to totally acclimate to American ways, but retain ways of thought and behavior from the places they left. In addition, many of them are not concerned about complying with American law, as illustrated by the massive number of them who did not enter the U.S. in accordance with American law and continue here illegally for years.

The article I mentioned had surprising facts, some of which I will share with you. In 2015, the average federal welfare benefits per immigrant household was $6,234 while the average federal welfare benefits per native household was only $4,431. That kind of trend was not a fluke for a single year. A chart of the percentage of households receiving cash, food stamps, or Medicaid 1994-2016 showed that the percentage of such help for noncitizens in every year was significantly greater than for citizens, especially those born in the U.S. In most years, the difference was as large as a factor of two or three.

In the world of limited resources, what is spent in one place cannot also be spent in another place. Seldom does one hear advocates for better treatment of and more benefits for immigrants acknowledge that such help to immigrants limits resources for U.S. citizens, especially those on the lower end of the economic scale. Those advocates are either blind to the facts or strangely unconcerned about poor American citizens.

Every nation legitimately is concerned about those who come into their land. Whether the concern relates to exploitation of its resources, consumption of its benefits, threats to the security and well-being of its people, or for some other reason. Unfortunately the sloppy and careless thinking about immigration that dominates public discussion and comments about this issue is typical of the sloppy partisan approach to discussion of significant issues in recent decades. Few seem capable of addressing facts about an issue comprehensively and considering the variety of views about the subject carefully and fairly. It is far easier to lambast a distorted misrepresentation of views other than your own than it is to seriously address reality. Too many good people are willing to do bad things for good causes; they often fail to acknowledge they are simply using the old "end justifies the means" approach that has been discredited repeatedly by decent people.

Immigration discussion needs to be realistic and to be done with courtesy and consideration for ALL who address it. Many advocates of issues are afraid to address things in that way because they may lose some support when people understand the issue better. So they behave with partisan enthusiasm and ignore reality's inconveniences.

Musing 86: Stoapl
(initially posted March 4, 2017)

I decided to add a new word to the English language: stoapl. It comes from an acronym for "Sad Tale of a Petty Life." I believe that I will be responsible for coining this word, although I do not expect it to become known by many others. Perhaps only the handful of people who read this musing will ever be exposed to it.

I believe the word is novel, at least in English. It is not listed in the Oxford English Dictionary (OED), which shows several times the number of words found in other unabridged English dictionaries. Nor did I find stoapl when I typed it into various web search engines. I used both the standard ones (Google, Yahoo, and Bing) as well as lesser known ones such as DuckDuckGo. So I concluded that indeed stoapl is not a word that has been given a meaning previously by others.

When the question of how stoapl should be pronounced arises, I leave that to the initiative of those who might choose to use the word orally. My own pronunciation of words is so atrocious that I would not want the way I say something to become a model for others. As a child, I went to special speech classes until I was in the fourth grade to try to help me to speak in ways that others could understand more easily. Others in that speech class had severe stuttering, lispering, and cluttering problems and possibly other serious speech afflictions. It is obvious I am not a good source for pronunciation guidance.

As you probably guessed, I decided to coin the word stoapl because of reflection on my own life. One of the things I dislike most about myself is my pettiness. It makes me feel despicable; and the petty things I have done in my life deserve that derogatory description and worse.

My pettiness has also been a major spiritual hindrance. Chapters 5-7 of the Gospel of Matthew contain the teachings of Jesus that we call the Sermon on the Mount. That portion of Scripture contains much that Christians consider central in Christianity. The *Lord's Prayer* is contained in it; as are the beatitudes and Jesus' comments that evil thoughts and intentions are as wrong as grievous acts such as murder and adultery. The ethical standards set forth in the Sermon on the Mount exceed what most of us even strive for; for example, it tells us not to expect God's forgiveness if we do not forgive others.

Of course, our natural reaction is to try to water down what Jesus says by the way we interpret the Sermon on the Mount; but that is simply one of our many foolish ways of failing to respond honestly to God's truth. Instead we should strive with all our might to comply with what Jesus says we should do.

That is where my pettiness puts a major barrier in my way. Let me illustrate this with what Jesus said in Matthew 5:23-24: "[23] So if you are offering your gift at the altar and there remember that your brother has something against you, [24] leave your gift there before the altar and go. First be reconciled to your brother, and then come and offer your gift." (ESV). In these verses, Jesus tells that getting things right with others (especially those that we might call "brother") is even more important than making an offering to God and takes priority over doing that.

Look at how my pettiness interferes with my obedience to this instruction from Jesus the Christ. It is I who has to realize that I have offended another. I am not the offended one. The comment earlier about our need to forgive others in order to expect God's forgiveness of us has specified my reaction when I am the offended one. No, this instruction is about my wrong doing. My pettiness makes it hard for me to admit my faults, especially as would be necessary when I go to the offended brother and seek to make things right so we can be reconciled.

Jesus says don't bother making an offering to God until I have gone to the offended one and made things right! Giving my time to God by going to church and being involved in religious activities, giving my money to Christian causes, etc. are to be on hold until I am reconciled with the one whom I have offended. My pettiness does not want the shame of behaving that way, and at the same time my pettiness does not want me to take the initiative and go to the offended brother to make things right. Unfortunately I am not always wise enough to ask God to help me deal with my pettiness; I need His help in that because I am such a petty person.

Unfortunately I am not the only person who fails to heed this instruction of Jesus as I should. Many churches have people within them with grievances toward others in the congregation that go for long periods without being addressed. No wonder Christianity in America is so anemic. We need to take Jesus seriously and do what He tells us to do in Matthew 5:23-24. I have told you the sad tale of my petty life in this regard; and I hope you will pray for me and encourage me not to let my pettiness be such a hindrance to me spiritually. I and others miss many blessings of God when I allow my pettiness to do that. I also hope stoapl does not apply to you as it does to me.

Musing 87: Bad Guides
(initially posted March 6, 2017)

Bad guides are dangerous. They will not help you get to where you need to be.

Some guides are bad because they are incompetent or uninformed; others are corrupt and will mislead you for their own gain. The worst of the bad guides are both incompetent and corrupt.

Sinclair Lewis, who in 1930 became the first American writer to win the Nobel Prize for literature, published *Elmer Gantry* in 1927, a novel about a hypocritical evangelical minister. Later Burt Lancaster won the Best Actor Oscar for his performance as Elmer Gantry in the 1960 movie based upon part of Lewis' novel. That novel and movie illustrated the danger of seeking spiritual guidance from a bad guide.

The fictional character of Elmer Gantry was neither the first bad guide spiritually nor the last one. The New Testament warned of false teachers (they existed then and have been around since). The second epistle of Peter says false teachers deny the Lord Jesus Christ, follow sensuality, and exploit others for greed using false words. The Apostle Paul provides similar warnings in his letters to Timothy and others. Consequences are dire for both the false teachers and for those led astray by them.

Unfortunately bad spiritual guidance abounds today (as it did two millennia ago) in spite of the material, technological, and social advances manifested in modern society. Perhaps I should explain my perspective on "spiritual" things since some may relegate such just to the realm of strictly religious activities and assume that they only pertain to things done within a church building or other religious edifice.

In my perspective, spiritual things have two primary aspects. First, they are what is beyond the material realm, although they can have major impact on material things. For example, the Creator is beyond the material realm (He is Spirit) and yet has a major impact on material things since He made and sustains all that is. Spiritual, as noted by the *Oxford English Dictionary (OED)* as part of its first definition for "spiritual," also applies to "higher moral qualities."

Of course there are false teachers in the religious field such as Frederick J. Eikerenkoetter II, better known as Reverend Ike, a promoter of "prosperity theology" who passed away in 2009, and others who ignore or deny clear truths from God's Word, the Bible. However, such are not my primary concern in this musing. Nor are atheists and agnostics who deny the Creator my primary concern here.

My primary concern in this musing is "civil religion" whose morality is contrary to clear teaching from the Christian Bible. By "civil religion" I mean both widespread social attitudes and things dictated by the law that are contrary to "high moral qualities" expressed by Biblical instructions and comments, especially those in the New Testament. I address a couple of these to illustrate the problem that this poses for people. The Bible is clear that both those promoting such ideals and those compliant with them will face God's judgment.

At present, acceptance of a woman's "right" to terminate a fetus without it being a medical necessity to save her life is widespread in America and legally permissible (even in some conditions when the fetus could live as a person outside the mother's womb). This aspect of civil religion is clearly at odds with Biblical teaching about the sanctity of life and contrary to widely accepted morality of past centuries. Neither the law nor medical science has explicitly identified when a fetus becomes a person with full civil rights beyond some definitions that identify a person as a human being who can survive outside a woman's womb. Medical evidence suggests for some (perhaps many) fetuses, such survival becomes possible after a fetus is 20-22 weeks old. Generally the law currently allows abortions for fetuses through week 24 without requiring medical necessity for the procedure. The unspiritual immorality of current practice is obvious.

History is full of things that have been socially and legally acceptable at times (such as slavery) that are now seen to be unspiritual and immoral. I hope the future will see abortion simply because a woman chooses not to let a fetus live in the same way.

Many people fail to keep their word or fulfill their promises; and many in America consider such to be acceptable. For example, the majority of couples who marry promise in solemn vows to be faithful (i.e., no sexual partner other than one's spouse) and for the union to be permanent. The abundance of adultery and divorce shows how little stigma attaches to failure to keep one's word since those guilty of such are seldom ostracized in a significant way.

Who are bad guides leading civil religion to be so abominable? They are pundits promoting such unspiritual approaches to life. Some may pontificate from pulpits. Others may corrupt minds of the young in academia.

Others may possess political leadership or media influence. Regardless of where the pundit may reside and function, he or she is a bad guide if that pundit urges things contrary to plain teachings of the Bible. Many different rationales are used to justify atrocities that follow ideas from bad guides. Unfortunately those rationales will not save anyone from the consequences that follow bad guidance.

What can we do? Each of us can turn to the Bible and get good guidance about spiritual things. Then we can be diligent personally to live in compliance with that good guidance, and let others know when we see things happening that are contrary to that good guidance. Such action by us as individuals could do a lot to correct our current problems

Musing 88: Benefit Cost
(initially posted March 8, 2017)

I spent decades as an analyst at the Applied Physics Laboratory (APL) of Johns Hopkins University. My role was to help in assessing proposed systems and modifications to systems employed in national defense. During those decades I used a wide variety of analysis techniques and became very much aware of what made analysis of an issue valid or possibly misleading.

A common problem that one encounters is incompleteness of the analysis. For example, proponents of an issue (whether it is a proposed new weapon system, changes in policy about welfare qualifications and requirements, or modifications to the way immigration is addressed) tend to focus on purported benefits for their ideas while not fully addressing the costs associated with what they propose. On the other hand, opponents of an issue often focus on the costs and minimize purported benefits or portray them in distorted ways.

What is needed for a good decision about an issue is a comprehensive analysis that fairly and factually portrays both benefits and costs (sometimes called "cost-benefit" analysis). Unfortunately that often does not get done; and we (our nation as well as individuals) suffer the consequences of decisions that are not the best, and sometimes not even good from any realistic perspective.

A common problem in decisions at both national and individual levels is failure to address benefit cost realistically. This was something that many individuals did (abetted by financial institutions and often encouraged by them to act foolishly financially) when those individuals tried to purchase homes beyond their ability to pay for. Most Americans are aware of the financial chaos that debacle has caused us in the past decade or so.

At the national level, the federal government (especially Congress) is well known for actions that they fail to pay for appropriately. The Affordable Care Act (ACA) is a recent example of such irresponsible behavior by our elected officials. In ACA, instead of admitting how much it would cost to implement and taxing appropriately to produce adequate funds to pay that cost (action Congress felt would be unwelcome by the public and possibly cost some of them their posh positions in Congress), Congress forced those providing health insurance to act in ways that were unwise for them businesswise to cover much of ACA costs. This hid those costs and did not require them to be paid by our taxes, but it made aspects of the medical insurance business unprofitable. The consequences have been increases in charges from medical insurance firms and the withdrawal of a number of them from aspects of the health insurance business. I consider this a classic example of the failure to make public an honest analysis of benefit cost.

Congress was aware of the basic problem: that they were unwilling to require adequate tax revenues to pay for purported ACA benefits. They simply passed the buck by forcing private industry to bear the cost Congress was unwilling to pay. Whether Congress had all the information a decent cost benefit analysis would have provided and chose to act in the despicable way it did, I do not know. Certainly the use of law and regulation to force private industry to pay for benefits decided by the government instead of government collecting the needed money by taxes is contrary to the basic ideas underlying our republic. I believe Congress realized that trying to do that properly would create such an uproar from the public over the additional taxation (putting their political futures in jeopardy) that Congress chose to act in the dastardly way it did.

Unfortunately our political leadership has behaved so badly for such a long time that public trust and appreciation of those in Congress is so low (just 8% in 2015) that even such atrocious behavior as in ACA is unlikely to reduce it farther. In the early days of our republic, those in leadership roles such as the early members of Congress were held in much higher regard. Perhaps they had not developed the conniving ways of contemporary "professional politicians" (the average length of service in both houses of Congress has more than doubled in the past century as the U.S. is now governed mainly by professional politicians instead of citizens taking a break from their normal business for a stint of public service – such accounts in part for the abundance of self-serving abuse the nation suffers from its professional politicians).

What do I propose in this musing? Why did I bother to write it?

My purpose is simple. I hope to encourage others to demand (as I try to do) a full accounting of costs for a benefit proposed by advocates of issues. Without such, I am very reluctant to give my support for an issue. In a fantasy world without resource limitations, one could support any and every issue that proposed benefits for some (or even all) since doing so would not have any negative implications for other things one might want to do. However, I live in the real world with resource limitations; and what is possible in a fantasy world could be bad in the real world.

The benefit obtained could cost so much that far more important benefits (possibly even necessities) could not be afforded because of resources spent on the other benefit.

Many advocates fail to appreciate resource limitations and the importance of understanding benefit costs for good decisions in the real world. Those advocates are often unwilling to admit potential adverse consequences from what they propose. Likewise sometimes opponents of an issue do not deal fairly with its claims. Neither approach is good, either for the individual or for the nation.

Musing 89: Curiosities
(initially posted March 10, 2017)

As many serious Christians know, in reference to the Old Testament Scripture the New Testament writers quote mainly from the *Septuagint* (often abbreviated as *LXX*) instead of the Hebrew Masoretic Text (as indicated when the wording of the passages differs a bit in the material quoted). The 39 books of the Scripture contained in the Masoretic Text of Hebrew Old Testament were written originally between 1500 and 400 B.C. However the oldest extant copy of the Masoretic Text was made about 900 A.D. <u>It is possible that editorial changes were introduced during the centuries from the time of the original writing to the oldest extant copies.</u>

The *Septuagint* is a translation of the Hebrew Scriptures into Greek that was made a couple of centuries before Christ. It was widely used by Jews and non-Jews until the early centuries of the current era when Judaism stopped extensive use of the Septuagint to distinguish Judaism from Christianity which by the end of the first century had become predominately a religion practiced by Gentiles. The oldest extant copies of the *Septuagint* come from the third and fourth centuries since Christ, which makes those copies more than 500 years older than the oldest copy of the Masoretic text. <u>It is possible that the *Septuagint* in places may represent an older reading to the Hebrew Scripture than does the Masoretic Text.</u>

The story of David and Goliath illustrates this. Goliath was a giant of a man, and David slew him in battle. The Masoretic Text of 1 Samuel 17:4 says Goliath was "6 cubits and a span" tall. A cubit is the length from elbow to fingertip (18-20 inches) and a span is 4-6 inches, the width of a person's hand. This makes Goliath something over 9 feet tall, a human height for which history has no physical record. On the other hand, the *Septuagint* says Goliath was only 4 cubits and a span, which would make Goliath about 7 feet tall (a very large man, especially in ancient times when people were shorter than today – a height for which there is historical record of others being that tall). The only Hebrew text of 1 Samuel 17:4 among the Dead Sea Scrolls (it was written a little before the time of Christ which makes it centuries older than either the Masoretic Text or the Septuagint) also says 4 cubits and a span. It is likely that the reading of the Masoretic Text about Goliath's height is an editorial modification to what the Scripture originally said that was made in the centuries between the date of the of the oldest extant copy of the Masoretic Text and the age of the oldest extant copy of the Septuagint.

This kind of curiosity has caused me to decide to read the whole *Septuagint* (something I have not done before). In my study of New Testament quotations from the Old Testament, I looked at differences between the Masoretic Text and the *Septuagint* that occur in those quotations, and long ago I read the *Apocrypha* (Jewish historical books dealing with things in the centuries between 400 B.C. and a century or so before Christ) which is included in the *Septuagint* (also in Bibles of Catholics and Orthodox Christians – the *Apocrypha* also was included in the *King James Version* of the Bible for the first two centuries after it was initially published in 1611 A.D.).

I just started my plan to read through the *Septuagint* and found a curiosity already. In Genesis 4:21. That verse in the Masoretic Text indicates that musical instruments (harp and flute/pipe) were originated by a descendent of Cain (the son of Adam and Eve who murdered his brother Abel). In that verse, the Septuagint identifies the same man (Jubal) descended from Cain as the Masoretic Text but expands what he invented from the musical instruments (harp) to include the poetry/lyrics (psaltery) that go with the music.

Such curiosities amuse and interest me. Sometimes they have no more significance than to provide a moment of release from the cares of daily life as I laugh within at the curiosity. Other times the curiosity may be more significant. For example in the case of Goliath's height, a 7 foot tall man in the age of 5 feet tall men gives more credence to Biblical accuracy historically than the story of a 9 foot giant (a height that current history has no physical evidence of ever being achieved by a human being).

My attraction to curiosities in this case has an added benefit. It will keep me in the Scripture more than I might be otherwise. I will see what I read in the *Septuagint* (probably a handful of chapters most days), and I will also spend time in the traditional Old Testament based upon the Hebrew Masoretic Text to refresh my memory of what it says so I will detect curiosities as they come along. Few things contribute more to spiritual vitality for the Christian than time spent in God's Word, reflecting on it and its application in one's life.

Hence I am glad for my interest in curiosities because in this instance that interest will have a positive impact on me spiritually. Unfortunately, others and I may find our interests pulling us away from God and proper living instead of drawing us closer to Him. We understand how carnal interests do that, whether the interests are sexual or the ones related to pride and status; other times the interests themselves are not bad, but excessive attention to them is (e.g., excessive time and effort spent in sports). I am thankful when my interests are spiritually helpful.

Musing 90: Need For Clarity
(initially posted March 13, 2017)

There is a great deal of turmoil in the U.S. at present over healthcare and much of it is centered on the Affordable Care Act (ACA, also known as ObamaCare). Neither proponents nor opponents of ACA have been very clear about fundamental principles involved, at least not in the materials I have seen. This musing discusses a fundamental issue that seldom gets addressed.

That fundamental issue is who is responsible for a person's health care. Let me limit the scope of my discussion (simply to accommodate the thousand word limit I impose on my musings) to deal only with mentally competent adults. This leaves out consideration of health care for minors and those without mental competency. Of course, I know some ladies who are convinced that no male has a correctly functioning brain, but I will not go to that extreme although I admit that we males often give females plenty of reasons to think that way about us.

How would you feel if a stranger walked up to you on the street and handed you a medical bill for treatment he had undergone and demanded, "Pay this bill for my treatment." Add to that a big monster with him to make you pay his bill. This scenario makes most of us gasp, or laugh. Who could envision such a ridiculous situation?

However, functionally that is what ObamaCare does; the monster is the U.S. government who insists people pay the bills of others. The fundament principles involved need to be addressed explicitly in public discussions of this controversial program; and those principles have not been discussed in what I have seen or heard.

The first question articulated by a human being addressed this very issue. Some place east of Eden (we do not know where exactly) after Adam and Eve had been expelled from the Garden of Eden, God asked a man a question. The man replied with a question of his own instead of answering God's question. I believe that man's question qualifies as the first question asked by a person. Certainly it is the first human question recorded in the Bible. Of course, as those knowledgeable about the Bible know, the man's question was, "Am I my brother's keeper?" The person who spoke it was Cain; he said it shortly after he murdered his brother Abel.

It seems to me that question is pertinent to a fundamental issue in healthcare? Who is responsible? The individual him or herself? Or others? ObamaCare (and many other public endeavors) make tremendous assumptions about such without being explicit about the fundamental principles involved. We, the people, should demand clarity in this regard. If one does not get fundamental principles correct, it is very easy to get into big trouble.

We can all think of circumstances where another should be responsible for the medical care of someone. If a person is run over by a drunk driver and requires extensive treatment, certainly the drunk who caused that situation should be required to pay for all such expenses (although usually it will be the insurance company used by the drunk, and then the government often has to step in to cover a lot of costs that the drunk and insurance company cannot or will not pay); it is also likely that the injured victim will be out a lot also.

For the moment, let's ignore such situations. Let us just think about a simpler case. An adult who engages in behaviors that are likely to incur extensive medical expenses. It could be an adrenaline addict who indulges in risky sporting activities and incurs substantial injuries. It could be a person who indulges in unsafe sex repeatedly and acquires sexually transmitted diseases. It could be a person who smokes extensively. Or it could be a person who fails to exercise and overeats, etc. etc. etc. Who should pay the bill for medical treatment of that person? Just the person him or herself? Or should others in the community be forced by the government to pay medical expenses for such foolish behavior? Whether it is paid directly by taxes to get adequate money to cover those medical costs in government programs, or by government regulations that force medical insurers to accept such clients and then charge their other customers rates to provide the funds to allow them to pay the medical expenses of the irresponsible people.

I have not heard or seen much discussion of such fundamental issues in healthcare discussions. I see a lot about unmet medical needs of people, but little discussion about individual responsibility to behave wisely if others are to pay medical costs for that person. In my opinion, it's long past time for the authorities and proponents of medical care for the needy to address such fundamental issues explicitly so that good decisions can be made about how we deal with health care.

This musing has a limited perspective: the need to discuss fundamental principles in considerations of health care. I have only addressed a simple kind of case to illustrate the kinds of fundamental principles that need to be addressed. I understand that there are special considerations for those who are not competent (such as the young or those with mental deficiencies) and those who are needy because of their economic situations. Those situations also need attention, but they can more readily be addressed properly when due attention has been given to the kinds of fundamental principles addressed in this musing.

I hope those who read this musing will encourage discussion of healthcare to include full consideration of such fundamental principles.

Musing 91: Advantage-Disadvantage (initially posted March 16, 2017)

Some people have advantages and others are disadvantaged. Often both conditions apply to the same person. I will illustrate this with myself, and then share a few thoughts about the advantage-disadvantage condition.

I was blessed with a mild academic advantage. According to an individualized IQ test I took as a high school senior and my scores on the battery of tests I took after enlisting in the U.S. Army a few years later, I was in the top 1% academically. Hence I was considered to have an academic advantage. I was at the one in a hundred level academically. However during much of my adult life, I was at an academic disadvantage. In college, most of those in my classes were at the one in a thousand (or more) level. Most of my associates in my professional career at the Johns Hopkins University Applied Physics Laboratory were both more gifted intellectually and better educated than I. So while with an intellectual advantage over many people, I was at an intellectual and academic disadvantage with those with whom I competed for position and with whom I was compared by my peers professionally. This academic disadvantage was coupled with being at a social disadvantage since most of my peers were more likeable personalities than I and more couth socially than I. I fully understand what it is to be at the bottom of the barrel, the runt of the litter, or some other expression for the least capable of a group.

Of course, it helped (at least relative to my attitude about my situation) that I was mainly unaware of my disadvantage since for much of my life I was too limited in my perceptiveness to be aware of my situation. Whether that lack of awareness came from arrogance or some kind of deficiency in perceptiveness, I do not know. One could say that I was like the guy in the old joke. He had fallen off a tall building and the people looking out their windows in horror at his plight would hear him say as he passed by "Okay thus far." However, he made no comment after the big splat as he hit the ground.

Unfortunately today there are many advantaged-disadvantaged who are encouraged to focus on their disadvantage and see themselves as a victim of some sort. I think that is bad for them and also harms our society. Those who go about emphasizing such disadvantages are a bane.

Let me tell the story of a person who had a variety of professional disadvantages, some of which are often championed as debilitating disadvantages. This person was female during the middle have of the 20th century. She was also too old and out of shape to be accepted in the Navy when she tried to enlist initially during World War II. Those disadvantages (female, old, out of shape) could have shelved her if she had viewed herself as a disadvantaged victim (which is how many are encouraged to view their disadvantages). Instead Grace Hopper used her advantages of intelligence and education to get a waver which allowed her to enlist in the WAVES in 1943. She is known for the work she did for the Navy on computers at Harvard during the war; she ended up as a Rear Admiral who served until she was almost 80 (she was the oldest active duty officer in the Navy when she retired in 1986).

There are many people who have a variety of disadvantages (racially, gender-wise, educationally, physically, etc.). They have options about the way they view their disadvantages. Do they consider themselves primarily victims because of their disadvantages and seek special privileges and opportunities because of their disadvantages (which is how many who are proponents for the disadvantages or in the media encourage them to do)? Or do they act like Grace Hopper and build upon their advantages and creatively strive to achieve their goals?

Most of the people I know who are disadvantaged in various ways also have some advantages. Which the person chooses to focus upon and emphasizes (the advantage or the disadvantage) often has a major impact on whether or not the person is successful in achieving his or her goals.

Before people lambast me as a naïve and unrealistic idealist, be aware that I have been involved with many in jails and prisons over the past four decades. Those folks often have a ton of disadvantages. In addition to the stigma attached to having been in jail or prison, many have serious mental problems, bad job and credit histories, emotional issues from being abused, etc. However, even these people have a choice for how they view themselves. Do they see themselves primarily as disadvantaged victims from their past and their problems? Or do they emphasize their advantages (whatever and however small such may be)? Which they choose makes a big difference in how they might progress toward their goals.

Actually most of us are in the advantaged-disadvantaged condition. We too have the same choice as those I have mentioned. Do we view ourselves principally as disadvantaged victims? Or do we focus on our advantages and use them to propel us forward.

The choice is never an easy one. Often there are people encouraging the victim view. Please don't take that approach. It will hurt both you and others. Be bold. Work your advantages. Of course, it may take a while (just as it took Grace Hopper a year or two to get into the Navy); but in the end I believe you will be glad for making that choice. Try it and see.

Musing 92: LXX Reflections
(initially posted March 18, 2017)

In a previous musing (#89-Curiosities20170310) I mentioned that I had become of aware of differences between the Septuagint (often referenced as LXX, a Greek translation of the Hebrew Scriptures from a few centuries before Christ) and the Masoretic Text (the traditional Hebrew text of the Jewish Scriptures—oldest copy of which is about 600 years later than the oldest copy of the LXX). The specific difference I mentioned was about the height of Goliath.

I said that my curiosity was peaked and I had decided to read the LXX in total (previous I had only read the Apocrypha and the Old Testament passages quoted in the New Testament). I started reading and now am in the early portion of Exodus. This musing was stimulated by some differences between the LXX and the Masoretic Text which struck me as I read (when I read something that either does not agree with my memory of that passage from my memory of the Bible which is mainly based upon the Masoretic Text) peaks my curiosity, I compare the two.

That happened a couple of times recently. First in Exodus 2:25. Bible translations based upon the Masoretic Text say God knew about the afflictions of the Hebrews as slaves in Egypt before Moses delivered them; the final phrase of that verse expands on God's knowledge of their situation (being expressed in various ways by different translations of that verse). The LXX does not talk more about God's knowing of the Hebrews' plight in the final part of the verse; instead it indicates knowledge about God became known to the Hebrews.

The difference here between the Masoretic Text and the LXX is merely the aspect of the verb used (a verb that occurs more than 900 times in the Hebrew Old Testament and which appears in every aspect of the verb). So the physical difference between the Hebrew of the Masoretic Text and that used by the LXX would have been very small. However, that difference set my mind roaming on a path it had not been on before. It caused me to ask, What did the Hebrews know about God before Moses delivered them from their slavery in Egypt and gave them the law with its description of religious rituals for the Jewish people? I will give that question attention over the next week or two.

The next curiosity as I read Exodus in the LXX came in Chapter 3. As God talks to Moses at the burning bush, He tells Moses to bring the Hebrew people from Egypt to the land where various peoples live. The Masoretic Text list six groups living there (five of which seem to have descended from Canaan, grandson of Noah through Ham), but the LXX lists seven groups. Of course, there's always a spelling challenge. A word in Hebrew has to be translated into English for what we find in the Bibles we read; the LXX starts with that Hebrew word and translates it into Greek and then it gets put into English. It is even more complicated because the original Hebrew only had consonants written; vowels assumed were added much later. However, that did not prevent me from easily discovering which people are the ones only mentioned in the LXX.

The people living where Moses was to take the Israelites after delivering them from Egypt that are included in the LXX but omitted from the Masoretic Text were the Girgashites (also descendants of Canaan, grandson of Noah through Ham). They are included in the list of people living in the land that the Israelites went to from Egypt in the book of *Judith* (a deuterocanonical book written a century or two before Christ and included in the Apocrypha).

As I was musing on these things, I came across another curious difference between the LXX and the Masoretic Text. This occurs in 1 Samuel 1:24. The Masoretic Text said Hannah (mother of Samuel) brought "three bulls" to Eli as an offering; the LXX says she brought "a three-year old bull." The early manuscripts were written without spacing between words. The difference between "three bulls" and one "three-year old bull" is just a matter of where you divide the letters into words. The Masoretic Text had divided them one letter different than they were divided in the text that LXX translators used. It also seems that this verse in the Dead Sea Scrolls supports the LXX translation.

These differences between the Masoretic Text about the height of Goliath, the number of bulls that Hannah brought, or the inclusion of Girgashites as inhabitants of the land along with the six other groups mentioned are interesting but not of major significance spiritually or in what the Scriptures tell us about God. In fact, about 95% of Biblical text found in the Dead Sea Scrolls (all of which are about a thousand years older than the oldest copy of the Masoretic Text) agree with the Masoretic Text verbatim (showing its reliability); however, the Dead Sea Scrolls usually support the LXX where it differs from the Masoretic Text. A major finding from the Dead Sea Scrolls is that there was more diversity in the first century in regard to Scriptures used and accepted by the Jews than had been previously thought.

I enjoy the things I discover when I pursue my curiosities, and think some of those things might even be important for me. I am glad for the curiosities I discover as I read the LXX because they cause me to think more deeply and carefully about God's Word as it is presented to us in the Bible.

Musing 93: Before Moses
(initially posted March 20, 2017)

In the previous musing, I noted that reading Exodus 2:25 in the Septuagint stimulated me to ask what the Hebrews knew about God and what their religious rituals were before Moses. God gave the Israelites His law and His direction for them as a people through Moses, as presented in the Torah (the first five books of the Old Testament). Moses wrote the Torah about 1400 B.C. (or a bit latter, depending upon the date you ascribe to the life of Moses).

The book of Genesis describes God as having communication with Adam, Noah, Abraham, and Jacob (Israel) as well as with others; however no extensive description of how to live (such as in the Mosaic law) or specification of religious rituals (as also specified by the Torah) is found in the book of Genesis nor in the early chapters of Exodus (before Moses returns to Egypt to free the Hebrews from Pharaoh's slavery).

The Apostle Paul tells us that creation reveals enough about God so that no one can stand before God and claim to have lived up to the standard God expects which is revealed simply by His creation (Romans 1:18-32). The beginning of Genesis tells how Adam and Eve ate of the tree of knowledge of good and evil; presumably such knowledge of good and evil has passed on to us as descendants of Adam and Eve by our conscience. Of course, some people have defective consciences, just as other parts of people are defective in various ways (such as a person born blind, or with some other medical disorder).

Thus, at a minimum, the Hebrews before Moses had the knowledge of God and His ways revealed by His creation, and the knowledge of good and evil from conscience. The people lived in families and communities; so they had guidance that those with properly functioning consciences might provide. These two aspects of Hebrew life before Moses provide a solid foundation of knowledge about God and His ways for the Hebrews before Moses came to Egypt to free them from Pharaoh's grip.

In addition, Hebrews probably knew their heritage from Abraham: that God at times communicated directly with a person (such as Abraham) and that trust in God (faith) was the true basis for righteousness. They probably knew that blood was required in offerings to God from the example provided by Abraham and his descendants. They knew God made covenants (agreements, pacts, deals) with people at times, as He did with

Abraham. They perhaps knew of God's promise of a land for them. Thus, when Moses presented a covenant from God for the Hebrew people, it was not a new concept for them. They knew religious rituals (such as circumcision) were sometimes part of a covenant with God, even when they failed to do it faithfully (as noted in Joshua, the young men who survived the 40 years of wandering after the people left Egypt had not been circumcised – Joshua had to delay the assault on Jericho for the men to be circumcised and to heal from that, Joshua 5:2-9).

Apparently the Hebrew people had maintained their tribal heritage and had a political structure with recognized leaders (their elders). I suspect that such impacted their understanding and practice religiously. Basic moral and spiritual training was probably expected by the household head, and the community structure with guidance from the leaders of the tribe would supplement that. There is no indication in the Bible of exactly what that may have been.

The Biblical history from Abraham to the time Moses returned to Egypt to free his people gives no indication of how frequently any religious activity (such as prayer, offering, etc.) was done. No set schedule for worship or festivals is noted. The only specific religious ritual mentioned is circumcision, and how extensively it was practiced by the Hebrews before Moses gave them God's detailed law is unclear.

Thus I conclude that what the Hebrews knew about God before Moses came to free them was 1) what is revealed in nature, 2) what the consciences says about good and evil, and 3) tradition about their ancestors from Abraham to their day. It is important to remember that they lived in a time when there were many ideas about gods, and most peoples and localities had their own gods. Sometimes practices associated with such gods were atrocious.

How the Hebrews dealt with such before Moses returned to Egypt is unclear, but it is perhaps helpful to note that we live in a somewhat similar situation. There are a number of ideas about god competing with what the Bible tells us about the true God. In addition there are the ideas of civil religion in America, which says many things contrary to clear teachings of the Bible. We face the same challenge as the Hebrews before Moses. Do we just accommodate to our environment and culture? Or do we dare to hold firmly to Biblical revelation about God, His salvation through Jesus, and what the Bible says is the way to think and behave that pleases Him? Such puts me in a frightening situation: as the Bible clearly states and those with spiritual insight claim, it costs to be a disciple of Jesus of Nazareth. The cheap grace promoted by many elements of contemporary Christianity in America has little to do with the real gospel presented in the New Testament.

You do not have to take my word for that. A few hours reading the Gospels and Epistles of the New Testament will make it quite clear to you. The question we face is simple: How do we respond?

Musing 94: Insights
(initially posted March 23, 2017)

This morning as I read Exodus 14 & 15 in the Septuagint, I had several insights. These insights did not come because of the way the Septuagint describes the events (its description is basically no different in this passage than what is in the Bible translations that most of us normally read which are based upon the Masoretic Text, the traditional Hebrew text of the Old Testament). As noted in an earlier musing I decided to read the Old Testament in an English translation of the Septuagint (a Greek translation of the Hebrew Old Testament made a century or two before Christ and which was the primary version of the Old Testament used by early Christians).

The significant insight was to note that the Exodus 14:19 said it was The Angel of the Lord which had been guiding the people of Israel as they were leaving Egypt that went and blocked Pharaoh and his army as they pursued the Israelites. The pillar of cloud that had been used by God to guide the Israelites also was placed between the Egyptians and the Israelites and they were plunged into such darkness the Egyptians could not even see one another.

You know the story. God opened a way through the Red Sea and the Israelites passed through.

Then God removed the cloud and darkness and the Egyptians pursued the Israelites, but the Red Sea closed on them and they all drowned.

If I had noticed the role of The Angel of the Lord before, I had forgotten that. I suspect I had been aware of it in the past because it is so significant. I think that I did not remember that is just one among many examples of things I have forgotten that I once knew.

Why do I consider this so important? Good question, and there is a good answer to that question. It concerns the identity of The Angel of the Lord. When one considers the various places in the Old Testament where it says "the" angel of the Lord (in contrast to an angel without the definite article "the"), it is clear that the being that is referenced is different from the normal messengers from God that we call angels. This Being has divine attributes. Many Bible scholars believe that The Angel of the Lord is a theophany, and in fact was the Second Person of the Trinity, the Son of God, manifesting God to man. I think they are right.

You might want to check that out for yourself.

In this case, the comments in Exodus 14 & 15 indicate that it was the Second Person of the Trinity, the One Who later in history would become the Christ (the Messiah), that was guiding the Israelites and protecting them from the pursuing forces of Egypt. That is the significant insight from my reading this morning.

The other two insights that I will mention here are not so significant, but I think they enriched me. At the beginning of Exodus 15, Moses and the children of Israel sang a song of praise and thanksgiving to God. I believe this is the first song presented in the Bible.

We normally think of God giving His law and commandments to Moses for the people of Israel when they were at Mount Sinai. They did not get to Mount Sinai until a couple of months after they crossed the Red Sea. Exodus 15:25 notes that God gave the people some kind of instruction at Marah (and this was a month or more before they got to Sinai) even though they had begun to complain about the way God was treating them. The insight that struck me was that God had given the Israelites some kind of explicit guidance before the got to Sinai. That too is something I either had not noticed before or else it merely was no longer retained by my faulty memory.

Such gives me motivation to read and re-read the Bible. Things I had missed (or forgotten) before now might be noticed in this reading; in either case my noticing it this time will help me to live a more god-pleasing life now.

I was reminded of how foolish the Israelites were, and that always encourages me because I am often foolish in ways similar to them. They had seen God do amazing things. He was guiding them by a pillar of cloud by day and a pillar of fire by night. He had opened the Red Sea for them and destroyed Pharaoh and his army. Yet now, just days later, at most a month after crossing the Red Sea, they are complaining about the God who delivered them from their slavery in Egypt. Their behavior always amazes me when I read about it or think about it.

Then I usually think of how I so often behave just as foolishly. Forgetting or ignoring that every thought and deed is fully known by God. That things He wants me to do or not do are well described in the Scripture. That His promises are always true. Etc. Etc.

I'm glad that I'm reading the Septuagint. The translation I am reading uses different words than the more familiar ones in the Bible translations I normally read, and that makes the material fresh in a way. And it causes me to look again at how my usual translation describes the passage at times when I have a question about something. So I benefit a great deal from my reading in the Septuagint.

Thank you for letting me share these thoughts.

Musing 95: Abortion Chaos Part One (initially posted March 26, 2017)

This is the first part of a three-part musing. This subject is too extensive for treatment in a single thousand word musing. Abortion is a subject people have very strong feelings about. Pro-abortion advocates emphasize a woman's right to choose what is done with her body and many prefer the term Pro-choice for their position. Anti-abortion advocates emphasize moral and spiritual aspects of abortion believing removal of a fetus from the woman's body terminates the life of a person.

Unfortunately materials I see or hear about abortion usually treat so few of the critical issues of this contentious topic that I have little confidence in validity of conclusions reached by those presenting the material. I am not expert on this subject; nor am I aware fully of the extensive literature on abortion. However, because discussion of this subject in the media is so limited in scope of issues addressed (as that I have seen), then I suspect there may be no comprehensive treatment of the topic which addresses most or all pertinent abortion issues. Such lack may be the reason heated controversy about abortion continues.

My comments in a few musings will not provide such a comprehensive treatment, but I can identify a reasonably comprehensive list of aspects of abortion that such a comprehensive treatment of abortion would address. Then I would urge people on all sides of abortion discussions to withhold final judgment on abortion until they have been exposed to careful and extensive treatment of the issues in all those aspects.

It is likely the reader will come to some conclusion about my personal position on abortion from what I say in musings on Abortion Chaos, but I hope the reader will appreciate the importance of taking a comprehensive approach to this contentious subject in order to reach a valid conclusion whether or not the reader holds similar views on abortion to those the reader thinks I hold. For important issues such as abortion, sound-byte slogans seldom lead to valid conclusions. For example, a sound-byte slogan about freedom of speech implies anyone can say anything at any time. We know it would be bad for one to cry "FIRE" in a crowded theater when there was no fire. People could be hurt or even killed in the ensuing panic. Likewise many would consider prohibition against "hate speech" or "inciting to riot" as proper restrictions on speech. These are the kinds of things that get overlooked unless an issue is treated comprehensively.

America needs to be able to draw valid conclusions about abortion issues, but I do not think it can do that until the subject is addressed comprehensively (I do not think actions by our politicians and courts have been based on such comprehensive considerations so valid conclusions have yet to be reached). Unfortunately some think one aspect of abortion issues is so important that nothing else matters, whether the "else" is murder or condemning a mother and child to a horrible situation. I think such an approach is wrong; all aspects of abortion need to be considered if we are to reach a valid conclusion.

Here is a list of aspects of the abortion issue that I suggest as a minimum for a comprehensive treatment of abortion (the seven aspects are listed in the order they will be addressed in my musing): personal, social, financial, medical, legal, ethical/spiritual, and political. If you know of a comprehensive treatment of abortion addressing these seven aspects (either in a single source or in a collection of sources), please tell me and explain how I can get access to them so I can have the information I seek for a valid final conclusion about abortion.

Personal Aspect: The primary argument I hear for abortion is based upon giving the woman choice about what is done to her body. For the past century and a bit, there has been great emphasis on female rights: to have the same legal rights as men in regard to education, voting, property ownership, etc.; to receive the same level of compensation in employment as men in business; and to be the ultimate chooser in what she does or is done to her. Emphasis on a woman's choice in regard to abortion should be seen in this larger context of emphasis on female rights.

The impact on a woman for having or not having an abortion medically, psychologically, and relative to her future also needs to be considered. There are financial costs to the individual: either for the abortion, for the birth, and for rearing a child. There are risks medically both in abortion and birth. There may be psychological impacts of the choice made by the woman. Etc. These impacts need to be considered.

Historically some women have chosen to have abortions even when such was not allowed by the legal or cultural situation. The often unsafe condition for such behavior has been put forth as an argument for legalization of abortion by some. Such too needs to be considered.

I do not address every perspective on the seven aspects of abortion that I suggest as a minimum for a comprehensive treatment of abortion; but a comprehensive treatment will consider all the aspects I mention and do so in significant detail. Each of the next two musings in this three-part musing will treat three of the aspects suggested for a comprehensive treatment of abortion.

It is obvious that many parts of the abortion issue impact more than one of the seven aspects identified above; some will be treated in discussion of only one aspect, and others in more than one aspect.

Musing 96: Abortion Chaos Part Two (initially posted March 27, 2017)

This is the second part of a three-part musing. Abortion Chaos is too extensive for treatment in a single thousand word musing. The first part dealt with the need for comprehensive treatment of abortion so valid conclusions may be reached about abortion and with the first of the seven abortion aspects (personal, social, financial, medical, legal, ethical/spiritual, and political) needing comprehensive assessment for a valid conclusion on abortion. This musing part will address three of the remaining six aspects (social, financial, and medical) and the third musing part will address the remaining three aspects (legal, ethical/spiritual, and political).

Social: Social aspects of abortion are many and varied. They concern demographics, political blocs, economic and cultural acceptance, etc. If some racial or ethnic groups experience substantially different rates of abortions it can impact representation of that group within the nation. Abortion rates several times higher for blacks than for members of other racial and ethnic groups significantly limit growth of the black population in America (whether that is positive or negative depends on one's perspective). Black women's 19 million abortions may have limited black political influence; certainly it has reduced criminal justice costs (a positive impact socially) by preventing a number of violent crimes (if those whose births were prevented would have committed crimes at the rate done by blacks, a rate far higher than for other races).

A century ago abortion was considered wrong and avoided by most Americans; unwanted babies were handled in various ways (some by charities, some reared by their mothers or other family, etc.). For the past half-century, many Americans have not viewed abortions negatively; now about 20% of pregnancies end in abortion (more than 1% of which, close to 7,000 in a year, occur after 21 weeks of gestation, a point in pregnancy where the fetus may be capable of surviving outside the womb). Abortion allows women to avoid the stigma of unmarried pregnancy and the economic stress from costs of rearing the child, etc. Also the U.S. has not had to expand its infrastructure (schools, hospitals, lodging, etc.) to accommodate those who would have been born without the nearly 60 million abortions reported in the U.S. since the Roe vs. Wade decision by the Supreme Court in 1973.

I will leave additional identification and discussion of abortion's social aspects to others.

Financial: Abortion generally saves someone money. Cost of an abortion is lower than cost of a live birth. Most abortions (over 90%) are in the first trimester; hence the woman typically has far lower pre-procedure costs. Average cost of an abortion procedure is only about half the cost of a live birth procedure when there are no serious complications; but the information I could find on-line indicated a serious complication in about 2% of abortions vice a little over 1% for live births.

Criminal justice system savings from fewer prospective criminals being born was noted earlier. At current cost of around $50,000 a year (or more) to incarcerate a felon, savings from an estimated 4 million fewer incarcerations because of abortions (based upon current incarceration `rates by race and the racial distribution reported for abortions), perhaps $400 billion dollars have been saved if each one incarcerated spent just two years behind bars. Most of do not realize how much the nation has benefited from legalization of abortion (60 million fewer people).

From a society perspective, abortion saves a lot financially. In January 2017, CNN reported that families can expect to spend $12,350 to $14,000 a year to rear a child to age 18. With 60 million abortions since 1973, abortion has saved the nation a ton of money. From surveys reported on the web, about a fifth of women who have abortions said they could not afford to have a baby. The only other reason cited by about the same percent of women was "not ready for the responsibility" (particularly from very young women). No other reason listed in the surveys had anywhere near the percentage of these two reasons.

With the many contraceptive methods available today, it is surprising that nearly 20% of pregnancies end in abortion. One would think contraception would be preferred by women who did not want to have a child in her present circumstances.

Medical: Medical costs and frequency of severe complications for abortions were noted above. The health danger to women from illegal abortions was often mentioned in debates about legalization of abortion. There are current efforts to require that abortion clinics comply with the same health and safety standards as other outpatient medical facilities. At present such is not required in all jurisdictions. This raises questions about possible health danger for 10,000-plus women each year getting abortions who experience severe complications. This factor needs thorough consideration.

Cases of abortion providers selling fetal material from abortion without informed consent from the woman have been reported; and without financial compensation to her for such. This too deserves consideration from both medical and financial perspectives. Greed and inappropriate practices of some abortion providers have been noted by some.

This musing has illustrated the kinds of concerns that should be addressed in consideration of three aspects of abortion. The third and final musing on Abortion Chaos will address three more aspects. I hope these musing on Abortion Chaos will cause you to delay a final decision about abortion until all significant aspects of abortion have been addressed in a comprehensive and careful way. Only after such has been done do I believe valid conclusions about abortion can be reached. I hope you will encourage such a comprehensive examination of this important and contentious topic.

Musing 97: Abortion Chaos Part Three (initially posted March 28, 2017)

This is the third part of a three-part musing. Abortion Chaos is too extensive for treatment in a single thousand word musing. The first part dealt with the need for comprehensive treatment of abortion so valid conclusions may be reached about abortion and with the first of the seven abortion aspects (personal, social, financial, medical, legal, ethical/spiritual, and political) needing comprehensive assessment for a valid conclusion on abortion. The second part addressed three aspects (social, financial, and medical). This third musing part addresses the remaining three aspects (legal, ethical/spiritual, and political).

My goal is to encourage a comprehensive assessment of abortion so adequate information becomes available to support valid decisions about abortion. I only use valid information from reliable sources in my musings, but I am not expert in all areas that I mention. Hence when a careful comprehensive assessment is done by experts in the area, fully reliable information will be available about things.

Legal: The 1973 Roe vs. Wade decision basically legalized abortion when such was not necessary medically to save the woman's life. States have a variety of laws related to abortion. Those laws address attending physician and medical facility requirements, gestation limits (9 states and DC have no gestation limits; most states only allow abortions to the 24-26th week of gestation, and some even less), state-mandated counseling prior to abortion, waiting period prior to abortion, parental involvement in abortion for minors, insurance and government payments for abortion, and medical justifications for abortion. The issue of abortion when the fetus can survive outside the womb is murky at present, but could make abortion at some stage of gestation an illegal taking of a life.

Obviously states with more lenient laws attract people who want abortions but live where the woman's particular situation prevents a legal abortion. Modern transportation capabilities make it relatively easy for a woman to go to another state just to have an abortion. That kind of factor also needs to be addressed in a comprehensive assessment of abortion.

Ethical/spiritual: Ignoring the issue for adherents to a particular ethical or religious persuasion whose precepts preclude involvement in medical procedures such as abortion (such as some Christian Scientists), the primary ethical and spiritual issue concerns when the fetus becomes a person. Medical science currently cannot answer that question and the law is murky. For many, the legal definition of a person is basically a human being who can live outside the womb (with medical assistance if needed). Theologians over the years have debated when a living soul (i.e., a person) was created. Some think all souls were made before creation of the universe; they just wait somewhere until they are joined to a human body. What happens to a soul destined for a body that never comes to life because the fetus was aborted is difficult to answer. Others think the person begins at conception, and others think it occurs later in the pregnancy. Some states restrict abortion after the first heart beat has been detected, Capability for a fetus to survive as a baby outside the womb may occur as early as the 21st week of gestation, and medical advances may permit that to occur even earlier as time goes by. Essentially everyone agrees an infant is a living person by the time it draws its first breath of air after full term gestation.

In general, it seems to be the legal consensus that a living person has the same rights whether one minute old, one day old, or one month old. That means it is illegal to terminate the life of a living person, or to damage the person physically (unless such is a medical necessity). Thus, the question of when the fetus becomes a person is critical; it can make what some would simply call a medical procedure to be considered as an illegal termination of a life (which can be prosecuted as murder or manslaughter). Then the issue gets more complex. Are only the medical personnel performing the abortion liable to prosecution? Or is the one deciding to get an abortion also liable? And what about liability of the one paying for the procedure?

In other illegal termination of a person's life, all of those would be liable: the killer, the one hiring the killer, and the one deciding that the person should be terminated. There often are fuzzy, sentimental, and silly things said in discussing this topic. That is one of the reasons why a careful and comprehensive assessment of all aspects of abortion is needed.

Political: Politicians often cater to groups that are for or against something to create a base of supporters. This has happened with abortion, as it has with other topics. Politicians run the gamut on abortion from avid supporters to avid opponents with some in the middle even trying to avoid being penned down about abortion. Abortion issues politically go far beyond the pro-choice and life termination issues that get the most public attention. Abortion impinges state rights vs federal authority, healthcare regulations, financial and insurance arrangements, and fundamental issues such as what is a person and rights of privacy.

Thus, politically abortion is like an octopus with tentacles reaching into a variety of areas. As such, one can expect that most politicians will have a mixed perspective on abortion issues, supporting in some areas and opposing in others because of the variety of significant interests among the politician's supporters.

This ends my three-part musing about Abortion Chaos. I need a thorough discussion of all aspects of abortion as a basis for a valid decision about abortion. You do also.

Musing 98: The Demise of R&B (initially posted March 31, 2017)

It is quite possible that I will be chastised for the title of this musing: "The Demise of R&B" or the shorter version indicated by the file name (R&B-Demise). I may be told that the musical genre of Rhythm and Blues (which is often referenced as R&B) is alive and well; and I would agree. Then I would note that there are other associations for R&B than that of Rhythm and Blues.

It is easy to find about a dozen meanings for R&B from the internet. Such include common items like "room and board" as well as media references such as R&B use for the cartoon characters of Rocky and Bullwinkle. Unfortunately, none of the connotations for R&B I found in acronym lists was what I meant by R&B in the title for this musing.

I use R&B in this musing title as reference to a "rag and bone" man. I believe the term first appeared around 1850; it was applied to those on the bottom of the social barrel who scoured English cities for things no one wanted that they might sell. In particular they sought rags to sell to papermakers; bone also went to the papermakers because bone provided some of the chemicals used in paper making. It is thought their concentration on rag and bone is the reason these scavengers were given that label. For a couple of centuries before that, papermaker appetite for linen (even in rag scraps) was so great that laws were passed forbidding wrapping corpses in linen for burial (so more linen would be available to paper makers) and contracts were made with those in Egypt to obtain mummy wrappings for their linen.

This reliable market for rags certainly gave those scavenging the junk of society a reason to focus on things (rag and bone) that papermakers would buy. Ironically it appears that the term "rag and bone man" originated about the same time (mid-19th century) that technology would dramatically decrease the demand for rags by paper makers. It was about that time that it was figured out how to make paper effectively from wood pulp; this reduced papermakers' appetite for linen dramatically.

Previously papermaker demand for rags had been so great that it created social problems. It is thought that the 1636 outbreak of the Black Death in England was triggered by contaminated rags imported for paper making. During the American Revolution it was feared that paper makers would not have sufficient rag to produce enough paper of weapon quality (i.e., cartridge paper to hold gunpowder) to fully support the colonial rebellion against England.

The rag and bone label was taken by a pair of young men in the fashion industry in 2002 for their line of stylish casual clothes (Rag and Bone for men); it is also the name of a British band (Rag'n'Bone) gaining prominence this year.

I'm told that rag and bone men were often seen in England, coming to homes asking for any kind of junk that they might dispose of by selling it or just removing it as well as scouring the cities for such until mid-20th century. Then they began to fade away and few still exist. They were popularized by a BBC TV series in England during the 1960s and 1970s (*Steptoe and Son*); a similar sitcom in the U.S. based upon the BBC series (*Sanford and Son*) also was shown in the 1970s.

The demise of rag and bone men provides an example of a significant social problem: disappearance of an occupation that once was prominent. Rag and bone men were around for several centuries. Other occupations that have disappeared did not last so long. Think, for example, of elevator operators and switch board operators; they lasted less than a century.

The problem such occupation demise poses is two-fold. First, how will the necessities of life for the person (and his or her family) be provided without that occupation? And second, how can society evolve so that meaningful employment is available for all? We all need something to do (the adage about idle hands being the Devil's playground contains a lot of insight, as I know from years of conversations with inmates and former inmates).

No, I am not going to promote my vision for utopia and urge you to adopt it. I would not enjoy living in either Thomas Moore's utopia (he coined the term *utopia* in the 16th century) or Plato's ideal society (indicated by *The Republic*). I have not the wit to develop a viable concept for a better society than what we have (which I know has many warts). The problem, from my perspective, is the nature of the people who would inhabit any ideal society.

The Bible tells us that people are born with a sin nature; corruptness from human's sin nature causes even the best human society to be a mess. History has no example (that I know about) of a society in which a majority of the population committed themselves to the Lord Jesus Christ and lived mainly in obedience to the revealed will of God in the Bible for an extended period of time. Certainly America has not done that at any time in its history (the portion of the population that gives indication of serious commitment to Jesus is only a portion of church members, that membership being something between less than 20% of the population in colonial times to about two-thirds of the population in the 20th century). Hence I think it unlikely a suitable population for an ideal society will exist prior to the return of Christ.

Musing 99: Sensitivities (April 1, 2017)

April 1st is called April Fools' Day (or All Fools' Day by some); it is a time for pranks and jokes. Setting a time when pranks and jokes are expected, and perhaps tolerated more than usual, has been a custom in many countries for decades, some would say for centuries. While this musing is not intended as a prank or joke; however, because it addresses a type of behavior that seems quite foolish to me, this time of year is especially an appropriate time for me to post it.

The foolish behavior I have in mind is what I call "sensitivities," by which I refer to rather extreme sensitivity responses. This behavior manifests itself in a multitude of ways, some more serious than others. A news broadcast addressing concerns about civilian causalities in the war on ISIS stimulated me to post this musing.

Extreme sensitivity about status and insults was a primary stimulus for duels for a number of centuries. Currently extreme sensitivities in regard to speech about race and gender cause some to abandon freedom of speech as they censor and punish offensive expressions. Such is being done even by those who should be strong advocates of free speech which is enshrined in our Constitution's Bill of Rights; our universities with their speech codes and our legal system with its criminalization of various kinds of speech are guilty in this regard.

The real world is a nasty place. It has many unpleasant aspects. It is foolish to assume such is not so. Extreme sensitivities can cause actions that are foolish in that they are inconsistent with the nastiness of reality. For example, if free speech is important, as I and the Constitution think it is, then nasty things will be said at times. That forces a decision, is free speech important enough for tolerance of utterance of nasty things. If not, then free speech must not be very important. History shows repeated examples of regimes that would not tolerate free speech; I would not like to live in such, but I fear that America is moving in that direction because of its excessive sensitivities. Tolerance of nasty speech is far better than the loss of free speech.

I said this musing was stimulated by a radio broadcast addressing civilian casualties in the war against ISIS. As I said, the real world is a nasty place. It has been long noted that "war is hell." That phrase is often attributed to William Tecumseh Sherman, famous for his march to the sea through Georgia in the Civil War. It is thought that Sherman said "war is hell" a number of times in speeches, but the phrase cannot be found among any of his written communications, including his personal correspondence. Regardless of its origin, the phrase captures the nasty reality of war. Not just combatants get hurt; civilians (non-combatants) are injured and killed, and their possessions may be taken or destroyed.

Current sensibilities bemoan that reality and efforts to curb civilian casualties are encouraged, even efforts than can limit or even nullify military effectiveness. When leaders believe a serious risk is posed to the nation, they are willing to authorize effective military actions, even those which cause immense civilian casualties. During WWII, strategic bombing was used to crimple Axis industrial capacity and its infrastructure. At times, civilian casualties exceeded 10,000 killed in a single day. This happened both in Europe (e.g., Dresden in mid-February 1945) and in Japan (e.g., Tokyo on March 9-10, 1945).

Modern military leaders prefer not to harm civilians; they don't want to waste resources on them nor create unnecessary attitude problems for the future, after the enemy has been overcome. However, military leaders are realistic and know that sometimes steps to minimize civilian casualties reduce the effectiveness of military actions, which may prolong the conflict and cause the total number of casualties over the conflict to be greater than they might be if the most effective military approach were taken.

The radio broadcast that stimulated this musing expressed grief at civilian casualties and encouraged actions to reduce such casualties, but without serious discussion of the impact of their suggestions on the military effectiveness of following their suggestions. This kind of sentimental approach is characteristic of excessive sensitivity. A pertinent analogy is the refusal of a patient for amputation of a limb with gangrene because the patient did not want to lose the limb. Perhaps such a patient should be asked if being buried with a whole body would be preferable to an amputation. The real world is a nasty place.

I hope we will be mature enough to deal with reality, and curb the problems that come from accommodating excessive sensitivities far too much. We should strive to always emphasize the more important things: free speech in the example noted, and military effectiveness to allow the war against ISIS to be won.

For a couple of decades, excessive sensitivities in various areas have been tolerated, much to our detriment in my opinion. I believe it is time for us to regain our common sense and deal with the nasty real world, emphasizing truly important things such as free speech far more than contemporary dictates of political correctness.

It is far past time for those who should be in the forefront of encouraging emphasis on the really important things of life (religious organizations, our universities, and our legal system) to get off their duffs and do what should be done to enable us to make the best of the nasty real world. That can only be done when the really important things always get top priority.

Musing 100: Stupidities (initially posted April 3, 2017)

When I was young, comic skits often would contain a bit of dialogue showing the tendency of people to say stupid things. For example, one comic in a two person skit might say, "Yesterday I want to Old John's funeral." The other comic would say, "Is Old John dead?" Then the first comic would reply, "I hope so since they buried him." People are very prone to such stupidities as asking if the person of the funeral is dead. Usually they simply are expressing surprise; few actually question the reality of the person's death, except in mystery stories and spy movies. Unfortunately, not all common stupidities are as harmless as asking if a person is dead when hearing about the person's funeral. This musing is about such stupidities.

Abundance of more serious examples of stupidity is illustrated by a number of ads on TV about auto insurance. Either the advertisers are stupid or the ads are based upon the assumption that viewers are stupid. The ads criticize a person's choice of auto insurance because it would not pay for the full price of a wrecked new car. Any sensible person knows every insurance company has a multitude of policies, and that the ones that cover more also cost more. Every auto insurance company wants to make money, and they set the cost of their policies so that they make a profit on them. Most people choose the policy they think best for them based upon policy cost and the extent of its coverage. The insurance company may make more on a more expensive policy than on a less expensive one. So either the person buying the policy is stupid about insurance or prone to bad decisions, or the ad is a typical spiel of a huckster. The abundance of presentations of the kind of ads referenced here is a dismal indication of an abundance of stupidity in America.

The two examples noted show stupidity in how people talk and in a financial arena (auto insurance). Unfortunately there is an abundance of stupidity in America with far more serious consequences than verbal embarrassment or the loss of some dollars. The remainder of this musing will address that area of stupidity.

The area of stupidity with the greatest impact is in the spiritual arena. The Creator of the reality in which we live exists and amazingly is interested in people even though we occupy a very tiny speck of His creation. The Creator has chosen to inform people about Himself in multiple ways, the most important of which are through His creation and through revelation of Himself in human history as reported in the Bible. Most people in America know this.

The information about God from His creation and from the Bible tells us the kind of being He is and what pleases Him and what displeases Him. That information also warns of eternal consequences arising from a person's relationship to God, and notes that those consequences are more important than whatever wealth or enjoyment one might obtain while living here on the earth. The vast majority of people in the U.S. basically ignore God, and that is the most serious stupidity one can engage in. Its consequences are eternal and most significant.

How can I say that most Americans ignore God when a majority of Americans belong to a Christian church? That is a very reasonable question. Of the church members you know, how many seem to try to live in ways that the Bible clearly says pleases God? You can get a basic synopsis of that kind of life from Jesus' Sermon on the Mount (Matthew 5-7). The majority of church members I know might give lip service to trying to please Jesus, but the way they think, talk, and act does not indicate they try very hard to do what He said. Perhaps you know a different kind of people than I do, but I doubt it.

In my life time, many attitudes in America have changed from nominal acceptance of the Bible as a reliable guide to godly living to explicit rejection of the Biblical perspective in a number of areas (as demonstrated repeatedly by various opinion polls and by changes in America's laws). This is another indication of the spiritual stupidity I address in this musing.

People buy insurance to protect from the consequences of calamity: a horrible auto accident, major storm damage to a home, an unexpectedly youthful death of a spouse or parent, etc. Wise and prudent selection of the kind of insurance policy one buys is smart; failure to prepare for possible calamity is foolish, what I call a stupidity.

Spiritually those who fail to take God seriously and respond to Him in the way His revelation (the Bible) says pleases Him are not wise. I call it the most significant stupidity. God's revelation tells us that He loves people and wants to save them from the consequences of their wrong doings. Jesus came to make such salvation possible, and what pleases God most is acceptance of Jesus as the Savior and trying to live in ways that please Him. The Gospel of John and the Apostle Paul's letter to the Romans give a nutshell explanation for how to have a relationship with God that pleases Him and will bring an eternity of bliss. That is a stark contrast to the dismal eternal future for those that miss God's salvation by spiritual stupidity.

I hope you to too wise to follow the path of most Americans because it is a path of spiritual stupidity, and its eternal consequences are dire.

Musing 101: Truth
(initially posted April 6, 2017)

An April issue of *Time* magazine asked on its cover, "Is Truth Dead?" *Time* is not the first to have questions about truth, as every student of epistemology (the branch of philosophy concerned with the theory of knowledge) knows. A couple of millennia ago, a Roman governor named Pilate sarcastically said "What is truth?" during his trial of Jesus the Christ.

Many think Diogenes, founder of the ancient Greek sect of Cynics who is famous for his search for an honest man on the streets of Athens with a lantern in daylight, may not have known what to look for since he was run out of town for counterfeiting. *Time* magazine may have a similar problem given *Time's* history (a cover of an April 1966 issue of *Time* asked "Is God Dead?").

The issue of what is truth and how can one discover if something is true and what level of confidence one can have in a conclusion that something is true is not a trivial subject. A recent issue of *New Scientist* (a weekly English-language international science magazine with a fairly good reputation) contained ten features (i.e., articles) related to knowledge: what it is, how to tell truth from lies, why we'll never know everything, etc.

A popular 1940 song with lyrics by Johnny Mercer has been performed by many famous artists over the years. That song says wise men know that "fools rush in where angels fear to tread." In this musing, I may emulate one in love described by that song by rushing in and sharing my comments about truth. It is not an easy subject to discuss.

When I was a youngster, for a while my mother worked part-time in the concession stand in a theater. After school, I had to travel to the theater (first a bus and then on a street car). I would spend a few hours in the theater watching whatever was showing until my mother's shift was over. Then we would go home. That meant I saw some movies several times, one of which was a 1952 movie starring Burt Lancaster, *The Crimson Pirate*. In that movie, several times the pirate hero played by Lancaster said, "Believe nothing that you read, and only half of what you see." Of course, such warnings have come from many before being uttered in *The Crimson Pirate* movie, from such notables as Edgar Allen Poe and Benjamin Franklin among others.

The current furor over truth and its limited appearance in public discourse, especially in political arenas, is probably just an ideological fad because from my perception of historical conditions things are little different today than they usually are. Consistent and general ethical behavior of people is sadly lacking in every period of history and in every society that I know about, especially from those seeking an advantage over others emotionally, socially, economically, or politically. The first century Roman governor Pilate is just a well-known sceptic about truth from his comment during the trial of Jesus; he repeatedly declares Jesus is innocent and then condemns Him to death by crucifixion.

Search for truth requires both honesty and good sense. It also requires humility in that often the available evidence will be inadequate for a decision about the truthfulness of something. That reality bothers many people. Some it discourages; and they may assume that one cannot really know truth since one cannot know the truth about all things of interest to that person. Others simply decide to determine something's veracity based upon one's perspective, philosophy, opinion, desires, or some other basis than objective and logical demonstration of the veracity of that something.

I would urge you to be one of the rare individuals who is truly concerned about truth, and to pursue truth vigorously with honesty, good sense, and patient humility. You are unlikely to determine the truth of all things that interest you, but you should be able to determine the veracity of some of them.

In your search for truth, I hope you will be wise enough to realize that veracity of some things is more important than the veracity of other things. A simple illustration of this is the following. It is more important to know the veracity of a label on a bottle that says POISON if you might drink something from that bottle than it is to know whether rumors about the physical condition of one of your sports heroes are true. Such recognition of relative importance of veracity can help you to allocate your efforts in determining truthfulness appropriately.

Veracity of things that might cause you to act or not act is more important than the veracity of things that have no specific impact on what you do. Likewise veracity of things that have significant potential impact on you or others important to you is always of high importance. Acceptance of this perspective should have two definite implications for a person. First, since we seldom have time or resources to determine the veracity of many things, we must decide what sources we generally consider credible and pay more attention to them than to other sources. Second, we should not neglect spiritual aspects of life in our search for truth since that has potential eternal consequences. Unfortunately many in our society are not wise about this; they treat truth about spiritual things in a cavalier manner. That careless approach to something with potential eternal consequences is most unwise, yet it is probably something that characterizes the majority of Americans. I hope you are not among that foolish group.

My thousand word limit for musings prevents me from saying more on this subject.

Musing 102: The Big C
(initially posted April 8, 2017)

Cancer, the big C, horrifies many. The word cancer carries such emotional impact for many that they have a hard time dealing with it reasonably. Some will opt immediately for the most aggressive treatment without giving serious consideration to alternative ways of dealing with the cancer.

I understand the impact of hearing a doctor say that biopsy results indicated I have prostate cancer. Ten years ago I had that experience. Others I know went straight to surgery or radiation to deal with their prostate cancer. I did not do that. I investigated outcomes for men my age with prostate cancer of the sort my cancer seems to be. I discovered that the limited information available showed no difference in life expectancy outcomes for the various ways of dealing with prostate cancer (surgery, radiation of various sorts, and watchful waiting). I've opted for the watchful waiting and thus for the past decade I have been a "cancer endurer," in contrast to a "cancer survivor" (a term usually applied to people who no longer have cancer having survived both cancer and treatment to deal with the cancer). I chose the watchful waiting approach because it avoided side effects associated with the various other ways of dealing with prostate cancer and it also avoided a lot of medical expense. Of course, my kind of prostate cancer is asymptomatic (i.e., no pain); my choice probably would have been different if my cancer caused the kind of pain many cancers cause.

During my choice about my response to being told I had cancer, I prayed for guidance and also asked God to heal me. I believe He has guided me in my response to the cancer, but He has not chosen to heal me. Sometimes God heals in response to prayer; He may do that through medical treatment or independently in what appears to us as miraculous. Sometimes He does not choose to heal, even though many people pray for a particular person to be healed.

It is good that God does not respond to every prayer the way we want. Think how crowded it would be and how many social problems would exist from several times as many people because God responded to every prayer for healing so that people did not die before reaching or going far beyond a hundred years of age. I'm glad God is so much wiser than we are in the way He responds to our prayers.

Three days ago again I heard my doctor say, "You have cancer." This time it is a skin cancer. The next day I saw a dermatologist. Both my primary care physician and the dermatologist believe it is a basal cell cancer; the biopsy will say what kind of cancer it is. Now I am walking around with an extra hole in my head, although I suspect it is just a hole in my epidermis. I doubt that the dermatologist could have penetrated my hard head with the small hand tool he used to remove the offensive tissue.

My responses to hearing my doctor say, "You have cancer," were not the hysterical kind of response reported for some for a variety of reasons. In part my response comes from my personality. I am not as emotional as some I know. In part my response came from some awareness of the medical situation in regard to prostate and skin cancers. And in part my response comes my knowledge of what lies beyond this life.

The Bible is very clear about this point. Those who have trusted Christ to be their Savior and have been born again by the work of God's Holy Spirit go to be with God when they leave the earth. So in one sense, death is something I look forward to because things will be far better for me then (regardless of how wonderful things might be for me here on earth at that time). Of course, I have concern about dying, concern that the process of dying may be both painful, unpleasant, and take quite a while. I also have concern that my loved ones may face some difficulties after I die because they now have to do things I formally did and because the cost of my dying could hurt them financially.

I know others will also hear the "Big C" word from doctors. They cannot do much about the emotionality of their personality, but they can determine ahead of time to become informed about options of life expectancy outcomes before they make a decision so that their decision can be made wisely and not be just an emotional response. Also, I hope they will pray for wisdom and God's guidance so that they make a wise decision. If they do not have an assurance of their eternal destiny, I hope that hearing the doctor say "You have cancer" will spur them to go to Jesus Christ for His salvation. Jesus is so loving that He is happy to receive you even if your motivation is to avoid the possibility of eternal separation from God.

If you don't know how to connect with Jesus for salvation, ask a Christian friend you know whom you would classify as "born again." Your friend can tell you what to do. Reading the Gospel of John and book of Romans in the New Testament will also make it clear what you need to do.

It is horrible to hear "You have cancer," but hearing that does not have to destroy you. You might become a cancer survivor or like me, a cancer endurer, as you travel to your eternal destiny.

Musing 103: Rumination
(initially posted April 10, 2017)

Rumination is a word I seldom hear or see, and I suspect many do not know what it means. The *Oxford English Dictionary (OED)* defines rumination as "1. Contemplation, meditation; *pl.* Meditations, thoughts, reflections; 2. The action of chewing the cud." *Merriam-Webster* (on-line) defines rumination as "(transitive verb) 1. to go over in the mind repeatedly and often casually or slowly; 2. to chew repeatedly for an extended period; (intransitive verb) 1. to chew again what has been chewed slightly and swallowed : chew the cud; 2 to engage in contemplation : reflect." I suspect that most people are like me and ruminate a lot.

The medical community has defined a "rumination syndrome" as a physical disorder, particularly among children, in which the person brings up and re-chews partially digested food. Psychology also gives a particular connotation to rumination: repetitively going over a thought or problem without completion, and associates rumination with anxiety and depression.

This musing uses rumination simply for thinking about something a number of times, sometimes coming to a conclusion about it and sometimes not being able to reach a conclusion about it. The subject I address in this musing is the exodus of the Jews from Egypt under Moses and the forty years they spent before the Jews entered Canaan. This subject is mainly addressed in the part of the Bible that Jews call the *Torah* (the five books of Moses that begin the Old Testament: Genesis through Deuteronomy). Most of what I ruminate about comes from Exodus and Leviticus.

At Mount Sinai, God gave Moses instructions about how He wanted the people to behave (e.g., such as the Ten Commandments) and how they were to worship Him. These instructions include description of a tabernacle which would be central in their worship. The instructions also provide descriptions of what the religious leaders (e.g., priests) were to do and the various offerings to be made for individuals and for the people as a whole. The ruminations of this musing focus on logistics of offerings mentioned.

Exodus reports more than 600,000 men (males over twenty) along with their wives and children, plus their flocks, herds, and possessions. This crowd of a couple of million created enormous logistical problems (water, wood for cooking, fodder for animals, food for the people, etc.). Think of infrastructure required for a metropolitan area such as Austin, Kansas City, or Las Vegas (each of their populations is about two million) to get a feel for the magnitude of the logistic problem faced in the exodus.

Leviticus describes a variety of offerings for different purposes. The offering often was to be a young bull, a male goat, or a female goat. Such offerings were required to be burnt; normally Leviticus describes that as being done in or near the tabernacle. Sometimes the whole animal is burnt, and sometimes it seems to be divided into three portions (some for God, some for the priests, and some for those making the offering). The priest usually got the skin of the animal sacrificed. Some of the animal's blood was put in some way on specified things (such as horns of the altar) and the rest was poured out (e.g., at the foot of the altar).

Logistical questions about the offerings intrigue me. Assume that between the voluntary and the mandatory offerings each Jewish male made one burnt offering a year. That would require over 1600 burnt offerings a day for every day of the year (if they were evenly distributed throughout the year), about 70 offerings an hour if sacrificing 24 hours per day (more per hour if not 24/7)! All of this going on in or near the tabernacle! You can begin to see why I ruminate on logistics here.

How long would an offering take? An animal is led to the place of sacrifice, then killed, and possibly skinned. Wood has to be available for the fire to burn it. How long does it take to burn a young bull or a goat in a sacrifice? An offering would take at least a few hours but probably no more than two days (overnight is implied for some situations). About 3,300 priests provides one priest for each offering assuming two day max offering duration; perhaps the 20,000+ men of the priestly tribe from Levi could support such and all other priestly responsibilities.

Think of the blood volume. Each offering might produce 5-10 gallons of blood, hundreds of gallons of blood an hour for the 70 (or more) offerings each hour! What a mess! That's a lot of blood.

If it only required 1/10 cord of wood for each offering, a dozen cords of wood an hour are needed for the burnt offerings! Such is needed 24/7. Add in Sabbath rest requirements, and the hourly rates of things go up about 15%.

I do not know how the logistics required to implement instructions about offerings in Leviticus could have been met. I suspect Jews of the exodus ignored many of those instructions just as they ignored circumcising boy babies during the exodus (the book of Joshua in the Bible tells how Joshua delayed attacking Jericho so his men could be circumcised). However, since the sacrifices and offerings of the Old Testament are an object lesson about the seriousness of sin from God's perspective and foreshadow the great sacrifice of Jesus which makes our salvation possible, I'm impressed with how the massive volume of offerings suggested by Leviticus indicate that Christ's offering for us would be even greater, and that makes me appreciate what Jesus did for us even more. I hope you do too.

Musing 104-Why? Part One
(initially posted April 11, 2017)

WHY? is a question people often ask of God when calamity hits or when information seems to threaten one's beliefs. This musing is about such questions of WHY? Normally I address a topic in in a single musing, but for this topic I will use three musings; the topic is vitally important and not as widely addressed as it should be. Beware this topic involves disturbing ideas.

My first draft of the musing was made months ago. It hit me as I reviewed the draft musing that Easter week (Holy Week as some call it) was an appropriate time for the three musings addressing the WHY? question.

Technology advances have enabled modern medicine to understand better how people function. We're beginning to see how things happening in a person's brain can impact the person's thinking and behavior. A debate's beginning about one's ability to choose and act responsibly when normal brain processing is prevented by injury or biological conditions. The raises a question about "free will;" does everyone have "free will" (with associated responsibility for thoughts, words, and actions) all the time?

New terms are beginning to show up. One is "neurocriminality" (defined as "a neural basis to crime") used in the context of those committing violent crime repetitively. The word may have been coined by Adrian Raine, a leading authority on the biology of violence and a professor of Criminology, Psychiatry, and Psychology at the University of Pennsylvania. There's a relatively new discipline called "neurolaw" (a term coined by Sherrod Taylor in 1991 as "an emerging field of interdisciplinary study that explores effects of discoveries in neuroscience on legal rules and standards").

Why is this important? It's important because responsibility depends upon choice. If a person has no choice, is that person responsible for consequences of the choice? Suppose you mistakenly put an important paper in a shredder and it is destroyed. You would not blame the machine for doing what it was designed to do (if it performed properly). It has no responsibility for the mistake in destroying an important paper. Responsibility for that lies elsewhere.

The Bible is clear that God holds people responsible for evil choices they make. This is clearly stated by the Apostle Paul in Romans 1: 18-32 (as well as in many other passages in the Bible). However, it is also clear that some people have less capacity for choice than others. Young children do not have the same capability as adults. Those with severe mental limitations and various medical conditions have limited choice; for example, a person in an epileptic seizure (sometimes called a "fit") may damage and break things without consciously choosing to do so.

Modern technology has enabled brain scans to detect abnormalities (such as tumors) in brains of some convicted of multiple violent crimes. When the tumor was removed in one case, the person no longer behaved with the previous characteristic violence. The person behaved decently for years; then the violence returned as the tumor returned. When the tumor was removed again, the violent behavior also went away. In a situation such as this, should the person be held responsible for the violent behavior when it was evidently caused by the tumor in the brain that changed the way the person thought and acted?

This is an issue being discussed in various venues: courts, universities, and religious circles. I start my comments in a different place than some: they focus on the individual involved. Instead I start with a few comments about God.

First, how do I know about God? Why should my ideas be given more credence than someone else's? Today some people say everyone worships the same God, regardless of which religion they are in. I am always amazed that such hogwash exists in modern times. People who say that normally are only referring to the major religions and would not extend their comments to those worshipping an animal or a tribal deity. Sensible people understand that reality does not comply with or accommodate such hogwash. When there are significant differences in characteristics of the deity that different groups worship, they cannot all be dealing with the same being.

What I know about God comes from the Bible. It tells me of Jesus, the Son of God Who came to earth to make it possible for people to become acceptable to God. Since His coming to earth, there has been only one way to an acceptable relationship with God: that way is through Jesus. Any who do not recognize and accept Jesus as the Savior will not know God or be accepted by Him. Hard words for most people in the world, but true.

Second, what is God like? He is the all-powerful all-knowing One, nothing is impossible for Him. He is good, righteous, holy, and gracious. The Romans passage cited earlier indicates that God holds people responsible for living up to the level of revelation about God to which they have been exposed. Jesus made it possible for people who accept Him as Savior to be forgiven for wrongs they did. For those with limited capability to choose, God will do the right thing. I'm not so presumptuous as to presume what that right thing is; I trust how God deals with everyone will be just and right with full consideration of all aspects of their lives and capabilities. How glad I am that I will be dealt with mercifully because Jesus paid for all the evil of my life; otherwise I would expect nothing but God's righteous judgment.

I will continue musing about this topic in a future musing (WHY? Part Two).

Musing 105: WHY? Part Two
(initially posted April 12, 2017)

This musing is a continuation of the WHY? Part One musing. It addresses the issue of free will in the light of growing medical and scientific information about the impact of one's biological condition on the person's choices and behavior. The Part One musing introduced the topic and noted a few characteristics about God from the Bible. This musing begins at that point.

From a human perspective, God is not fair since all that is and all that happens is what God has chosen for the course of history for the universe and for our world. Certainly those born in America at this time with good health and are reared in a decent family with adequate resources are much more fortunate from a human perspective than one born elsewhere with physical and mental impairments into an abusive family in an impoverished community. Some might complain that God was not fair to treat to people so differently.

Such different treatment of people is specifically indicated in the Bible. In John 9, Jesus says the man born blind was that way so that God could be glorified when Jesus healed the man, enabling him to see. Likewise in Romans 9 Paul explains that God gave Jacob preference over his older brother Esau by choosing him before the boys were born. God chose those who would be saved in Christ before creation of the world (Ephesians 1:4).

The story of Job in the Old Testament tells of a godly man who experienced calamity: he lost his possessions, his children, and his health. Job asked why such horrible things happened to him. In chapter 38 of Job, God begins to respond to Job's WHY? question. God does not tell Job why He acted as He did; instead God asks Job what right he (a miserable speck of creation) has to reproach the Creator with such a question. Human comprehension is not capable of grasping the infinite set of things that God considers as He determines what He chooses to do. At the beginning of chapter 42 we find Job's response to God's comments; Job concludes with these words: "My ears had heard of you, but now my eyes have seen you. Therefore I despise myself and repent in dust and ashes." Job came to understand that his human perspective, limited by the finite reasoning of the human mind and his limited comprehension of the situation, gave him no right to question how God does things.

As noted in the previous musing, God is all powerful, all-knowing, good, and wise; what He does will be the right thing. Our human perspective, even on things that look wrong to us, is not a valid basis for criticizing God.

Think of the analogy of a mid-19th century African without modern medical information who brought a sick child to a medical missionary. The missionary diagnosed the problem as appendicitis. He knows the child's appendix has to be removed. The African watches as the missionary doctor appears to kill his child (by administering anesthetic). The African would see the missionary start to cut the child open. For a person without comprehension of modern medicine, it appears the missionary doctor is doing bad things; when in fact the missionary doctor saves the child's life. The African had to trust the missionary even though it looked like the missionary was doing evil things. We are in a similar situation as we look at the history that is unfolding about us. God appears to be doing bad things in the unfair way some people are treated. BUT He is not. He never makes a mistake.

Dealing with that reality is a hard thing for every serious Christian. When I see those whose lives are unimaginably hard because of their physical and mental condition or the circumstances in which they live, I struggle to keep my perspective and remind myself that God is indeed in control of history, every bit of it to the smallest detail – Jesus said a sparrow does not fall to the ground without God's awareness of it, and that even the number of hairs on our heads are numbered. Just as the 19th-century African in my analogy had to trust the medical missionary, so I need to trust God to be the God the Bible declares Him to be. He is all powerful and He does everything right.

It is in this situation that the Bible indicates God has made people responsible for their choices and behavior (that is what we mean by the term "free will"). It is true that a person's biology and circumstances can create pressures on the brain that appear to dictate choices and actions, just as an excessive amount of alcohol drunk can impact a person's thinking and behavior. God's judgment of people in such conditions will be appropriate, as well as wise, just, and right. Because we have such limited knowledge about such things, it is wise to follow Jesus' instructions in the Sermon on the Mount not to judge others.

As far as the appropriate way that society (i.e., the law) should deal with people of impaired choice capabilities and their actions, I think there are many more informed and wiser than I who are dealing with that. I, as a citizen, will try to comply with the guidance from the Apostles Paul and Peter to obey the laws of the land unless those laws cause me to deny God or worship something other than Him.

I will address a few more aspects of this topic in Part Three of this musing. This topic is hard and complex, but important.

Musing 106: WHY? Part Three
(initially posted April 13, 2017)

This musing is a continuation of the WHY? Part One and Part Two musings. It addresses the issue of free will in the light of growing medical and scientific information about the impact of one's biological condition on the person's choices and behavior. The Part One musing introduced the topic and noted a few characteristics about God from the Bible. The Part Two musing discussed the fact that God's actions in His creation may seem unfair in many situations. This musing begins after recognizing that we (mere created beings with finite limitations) have no right to criticize the Creator and have limited capability to properly understand actions of the Infinite One in acknowledgement that our comprehension of things is limited and incomplete. In this musing, I discuss a few additional aspects of the free will and contemporary biological knowledge topic.

It is important to realize limitations of our current knowledge. The first suggestion that much of the universe (more than 90% of it by reliable estimates) was outside the realm of direct observation by current technology occurred less than a century ago; now it is generally believed by scientists that the majority of our universe is Dark Matter or Dark Energy. Our direct observations of the inner workings of the human brain are likewise recent; X-rays of the brain were first done about a century ago, and computerized axial tomography (CAT or CT scanning) and magnetic resonance imaging (MRI) began less than half a century ago.

A great deal of progress has been made in gaining knowledge about normal functioning of the human brain, but there is substantial evidence that the brain operates differently in some people at some times. With over 80 billion neurons in the human brain, each of which can have thousands of connections (synapses) with other neurons, there are a very large number of alternative ways information (signals) can pass around the brain. It is known that sometimes when there has been physical injury to the brain (or surgical action) that the brain creates new pathways for signals when the original normal pathway is no longer possible.

What current medical science understands is how certain situations can have a major impact on a person's thinking and behavior (as it did with the man guilty of repeated violence with brain tumor mentioned in Part One of this musing), it has not shown that such brain situations always produce such thinking or behavior for a significant number of people. Hence the tendency to dismiss free will and say a person is simply a product of the way the brain functions in the situation, which some who reject spiritual realities have said, is quite unjustified by the present state of knowledge.

Scientific knowledge claims at times go far beyond what the evidence supports. A classic instance of such is the false claim that finger prints are unique. The falseness of that claim has been demonstrated repeatedly since automated processing of fingerprints became common. When automated systems have been applied to large numbers of fingerprints (i.e., thousands), a number of the prints will be identified as from the same person, even when it is known the collection of fingerprints are all from different people (such as those who worked for a given company). The number of fingerprints identified as the same will decrease as the number of criteria that must be satisfied in the search are increased. It has been demonstrated that at times fingerprints from the same person, even when taken on the same day, are not always identified as from the same person. Such problems also exist when experts are used to process the fingerprints as well as when automated systems are used. This contradicts the claim often put forth by forensic scientists about fingerprint uniqueness and the confidence that should be put in fingerprint identification.

Some of what I have seen in the literature about free will from those involved with neuroscience has the same flavor as the early erroneous claims for fingerprint uniqueness.

The Bible tells us that God holds us accountable for our decisions and actions. We do not know how He will evaluate those with limited mental capabilities, such as young children, those with brain injuries or disease, or those whose biology significantly hinders normal brain processes; but we do know that whatever God does will be right, just, and based upon full knowledge of everything related to the situation. It will be the appropriate judgment, regardless of how we mortals may look at it.

Human arrogance is something that God does not appreciate. That is demonstrated in God's response to the Tower of Babel (Genesis 11:1-8) as well as in Paul's comments in Romans 1:18-32. Human arrogance shows in human foolishness of trying to live without God and in people's criticism of how God works and what He does. I hope this three part musing about advances in medical science and the questions such raise about free will stimulate us (you and me) to seek to better understand God and how He acts, and cause us not to be so presumptuous as to criticize Him or advise Him about how things should be done. Let us recognize how little we may understand about things and the limitations of our finite reasoning; let such encourage us to appreciate God's mercy and grace in providing a way for people to have a proper relationship with Him through His Son, Jesus Christ the Savior.

The topic addressed in these three musings is complex and requires hard thinking; some people just ignore such. I thank you for the attention you have given the topic.

Musing 107: Publication of Pace Musings (initially posted April 14, 2017)

In April last year, I decided to post musings in my Facebook account and posted my first one on April 26th. This is the 107th one posted thus far, which works out to be a couple a week on the average. I've decided to publish the first year's worth of musings, and will do so on Kindle so I can charge just a nominal price for the collection of them. I will make that collection of musings all that I do by the end of this month, so the first year of musing will include all posted from April 26th last year through April 30th this year. That should be 120-130 musings. I plan to include a few words of introduction that explain my thousand word restriction to a musing and a topical index that will point one to particular musings that address a topic of interest to the person. I will announce when the book appears on Kindle; probably it will be in late-May.

Since today is Good Friday, instead of saying more about my publication plan, it is appropriate for this musing to address the tremendous event that this day commemorates: the death of Jesus that makes our salvation possible. It is the most astounding thing that ever happened, at least I believe it is.

The death of Jesus, the unique Son of God, is more amazing than creation. God is all powerful and all knowing. Bringing things from nothing into existence is what He did in creation, and that is amazing. As we have grown in our understanding of how vast His creation is (and how little of it we can observe or understand), it amazes us to think of the power it took to begin creation and the power that it takes to sustain all that is. This aspect of God is amazing.

Jesus said it was harder for a rich man to get into heaven than for a camel to go through the eye of a needle; He said this about a very good man, one who had kept the commandments Jesus mentioned. Jesus' disciples were astounded. If this good man could not qualify for heaven, no one could; they exclaimed, "Who then can get into heaven?" The Bible explains that it's not just the good rich man who cannot qualify for heaven by his own efforts; no one can because ALL HAVE SINNED AND FAILED TO LIVE UP TO GOD'S STANDARDS. Jesus could also have said it was harder for that camel to go through the needle's eye than for a poor man to get into heaven.

On Good Friday we commemorate what Jesus did to make it possible for God to forgive people for their sins and give them eternal life with Him: they have to do is commit themselves to Jesus in faith, trusting God to keep His promise to save them if they do that. It is amazing that God cares enough about humanity to make a way for people to be saved; I'm very glad He does. However, that amazing love of God is not as astounding to me as something else about the death of Jesus.

God is alive and holy. Those are two of His most significant characteristics. He is the source of all life. Sin (evil) and its consequences (death) are totally incompatible with God's nature. That sin and death could somehow enter the Godhead is to me the most amazing thing about the death of Jesus, more amazing to me than God's great power and knowledge in creation, even more amazing than His astounding love for people.

People often comment about the horrible physical agony that Jesus endured in crucifixion, and it was horrible beyond the imagination of most of us today; but when Jesus was on the earth thousands of people experienced that horrible agony because they were crucified. More amazing, and perhaps even more horrible from God's perspective, was that Jesus, the Second Person of the Godhead, experienced sin and death.

The Bible tells that somehow Jesus "Who had no sin was made to be sin for us, so that in Him we might become the righteousness of God." 2 Corinthians 5:21. He Who was life itself and as God the source of all life died. How astounding that God possibly risked His very existence as the holy One allowed both sin and death to enter His being when the Second Person of the Trinity was on the cross. That to me is the most amazing aspect of Easter, and the one for which I am most grateful for without that neither I nor anyone person would have a chance to be acceptable to God. How great our God is!

About thirty years ago, Leonard Cohen wrote a haunting melody that he named *Hallelujah*. Numerous noted vocalists have performed the song, with a variety of lyrics as Cohen himself did. The lyrics I like best were written a few years ago by Kelly Mooney. She replaced Cohen's lyrics when she was asked to sing *Hallelujah* at an Easter worship service. Perhaps you would find her revised words to *Hallelujah* very appropriate this year. You can hear her sing them and see them at https://www.youtube.com/watch?v=h350JjUsWKo. Her words are much more appropriate for Easter than any of the original versions of Cohen's *Hallelujah*. Mooney's words are often called the *Easter Version* or *Good Friday Meditation*.

May God bless you as you meditate of Jesus' death on the cross for us, and may you be wise enough to seek the salvation made possible by the death of Jesus Christ our Lord.

Musing 108: A Small Concept of God (initially posted April 15, 2017)

In recent years I have become increasingly aware that many people, even religious leaders, have an inadequate concept of God. A small concept of God has implications both for one's beliefs and for one's behavior. This musing discusses a few aspects of this common problem.

In 1940, a noted Christian of last century (C. S. Lewis) published a thoughtful book **The Problem of Pain**. In it, he illustrated the problem, a part of which I call a small concept of God. Lewis wrote, "What would really satisfy us would be a God who said of anything we happened to like, 'What does it matter so long as they are contented?' We want, in fact, not so much a Father in Heaven as a grandfather in heaven — a senile benevolence who, as they say, 'liked to see young people enjoying themselves' and whose plan for the universe was simply that it might be truly said at the end of each day, 'a good time was had by all'."

In these words Lewis noted the general problem that people prefer a god of their own making rather than the God revealed to us by His Creation and the Bible. This musing is about a particular aspect of that problem: the restriction of God to something we can explain and describe in human finite reasoning. That is the essence of what I call a small concept of God.

In **The Problem of Pain** Lewis wrestled with the challenge that abundant evil in the world poses for the concept of an all-powerful, all knowing, all capable God who is loving, good, just, and holy. Thoughtful Christians throughout the ages have had to grapple with that issue. It is an issue that cannot be resolved if one's concept of God is too small.

We must begin with recognition (a confession) that we are just a tiny speck in the vastness of God's creation whose awareness and knowledge is very limited and our capacity to understand is limited by our finite reasoning. Too often human arrogance, which God's dislike of was illustrated early in human history at the Tower of Babel, fails to recognize such limitations and presumes that everything can be judged properly by humans. This assumes that adequate knowledge is available for a sound decision and that the issue can be decided by finite reasoning.

How foolish people can be. It has only been in the past century that scientists have realized that the majority of the universe in which we live is outside our capability to observe or understand. We call that stuff Dark

Matter and Dark Energy; all we know is that it impacts the behavior of what we can observe (such as planets and stars). If our knowledge of the material world is so limited, isn't it rather presumptuous to assume we better understand the non-material world (which we generally describe by a word like "spiritual")?

The mathematics that address infinity, such as Infinite Set Theory, illustrate that finite reasoning does not always apply when infinity is involved. A fundamental principle of finite reasoning is that something is either A or it is not-A. When dealing with infinite sets, something can be both A and not-A at the same time! This is illustrated by the Cantor Point Set where a line segment is thrown away while being kept completely.

The God revealed in the Bible is an infinite being; and it is at least likely that aspects of reality (both spiritual and material) may be infinite. That puts such beyond the capability of finite human reasoning to judge properly. The combination of limited human knowledge and limited human comprehension is why the recognition/confession mentioned earlier is so important. What it means is that on our own we cannot make valid decisions in this area. What we can do is accept and believe what God has chosen to reveal to us about Himself and how things are.

Sometimes God's revelation will seem contradictory and impossible or wrong; but a wise person will believe it. For example, God reveals that He is a Three Persons in One God Being; that the Second Person of that Godhead is both divine and human; that God predestines all who will be saved while allowing people to have free will; that evil exists abundantly in the creation by a holy and all-powerful God; etc.

When our concept of God is aligned with the revelation of Him that He has given us in the Bible, we understand God is infinite and valid assessments of how things are must accommodate the complexities and contradictions associated with infinity. This can be hard for people because we are prone to force our concepts into the way we see things, judging by finite reasoning with incomplete and possibly incorrect information.

Ultimately each one of us is faced with a decision. Where do I put my ultimate trust? In what I think I know and my own finite reasoning about God and His behavior? Or in the revelation of God in the Bible? I recognize and confess my limitations as a poorly informed human with limited reasoning capacity and avoid the arrogance of placing my ideas above what God has chosen to reveal of Himself in the Bible. Some I know do the same, but others, unfortunately, do something different.

Any concept of God that does not fully accept ALL that the Bible reveals about God is a small concept; and that will limit one's capacity to properly understand both God's truth and the reality in which we live. May God give you wisdom in the choice you make.

Musing 109: Easter
(initially posted April 16, 2017)

Easter commemorates the most significant event in human history: the resurrection of Jesus. Although Christianity, the religion focused upon the Jewish Messiah (Christ) Jesus of Nazareth, started within Judaism, Christians soon switched their primary day of worship from the Jewish Sabbath to the Lord's Day (Sunday) in honor of Jesus' resurrection.

Most churches in America have a variety of special activities related to Easter. Many emphasize Lent, a forty day period in which people do things that prepare them to worship God more significantly than they might otherwise. Special names and significance have been attached to certain days during this period of time: Ash Wednesday (when Lent begins), Palm Sunday (the week before Easter commemorating Jesus' triumphal entry into Jerusalem), Maundy Thursday (commemorates the Last Supper shared by Jesus and His disciples), and Good Friday (commemorates the crucifixion of Jesus).

Easter Sunday is a day that many more people attend a Christian worship service than are usually present. Many churches find the number of people present on Easter is 2-3 time the usual number attending their services. Some churches add a service to their services that day; some have a sunrise service to acknowledge that Jesus came out of the grave early when He arose.

I am not inclined personally to special events of the liturgical year (such as those associated with Lent and Easter), but I am always glad for anything that causes people to give Jesus more attention and to be more responsive to Him. However I grieve at the way contemporary American society abuses religious holidays. Celebration of the Incarnation at Christmas is profaned by gross commercialization and the attention given to Santa, elves, reindeer, snowmen, and the Grinch. Likewise Easter's celebration of Jesus' resurrection is profaned by attention to the Easter bunny and eggs as part of welcoming Spring and by student excessive lasciviousness on Spring Break. Unfortunately these abuses of religious holidays make it hard for people to give Jesus the attention He deserves.

Years ago I discussed Easter with Dr. Wilbur H. Goss, Assistant Director of the Johns Hopkins University Applied Physics Laboratory (APL) where I worked for many years. Dr. Goss had been leader of the team developing the first flight of a successful supersonic ramjet in 1945 and led in development of the Navy's Talos air defense missile system. My talk with him about Easter occurred in the mid-1960s as he gave me a ride home after we both worked late one evening (my car pool had departed hours before).

Dr. Goss regularly attended a church in his community; I believe it was a Lutheran church. He recognized that the resurrection of Jesus was the critical fact of Christianity, but he did not believe it had happened. Consequently, he said that he never attended church on Easter. He attended church so he would be a constructive member of the community, but he would not be hypocritical by pretending to profess faith in the resurrection of Jesus by participating in an Easter service.

I told Dr. Goss that he was wise to recognize the resurrection as the crucial core of the Christian gospel, but he was wrong in not believing Jesus' resurrection to be true. I also told him that I appreciated his candor about his perspective. I prayed a number of times over the years that God would open Dr. Goss' eyes to the truth of Christ's resurrection, but I do not know if that ever happened. Dr. Goss passed away years ago.

Dr. Goss was a brilliant and well educated man, a good man morally, honest and ethical. He was aware of the Christian gospel and a frequent attender of Christian worship services, but at the time I spoke with him about Easter I would not say that he was a born-again Christian because of his disbelief about the resurrection of Jesus. The essential aspect of the resurrection in the Christian gospel is summarized by the Apostle Paul in his extended discussion of the resurrection of Jesus. In 1 Corinthians 15:17, Paul bluntly and plainly says "if Christ has not been raised, your faith is futile; you are still in your sins."

Many people are not so clear sighted as Dr. Goss. They do not grasp that the resurrection of Jesus is the essential core of the Christian gospel. The early church recognized the importance of the resurrection. The earliest formal statements summarizing the core truths of Christianity (such as the Apostles' Creed and the Nicene Creed) are very explicit about the resurrection of Jesus and its importance.

Each of us is faced with the resurrection of Jesus? Do we ignore it or deny it? Or do we believe that Jesus rose from death and believe it to be true? Then do we trust in Christ's resurrection enough to seek salvation for Jesus?

I knew a woman who said she believed airplanes could fly safely, but she would not trust an airplane enough to fly on one. Some people are that way about the resurrection of Jesus; verbal acknowledgement that Jesus rose from the dead, but no real trust in the risen Christ. Such a person should worry about the future.

I hope you are wise enough to believe that Jesus did rise from the grave; and that you will trust Jesus to save you. He can. There is no other way to become accepted by God than by trusting in what Jesus did for you when He died on the cross for your sins. His resurrection is proof that He can save. Thank God for His love. I hope you make that commitment to Christ if you have not already.

Musing 110: Folly
(initially posted April 16, 2017)

One of the most notable works of the Renaissance and which also played an important role in the beginnings of the Protestant Reformation was an essay written in Latin in 1509 by Desiderius Erasmus of Rotterdam during a week-long visit with his English friend Sir Thomas More at More's estate in Bucklersbury. That work, *In Praise of Folly*, is a satirical attack on contemporary superstitions and traditions of European society as well as on the Roman Catholic Church.

Critique of contemporary society and religion by one of the most widely recognized scholars of his day, even though done satirically, opened the door for similar criticisms from Luther and other leaders of the Protestant Reformation that began a decade or two after publication of *In Praise of Folly*. Erasmus was a Dutch/Netherlandish Renaissance humanist, Catholic priest, social critic, teacher, and theologian. Using humanist techniques for working on texts, he prepared important new Latin and Greek editions of the New Testament, which raised questions that would be influential in the Protestant Reformation and Catholic Counter-Reformation. His Greek New Testament was the first to be printed (1516); it became known as *Textus Receptus* and was the primary New Testament text used for the German Luther Bible and for the King James Version English translation.

In Erasmus' essay Folly herself stands before a crowd wearing the costume of a fool and says she will extol her virtues and merits. She is accompanied by a number of her attendants, including Philautia (Self-Love), Kolakia (Flattery), Lethe (Forgetfulness), and Anoia (Imbecility). You can imagine the way that a clever person like Erasmus could make fun of the foolishness of human behavior in all aspects of life, including the religious arena.

All of us are familiar with folly. It is presented to us repeated by the media. Think of the many sitcoms on TV. They show the consequences of folly after folly, and present such in a humorous way; but they usually are not candid about the reality of folly's consequences. Somehow the follies presented do not destroy the ones who behave so foolishly in the show. Unfortunately, reality is not so accommodating.

I limit a musing to a thousand words; it would take a thousand pages just to begin to address the many common examples of folly in contemporary America. I am not going to make a list of the names of the most devastating or the ones most often seen or the ones I dislike the most. Instead I discuss avoiding folly.

Unless your desire is to amuse all who know you by the calamities you bring upon yourself by folly, you will want to avoid folly by living wisely. My suggestions for how to do that are what the rest of this musing addresses.

First, be sensible. What do I mean? Whether you are a genius or dumb as a doorbell, you can use the good sense that God blessed you with. Use it ALL THE TIME. What are the kinds of things a sensible person does? He or she looks before leaping. He or she considers both long term and short term consequences of a decision or action. Too many forget to consider long term consequences when they opt for short term pleasures or benefit. That new car, extensive vacation, etc. could put you behind the 8-ball financially for a long time. Many people fail to weigh the costs and benefits of both long and short terms when making a decision.

Second, be careful about where you turn to for advice and guidance. Friends, family, school, internet, professionals, etc. can provide advice and guidance. Not every source is well-informed, honest, or helpful. Be very careful. Often it helps to get input from several different sources. When all the sources give roughly the same advice or guidance, you can generally trust it to be valid. However, remember that unless the advice or guidance is given by a source that FULLY understands your situation and what you want, the advice or guidance may not be helpful; it even could be harmful.

Finally, remember that there is more to life than the here-and-now of the material world. Do not neglect the eternal and spiritual dimensions of life. Remember that you are as likely to get bum advice and guidance in that area as you are in other areas of life. America currently is in spiritual turmoil. Ideas of secular humanism have infiltrated many aspects of contemporary education and media, and those ideas can be harmful as well as helpful. Religious diversity is growing rapidly in the U.S., with those who basically dismiss the importance of religion in their lives as one of the fastest growing segments.

If you want input from me about this, I will point you to Jesus the Christ as He is revealed in the New Testament of the Christian Bible. Aligning yourself with Jesus and seeking to live in ways that please Him is probably the wisest thing a person can do. If you want to turn to someone to help, a godly friend or spiritual leader, choose someone whose life is characterized by what the New Testament describes as "the fruit of the Spirit" of God: love, joy, peace, forbearance, kindness, goodness, faithfulness, gentleness and self-control (Galatians 5:22-23). Beware of advice or guidance from those who do not manifest the fruit of the Spirit, regardless of their academic or religious credentials.

Folly is all about us: in the behavior of people we know and in our society; perhaps even in ourselves. Folly may amuse when in the life of another; but it is never a good thing for your own life.

Musing 111: Secular Humanism (initially posted April 18, 2017)

This subject is as difficult to handle as a porcupine. Whichever way one approaches it, one is likely to experience pain from puncture by quills. If I do not jump on secular humanism with both feet, some will criticize me for failing to defend my faith. If I do criticize secular humanism, I am likely to be labeled as a Neanderthal who is out of place in contemporary society. And, of course, either side might react to my ideas more forcefully than a few sharp words. So I will be very cautious in this musing.

As an English word, "secular" has a long history, with early usage eight centuries ago noted by the *Oxford English Dictionary (OED)*. The basic connotation of the word has always been "not associated with organized religion or religious activity." As an English word, "humanism" is more recent, just being used within the past couple of centuries (ala the *OED*). Its basic connotation has to do with humans.

Use of the two words together as "secular humanism" is alleged to have begun in the 1930s (although the Council for Secular Humanism website says the term was coined by advertising executive Rosser Reeves four decades before the 2002 article it quoted) and multiple connotations have been attached to the term. Some of the connotations come from its promoters and other connotations come from its opponents. "Secular humanism" is both viewed as a subset of some variety of Humanism and as a synonym for it. "Secular humanism" basically is an approach to life without regard to religious beliefs or perspective; in some manifestations secular humanism is antagonistic toward religion and in other manifestations it is not antagonistic. I think the comments in this musing will be appropriate with regard to any variety of secular humanism; hence it is not important for me to try to identify a particular variety of secular humanism that I address since I am addressing all aspects of it.

Definitions and descriptions of secular humanism that I found on the web from those promoting secular humanism (or at least favorably inclined toward it) emphasize it as an ethical system based upon the world of experience and objective; emphasizes science, human reasoning, and philosophy; and often is associated with atheism and agnosticism.

First, I should acknowledge the obvious. Christianity has failed to present to our society, actually to the world as a whole, compelling explanations of reality that make the Christian gospel something no sane or decent person would reject; and the church has not manifested consistent extensive godliness by its members to demonstrate unequivocally the power of Christ in their lives by showing the "fruit of the Spirit" (love, joy, peace, forbearance, kindness, goodness, faithfulness, gentleness and self-control) day in and day out through the vicissitudes of life. Before any Christian criticizes secular humanism for seeking a way of life apart from God and religious institutions, a confession should be made that the failure of God's people to provide overwhelming living evidence for the reality of God planted the seeds that blossomed into secular humanism.

Second, I would observe that those who base their view of life and ethics on observation of the reality in which we live and approach that scientifically, seeking rational explanation for how things are, have two fundamental problems that few seem to face honestly. First, there is no scientific proof that there is no God. There is only presumption and assumptions. The British comic from half a century ago, Benny Hill, frequently noted that to assume made an ass out of you and me. The other point is that finite human reasoning cannot be sure it draws correct conclusions when something infinite is involved. Those who do not understand how finite reasoning cannot always draw valid conclusions about infinite things can check out the Cantor Point Set (where a line segment is thrown away and kept completely at the same time because the line is infinitely dense) or other aspects of infinite mathematics. The scientifically aware know about limitations on logic (such as Godel illustrated) and observation (such as illustrated by the Heisenberg Uncertainty Principle). Secular humanists often fail to recognize the inherent problems of their way of approaching reality.

Finally, it is important to be responsible. I started with acknowledgement of the failure of Christians to live the godly lives we should. Now I ask if secular humanists will accept responsibility for consequences from implementation of some of the things that they advocate? A number of people wearing the label liberal have advocated actions to help the poor and needy, but want others to pay the costs for such. Some such seem unwilling to help the poor and needy unless others foot the bill for it. That attitude has always struck me as inferior to the attitude of the honorable men who signed the Declaration of Independence in 1776. The final sentence of that document is a promise among the signers, to "mutually pledge to each other our Lives, our Fortunes, and our Sacred Honor." Many of them did in fact sacrifice their lives and fortunes in service to our country.

I hope I do not walk away from this porcupine issue with too many quills stuck in me. I suspect both advocates of secular humanism and those opposed to it may be disappointed in what I have said. I have observed that discussions of contentious issues often fail to deal with fundamental aspects of the issue. Here I present what to me are fundamental aspects of this issue: Christian failure as a stimulus for secular humanism, and its failure to deal realistically with reality.

Musing 112: Biblical Inerrancy Perspective (initially posted April 19, 2017)

During the 20th century many Christian groups separated over the issue of Scriptural inspiration and Biblical inerrancy. The role of the Bible in the life of a growing and vibrant Christian, and the trust that should be placed in what the Bible says, is extremely important. At the same time dealing with God's truth honestly requires humility and candor, as well as commitment to Christ. This musing shares some of my thoughts on this subject.

Statements about the reliability of the Scripture need to address two very different aspects of the subject. The first aspect concerns the original documents, often called the "autographs," which were written by those God used to write different parts of the Bible. The second aspect concerns the Bibles you and I have and read.

Most formal statements about reliability of the Bible apply mainly to the original documents, the autographs. None of those exist today, at least as far as we know. The oldest documents derived from them that exist today were written centuries after the original documents and we have no knowledge of the way copies of copies connected the oldest extant document to the original one. General confidence that the oldest copy is basically what the original said comes from the presence of multiple copies in different geographic areas and of various translations related to the original document when those items are in basic agreement. It suggests that the original autograph is probably well represented by extant materials.

Based upon the above a person can have general confidence that the extant materials allow a reasonably accurate representation of the original, but that is a matter of belief – it cannot be proven to be the case. Few of us can read the oldest materials in the languages that they are in; so we rely on translation into English. Most major translations do a good job, and you can trust them to get the original message across clearly. Hence one can have general confidence in the trustworthiness of the Word of God as we read it in English.

Finally, we must realize that there may be some uncertainties in a few places in what the Bible says or what it means. For example, there are a few words of the original languages for which it is unclear exactly what that word meant originally. In addition, there are a few places where exactly what was said is uncertain. However, all very important things in the Bible are addressed clearly in multiple passages and there is no uncertainty about them.

Let me illustrate the kind of thing about which uncertainty exists. The height of Goliath who was killed by David is presented as six cubits and a span in the traditional Hebrew text of the Old Testament. One of the manuscripts among the Dead Sea Scrolls and the Septuagint translation of the Old Testament made a couple of centuries before Christ both say Goliath was only four cubits and a span tall. This is the kind of uncertainty that one can find in the Bible. How tall was Goliath? Six cubits and a span – or four cubits and a span? This shows why you can have general confidence that what you read in the Bible is the inspired Word of God and trust it as a reliable guide for how to relate properly to God and how to please Him.

Personally I am sorry that emphasis on doctrinal correctness such as inspiration and inerrancy of the Bible has separated so many followers of Jesus from one another. Such has hampered God's work through the church. Jesus prayed for His followers to have unity that would show the world that Jesus was sent by the Father; divisions because of things like Biblical inerrancy hinder that.

During the first couple of centuries after the ascension of Jesus, the church evolved from a sect of Jewish followers of Jesus in Judea and Galilee (which was opposed by Jewish religious and political leadership) to an collection of churches throughout the Roman Empire and beyond welcoming both Jew and Gentile from all aspects of society (in spite of opposition and persecution from the authorities and competition from multiple religions for the hearts and minds of people). God used the church in this impressive evangelistic expansion at the time when there was uncertainty about the content of both Old Testament and New Testament Scriptures. None of the formal synopses of Christian belief in the early church (such as the Apostles' Creed or the Didache) say anything about the inspiration or inerrancy of Scripture. They emphasized the good news (gospel) of Jesus' death and resurrection as God's way to save men and women through faith in Jesus, and the early church managed to deal well with the various heresies that arose during that period of time.

The Apostle Paul in 1 Corinthians 15 where he addresses the evidence for and importance of Christ's resurrection accepts those who are confused about the resurrection as brothers in Christ. Perhaps we should be careful about letting our emphasis on various doctrines, such as those related to Biblical inerrancy, separate followers of Jesus if we want to please the Lord, and if we want to let Him use us as He did the early church in spreading Christianity throughout the Roman Empire. That is a very challenging thought.

I hope the perspective presented in this musing reaffirms your trust in the reliability of the Bible, and encourages you to seek the kind of unity with other followers of Jesus that He prayed for. May God bless you as your serve Him.

Musing 113: Religious Labels (initially posted April 20, 2017)

As I have indicated before in my musings, I dislike labels because they mislead as well as characterize someone. However, I use them at times.

Recently I read parts of a 740 page tome by a Pulitzer Prize winning author (Frances Fitzgerald) that stimulated this musing. This 2017 book is *The Evangelicals: The Struggle to Shape America*. A number of religious labels are used in the book: liberal, evangelical, fundamentalist, neo-orthodox, etc.

I was provoked to ask myself, what label would I like to be applied to me?

I had to be creative because I did not think any of the labels commonly used truly fit me, odd ball that I am. So I picked "Biblical Christian" as a label I hoped would be appropriate for me.

Why did I pick "Biblical Christian" as the label I want to apply to me?

Christian has a wide variety of connotation, some of them ridiculous. For example, years ago when I worked at the Johns Hopkins University Applied Physics Laboratory I rode to and from work in a carpool for a little over a year. One of the four guys in the carpool was Jewish, but he said he considered himself to be a Christian because he believed in the Ten Commandments. I told him that the term Christian should only be used for those who accept Jesus Christ as the Divine Savior and believe in Him for salvation.

Unfortunately that restriction of the word Christian is not used by everyone. Many in the Middle East are said to consider all Americans as Christians. Some people use the term Christian merely to mean a person is courteous, polite, or helpful (which is connotation 5 for the adjective Christian in the *Oxford English Dictionary*). Most people, however, just mean one is associated with one of the Christian religious organizations when they apply the term Christian to a person.

Many people, including me, make a distinction between being a Christian because of association with a Christian religious group and being a Christian because a person has a living relationship with Jesus Christ for salvation. To provide clarity, people often add an adjective to Christian, such as "True Christian," "Born-again Christian," or "Committed Christian" when they want to describe a person whom they think has a saving relationship with Jesus.

In applying the label "Biblical Christian" to myself I mean that I recognize Jesus as the Divine Son of God Who is the Jewish Messiah (Christ) and that I trust what He did at Calvary to be the basis of salvation that God offers me through faith in Jesus Christ. That is the connotation I give to Christian in that label.

What connotation do I attach to "Biblical" in the label?

First by Biblical in the label Biblical Christian I mean that I accept the Bible as revelation from God. This musing is not the place to discuss which books are actually in the Bible (knowledgeable people are aware that the Bible used by Roman Catholics and those in Orthodox churches have Old Testament books not in the contemporary versions of most Protestant Bibles). Consequently I consider the Bible to have been inspired by God and therefore a reliable guide for what He wants us to know about Him and about how He wants us to behave (i.e., how we think and act).

Second by Biblical in the label Biblical Christian I mean that I try to understand and believe what the Bible says about God and the realty in which we live that He created. This is not easy since I try to correlate what God says in the Bible with what we currently understand about reality from history and science. It also is not easy since God is infinite and finite human reasoning cannot cope accurately with some aspects of infinite reality. For example, the Bible teaches God is a 3-in-1 Triune Being, that He simultaneously predestines who will believe in Him and be saved with human free will so the person can choose to believe in Him or not, that the Second Person of the Trinity (the Son of God) is both Divine and human, etc. Such things are impossible in finite reasoning; but the Bible (God's Word) tells us that such is reality.

Third by Biblical in the label Biblical Christian I mean that I try to comply with guidance in the Bible about what I should do, how I should live, and how I should think. I confess that I do such very imperfectly. Sometimes I fail to do things I should unintentionally. For example, I do not always pray for those that the Bible says I should pray for. Sometimes I choose to do things I should not do. For example, I may not tell the truth in order to avoid getting into trouble. Or I might not be forgiving when wrong is done to me. Of course, many of my failings to comply with Biblical guidance about how to live are far worse than these examples.

The Bible warns of the consequences of not complying with God's guidance about how we should live. Not only does one miss the blessings of a close relationship with God, some of the consequences of non-compliance with God's way are devastating for the individual and also for society. I fear for America in that regard because in my lifetime the general attitude of many in our country has become disrespectful and disdaining of God's guidance from the Bible.

I have explained my meaning of "Biblical Christian" as a religious label; it is what I hope is appropriate for me.

Musing 114: Stingy Liberals (initially posted April 21, 2017)

As noted in previous musings, I dislike labels because they usually are misleading. They may apply appropriately in one part of a person's life, but often the label is erroneously applied to other aspects of the person's life too. In addition, the same label means different things to different people. So I believe it is far better to fully describe what a person believes or does than to use a label as a shorthand to categorize the person because a label can be so misleading.

Given that perspective, why am I presenting a musing that uses a label ("liberal"). Am I just a hypocrite, doing what I criticize others for doing? Or am I too stupid to realize that I am using a label? Or might there be some other explanation?

I used the label "stingy liberals" for this musing as a shorthand description of some information that I wish to share with you. In December of 2014, the *AARP Bulletin* contained a graphic that showed the average charitable giving (defined as a percentage of adjusted gross income in 2012 based upon tax returns received by the IRS) for each state. The graphic was a map of the U.S. showing the states with five levels of shading: charitable giving of 1-1.99%, 2-2.99%, 3-3.99%, 4-4.99%, and 5% or more.

I was impressed by the graphic. From time to time I look at it to remind me how stingy most Americans are. They largely want the poor and needy to be helped, but only at the expense of others. I have felt this was particularly true of those who identify themselves as liberals, either socially or politically. My feeling about this was stimulated by observing public information about a number of notable political leaders who were considered liberal. Those liberal leaders often promoted legislation that provided help for the poor and needy at government expense, but when information about their personal finances was made public it showed they gave relatively little to charity and some of what they gave was self-aggrandizing (such as donation to a school for a building or such bearing the donor's name).

Media displays of the distribution of votes in the recent presidential election struck me as being similar to the map of charitable giving by state that I had seen in the *AARP Bulletin* from several years ago. There seems to be a correlation between the two.

I think many who did not vote for Mr. Trump would call themselves liberals; certainly the media and many others have applied that label to Democrats in general and to supporters of Mrs. Clinton. So in gross over-simplification, let me call the states which Mrs. Clinton won "liberal states." Bring to mind the maps you saw from the media after the election that showed which states voted for Trump and which ones voted for Clinton.

I simplified the map from the *AARP Bulletin* by reducing the shading from five levels to just three levels: less than 3%, 3-3.99 %, and 4% or more. There were 26 states in the lowest level, 16 in the middle category, and 8 in the top category. Most of the states in the lowest of the three levels of charitable giving were in New England and other parts of the Northeast from Virginia north, on the West Coast, and a few in the upper Midwest.

My memory of graphics from the media after the election associates most of those states with ones that voted for Clinton, states that one might classify as "liberal." Hence, I chose to use the label "stingy liberals" for this musing.

There are many fine people who would apply the term liberal to themselves in various ways. Some would apply it to themselves politically; others would apply it socially. Some might apply it theologically or religiously; and others might accept the label generally for all areas of their lives. However, as a group, from my observations, those who are liberal politically are less inclined to contribute to charity than others. Liberals seem to prefer that others foot the bill for the good they want to do; and generally try to use the power of the government to force others to fund help for the poor and needy through their taxes. Many of the stingy states shown in the *AARP* graphic are among the richest states (measured by average income for its residents) in the country.

You might want to decide if my label of "stingy liberals" is a valid one, or one that distorts things. Think about all the people you know who deserve the liberal label either socially or politically. Then think about what you know of their personal resource use to help the poor and needy, either though charitable donations or privately, such as giving a poor person (who is neither a friend nor an associate) money for a taxi to the hospital or driving the person to the hospital. Then decide what you think of their charitableness as a group; don't judge the whole group on the basis of a few remarkable ones you may know.

If you are ambitious, you can search the internet or the library and see what pollsters and professional writers have said about how charitableness varies with social class, political persuasion, occupation, age, religious affiliation, etc. Then you will be in a firm position to evaluate the validity (or lack of validity) for the label I use in this musing. I hope you would conclude I used the label fairly; but if not, I hope you will let me know so I can correct my misconceptions should such exist. Thank you.

Musing 115: The Early Church (initially posted April 22, 2017)

I have been fascinated for years by the early church, by which I mean Christianity in the first couple of centuries after the Day of Pentecost (the birth of the church) ten days after the ascension of Jesus the Christ into heaven. During the early church Christianity transformed from a Jewish sect in Judea and Galilee which was opposed and persecuted by Jewish authorities into a religion composed of both Jews and Gentiles drawn from every element of society (rich and poor, free and slave, male and female, any ethnic group) spread throughout the Roman Empire and beyond (Armenia, the Parthian Empire, and India). God worked through the early church in amazing ways in spite of transportation and communications limitations in antiquity.

Most communications at that time were face-to-face. Telecommunications did not exist, and it is believed that the percentage of the population which was literate was low, no more than 10-20% according to many scholars. In addition, writing materials were expensive. Typically papyrus sheets were about 16 inches square and could be glued together to form rolls of considerable length. More durable materials such as parchment and vellum came from animal skins; two-to-four sheets of parchment (or vellum) for use in a scroll could be obtained from the skin of a sheep or calf. Cost of a single sheet of papyrus varied, but outside Egypt where all papyrus was made papyrus was expensive (from a few hours of a common man's compensation to more than a day's wage) due to Egypt's monopoly on papyrus. I have been unable to discover what might have been the price for a parchment or vellum sheet in the first or second century. It is thought a typical scroll contained about twenty sheets. One of the Gospels probably took a bit more than that, but one of the New Testament epistles (two of the shorter ones) could have been written on such a scroll. For comparison, a scroll of the *Torah* (the first five books of the Old Testament, the books of Moses) is about 150 feet long, takes many months to copy, and usually weights 20-30 pounds.

Transportation during the early church was slow. Mainly people walked. Some might have an animal to ride. By foot or on an animal (riding or being pulled in a wheeled vehicle), a person might average 10-20 miles a day for a trip. It would be hard to do much more than that, especially since you might have to wait for a hazard such as wild animals or bandits to be dealt with as you go along your way. Those traveling from one coastal location to another might travel a bit faster if the winds were favorable; they might average 3-4 miles an hour for a trip that takes a day or two.

Given these very real limitations on communication and travel, how did a religion that was often opposed by local authorities in many places (and occasionally subject to Empire-wide persecution) manage to attract so many people to Christ in the presence of competing religions and counter social behaviors? The simple answer is "Nothing is impossible for God." However, I think we can see some behaviors by the early Christians that facilitated powerful work in and through them by God.

The available information about how Christians in the early church acted is limited; so what I say here is a combination of speculation and fact. I believe that my ideas are reasonably consistent with the limited information available about that era and Christianity in it.

First, those early Christians focused on the nature of God and salvation through Jesus Christ the Son of God. They were less likely to get caught up in promotion of secondary things, such as an important doctrine or social issue. This contrasts them markedly with the behavior of 20th century Christians in America where fights over doctrine (e.g., liberal vs conservative, emphasis on Biblical inspiration and inerrancy) and social issues (such as abortion and same-sex marriage) splintered Christendom. This point is illustrated in the earliest formal statements of Christian belief that characterized most of the church (such as *The Apostles' Creed* and *The Nicene Creed*) which I think captures the message of the early church to the non-Christians about it; guidance for how to live as a Christian presented to followers of Christ (such as presented in the New Testament epistles or *The Didache*) deal with those secondary matters. This difference between the early church and us is part of the reason I think God has not worked so powerfully among the modern church as He did through the early church.

Second, the early church was serious about its belief in Christ and the Christian Godhead, as illustrated by the many confined, beaten, and killed for being Christians (about 1 in 200 Christians were martyred in that era). Nor did the early church expect the government or society to conform to its ideas or force others to live by them; that stands in marked contrast to the way the church has often behaved in regard to government and society since Christianity became a recognized religion by the Roman government and in the late-fourth century designated as the religion of the Roman Empire. This problem has corrupted all forms of Christianity

(Catholic, Orthodox, and Protestant) over the years, and continues to do so. That also limits God's powerful working through the church.

I am sure that some, perhaps many, have a different view than mine about these things; I ask that all think about the early church and ask, "Why did God work so powerfully through them?"

Musing 116: First Christian Ministry to Prisoners (initially posted April 23, 2017)

Since I have been involved with Christian ministry to prisoners for more than four decades (my first ministry visit to a jail was in 1971 to the Fairfax County Jail in Virginia), this is a subject that has been important to me for a long time. My doctoral dissertation addressed chaplains in jails, prisons, and juvenile facilities. I have been involved in programs in a score of jails, prisons, juvenile facilities, and halfway (re-entry) houses over the years. Many years ago I even wrote a book on the subject.

When people talk about the history of Christian ministry to prisoners, they usually cite the 1488 establishment of the Order of Misericordin ("Beheading of St John") as the earliest formally organized ministry to prisoners. That Order of the Catholic Church was formed to have its members assist and console criminals condemned to death, accompanying them to the gallows, and provide religious services and Christian burial.

However, Christian ministry to prisoners began long before that, and I can pinpoint it exactly. Can you?

Christian ministry could not begin until after the church started; so the Day of Pentecost (ten days after the ascension of Jesus into heaven) was the earliest possible time for Christian ministry to prisoners. Earlier Jesus had talked about ministry to prisoners being ministry to Him in Matthew 25 and Isaiah had said the Messiah would proclaim liberty to the captives (which Jesus said was fulfilled in Him when He spoke in the synagogue at Nazareth, where He grew up, Luke 4:16ff), but those were comments about things for the future.

Acts 2 says there was a tremendous response to a sermon by Peter on the Day of Pentecost; some 3,000 people were added to those believing in Jesus. Those people then devoted themselves to Jesus and the apostles' teaching, worshipping God and taking care of one another. The result was that day by day others were saved and added to their number. Some time after that Peter and John went to the temple in Jerusalem at the hour of prayer, and God healed a lame man through their ministry (Acts 3). A crowd gathered and Peter preached Jesus to them. A lot of people who heard them believed, so that Acts 4 tells us that the number of men came to 5,000 (it is unclear whether this was just an increase from the 3,000 noted earlier or another 5,000 in addition to the earlier 3,000). Jewish religious leadership was upset by what was happening; they had

Peter and John arrested and put into custody until the next day when the Jewish leadership would examine Peter and John.

This incident is what I identify as the first instance of Christian ministry to prisoners. I am sure the Peter and John ministered to one another that night as they were in custody. If others were confined in the same place, they probably told them about Jesus too. This first instance of Christian ministry to prisoners probably happened within a few weeks after the church began on the Day of Pentecost; we do not know exactly how long after Pentecost it happened.

Christian ministry to prisoners by Christians who themselves were prisoners was the pattern of Christian ministry to prisoners during New Testament times and during the early church. The book of Acts and the letters of the Apostle Paul illustrate this a number of times. In doing that, Christians ministered to one another when confined and to other inmates. They also ministered to officials, as Paul and Silas did when confined in Philippi (leading the jailor and his household to salvation in Christ, Acts 16) and as Paul did before various Roman officials while a prisoner. Christians in the community were urged to remember their brothers and sisters who were confined as if they themselves were in their place (Hebrews 13:3); that instruction applies to us today as do other instructions in the New Testament.

As noted above, it would be more than a thousand years after the early church before Christians on the outside developed formal ministries to those confined in jails and prisons. Surprising things have resulted from ministry to prisoners (beyond the conversion of inmates and others associated with jails and prisons). It is said that the systematic way that members of the "Holy Club" of Oxford visited condemned felons housed in Oxford Castle, their regular services and fondness for a system, earned the name of Methodists for members of the Holy Club, two of whom were John and Charles Wesley. Many may not realize that the name of a prominent denomination, one that had perhaps more impact in spreading Christianity in the U.S. during the 19th century than any other, derived its name from Christian ministry to prisoners by its prominent founders.

Christian ministry to prisoners is an agonizing blessing. The blessing comes from seeing God work in inmate lives and the joy of being used by Him; the agony comes from the horrible pasts of so many prisoners, that so many prisoners choose not to let Christ save them and transform their lives, and the ones who turn to Christ but later fall away from Him.

Of course similar agonizing blessings can come in all kinds of Christian ministries and from our interactions with family and friends.

It is possible that reading this musing has caused you to ask questions or develop ideas relative to what God wants you to be doing with your life. If that is the case, I pray that you will be wise enough to respond positively to what God is leading you to do.

Musing 117: Coerced Morality (initially posted April 24, 2017)

Like most people I think, I uncritically accepted the social morality that I grew up with as proper. However, as I matured, I become critical of some things in our society and was glad to see various things addressed by my society, things such as a variety of discriminations.

As our nation has struggled with a variety of social transformations (such as legalization of same-sex marriage), I have been troubled by the lack of clarity about how we should determine what is proper for our society. There are several possibilities. Some suggest that anything natural should be acceptable in our society; I would hate to see humans allowed simply to behave like animals. I realize that some such behaviors might be an improvement for some people, but it is not an approach I would recommend. Some suggest a philosophical basis, such as the greatest good for the greatest number (however could that be determined?) or as expressed by our Declaration of Independence ("life, liberty, and the pursuit of happiness" – but some of that varies greatly among different people).

Others suggest a religious guide for our society. While that sounds good, history is filled with unsavory examples of bad experience with such. Currently we see that in Islamic nations enacting sharia. Spain in the days of the Spanish Inquisition was an unsavory implementation of the Christian religion by the ruling authorities. The Blue Laws of last century were a mild form of social coercion for religious reasons.

Some have said that Biblical morality should be enforced in the U.S. because our country is a "Christian" nation; but I have heard people who hold such a view criticize countries for enacting sharia, even though a much higher percentage of such countries are Moslem than the percentage of Christians here (according to church memberships) and a greater percentage of them participate in religious services each week than attend church each week in the U.S.

Historically less than a quarter of people in what became the U.S. during the 17th and 18th centuries were members of Christian churches or regularly attended Christian worship services; during most of the 19th century the portion of people belonging to churches and attending them regularly had climbed to 2 in 5, but it was only in the 20th century that more than half the population belonged to Christian churches and regularly attended Christian services. I think it is inappropriate to call the U.S. a Christian nation when there is seldom a week during which the majority of Americans have attended a Christian worship service.

I confess that I have been unable to decide what the most appropriate basis is for deciding what laws should shape a society. Most are surprised that I do not suggest it is wisest to base our morality on that revealed by the Bible to please God. Certainly I believe it would be better for people to behave in accord with Biblical morality than to do otherwise, but I have a spiritual reason for not wanting to coerce such in society by law. That reason is when Biblical ideas are coerced by law, God does not seem to work as powerfully though the church as He does in other situations.

The early church illustrates this. By the early church, I refer to the church's first couple of centuries from the birth of the church on the Day of Pentecost ten days after Jesus ascended into heaven. This is the period before Christianity had become an acceptable religion to the Roman government and before designation of Christianity as the official religion in the Roman Empire in the late-fourth century. During those two centuries the church transformed from a Jewish sect in Judea and Galilee into a religion involving both Jews and Gentiles from every social element (rich and poor, free and slave, male and female, of any ethnic group) throughout the Roman Empire and beyond (Armenia, the Parthian Empire, and India). In general, Christianity was opposed by local authorities and experienced some persecution Empire wide. The church tended to adopt a hierarchical administrative structure in keeping with the way most organizations functioned at that time, but it had no buildings dedicated for Christian use (the oldest known building for that purpose was at Dura Europos about 240 A.D.; that is near Salhiye, Syria – much of the original building was removed to Yale University in the 1930s; the site has now been ruined archaeology by Islamic State looting around 2012, over 3,750 looting pits, in their destruction of Christian historic sites in Syria). Christians met in private homes and public locations for their worship and fellowship. God worked in the early church in an amazingly powerful way.

I am not aware of God working in such powerful ways in places where Christians use political power (the law) to coerce Christian morality, not even in the various Awakenings in this country and its previous colonies. The early church overcame opposition and persecution (1 in 200 believers were martyred during this period) in the presence of competing religions and social behaviors greatly different from those advocated by the Bible.

The early church repeatedly demonstrated their commitment to Jesus, unity in the faith in Him, and genuine love for other believers.

I do not approve of Christian efforts to make our laws compatible with Biblical morality because I think that coercion limits the way God will use the church powerfully. Perhaps that happens because we try to force people into godly behavior instead of depending upon God to change hearts and minds so that people choose to live in godly ways to please God. What do you think?

Musing 118: Trump Opponents (initially posted April 24, 2017)

This is a rare musing in that it is the second one posted today; I think that has only happened once (maybe twice) before. I have several musing topics in the queue most of the time. I draft what I want to say and then review it several times over a period of days (and sometimes longer). This morning I felt it was very important to address this topic today (it had not been one in the queue); and so I am.

A number of people who did not want Mr. Trump to become president have been expressing their opposition to him in many ways. Some have taken political actions to block or hamper things President Trump is doing; others have taken to the courts to do the same; some have participated in various protests; and many have expressed their opposition to and concerns about President Trump's behavior, policies, and actions.

All of those things are permitted (if done in accordance to current laws) because we live in a free country that permits and even encourages such dissent. My comments in this musing are not a criticism of legitimate activities of dissent; nor are my comments arguments for or against President Trump's behaviors, policies, or actions. Instead my comments are specifically for Trump opponents who are Christian. Others are welcome to read what I say, but my comments are not directed at you.

If you are a Christian and oppose President Trump, my concern is not your reason for doing so and I will not address the reasons you do so; instead I ask if you are behaving in accord with New Testament guidance for Christians in reference to the government they live under. As a Christian, pleasing God by complying with Biblical instructions for Christians should be important to you. In this musing I share my understanding of things the Bible says in this regard.

Before I present the Biblical material, let me say that there are many things in contemporary law and in the way our governments (local, state, and federal) act that I believe are unwise, wrong, and harmful to some. There are things in our laws that are clearly contrary to Biblical instructions. What I present below as Biblical guidance applies as much to me as it does to anyone else.

In Mark 12 opponents of Jesus tried to trap Jesus by asking if Jews should pay Roman taxes (they thought He would either anger a lot of people or get into trouble with the Roman authorities). Instead Jesus said, Give to Caesar what is Caesar's and to God what is God's.

Other than the Roman coin used for taxes, Jesus did not explain what might be Caesar's. Trump opponents who are followers of Jesus should ask themselves, is their behavior consistent with this guidance from Jesus. Are they giving the government what is the government's? Thinking about what they might do differently (or did differently) in that regard with different government leadership might provide insights about the answer to that question.

The Apostle Paul addresses the Christian's responsibility to the government in Romans 13:1-7 and follows it with a few words in verses 8-10 about social relationships. As you read those verses, it is helpful to remember the specific situation in which they were written. This epistle is addressed to Christians in Rome. It probably was written in the late-50s from Corinth when Paul was in that city on his third missionary journey. That puts Paul's letter to the Christians in Rome during the early years of Nero's reign as head of the Roman Empire. Social conditions were atrocious according to modern standards. Perhaps half of the population (or more) in Rome were slaves. There was the horrific spectacle of slaughter in the arena as public entertainment and frequent crucifixions to discourage enemies of the state.

As you read what Paul says in Romans 13 think of the conditions in which those words were written and reflect on that as you view your own thoughts and actions. You can supplement what Paul says in Romans about a Christian's relationship to government (even the evil government of Nero) with what Paul later said to men he mentored in Christian leadership (2 Titus 3:1-2 & 1 Timothy 2:1-2). The Apostle Peter says something similar in 1 Peter 2:17.

It is easy to be aroused by what one feels the government or a leader is doing which is wrong and harmful. For the Christian, the issue is how to respond to such concern in a way that is consistent with Biblical guidance. Certainly one thing that a person should do is to pray for our leaders, and such prayer should include prayer for President Trump. I wonder how many of Christians who oppose Trump have prayed for him. Prayer, as some note, is more to help us get in tune with God and His ways than for us to advise or petition Him about something. If a Christian who opposes Trump has not been praying for him then I encourage that Christian to pray for him in order to live in ways that please God.

I would also encourage the Christians who oppose Trump to review their thoughts and actions in light of New Testament passages cited in this musing so they can be sure that their thoughts and actions are pleasing to the Lord. Jesus makes heavy demands on us. He tells us to love our enemies and do good to those who do bad things to us. He demands to be first in our lives. Wisdom says, "Obey God's Word." I hope you do.

Musing 119: Biblical Mysteries (initially posted April 25, 2017)

Biblical mysteries are not like a mystery detective story where clues are dropped as the story unfolds, often with the culprit only being revealed toward the end of the book. The word mystery (*musterion* in the Greek from *meuo*) appears a couple of dozen times in the New Testament. The core idea of the word is something secret that is made known to those on the inside. Basically the idea of a mystery in the Bible is that it is secret information that people normally do not know and could not know which God reveals primarily through His special revelation (the Scriptures).

In this musing I comment on half-a-dozen mysteries mentioned in the New Testament; those who wish to have a fuller grasp of the subject might get a Bible concordance and check out each instance of the word "mystery" (or "mysteries") in the New Testament. That will permit examination of ones I do not mention in this musing.

First I say a few words about the mystery of the kingdom of heaven (Matthew 13:1-52). This passage of Scripture contains several parables taught by Jesus. In verse 10, the disciples ask Jesus why He spoke in parables. He replied that they, the disciples to whom He would explain the parables, were to know the secrets/mysteries of the kingdom of heaven, but such would be hidden from others. Basically these parables reveal the mystery of the interim program of God for His people on earth between Christ's first and second advents.

Second I say a few words about the mystery of the blindness of Israel and God's purpose with Israel's blindness (Romans 11) as a way of bringing salvation to both Jews and Gentiles. The Old Testament is clear that the Jewish people, those descended from Abraham, were God's chosen people; they were chosen to be the race that the Messiah (the Christ) would come from. When Christ came, that people as a nation rejected Him, although some Jews believed in Him. In Romans, after spending 8 chapters explaining how God's plan of salvation works, Paul uses chapters 9-11 to explain what part the Jews play in God's plan. Chapter 11 addresses the way the Israel's spiritual blindness (a mystery) fits into God's plan.

Third, I say a few words about the mystery of the departure of the church at the end of this age, identified as a mystery in 1 Corinthians 15:51-57 and addressed again by Paul in another of his epistles, 1 Thessalonians 4:13-18. What the Scripture actually says about this subject is largely contained in these two short passages, but a multitude have written many books presenting their ideas, speculations, and insights about the departure of Christians from the earth when Christ returns. Much of what I have seen written about this subject goes far beyond what the Scripture actually says; so be careful about such. While it may be helpful and have beneficial insights, good-intentioned writing expressing the ideas of godly and well-education people does not have the same validity as the revealed Word of God in the Scripture.

Fourth, I say a few words about what Paul calls the "mystery of Christ" (Ephesians 3:4) which was made known to him by revelation, the mystery of the church as the body of Christ where Jew and Gentile become one new man in Christ (Ephesians 3:1-11; 2:11-22). From my perspective this mystery is perhaps the one which has the greatest impact on our world; it is how the manifold wisdom of God is made known to all, on earth and in the heavenly places. I encourage you to take time to read the two short passages noted carefully and to think deeply about them. Ask God to reveal the significances of the passages to you.

Fifth, I say a few words about a related mystery, the mystery of the church as the bride of Christ (Ephesians 5:25-32). Relationships between husbands and wives are always a challenge, and currently a subject of great emotion for many. I hope you will put aside any social bias or untoward emotions in this area and try to understand what the Apostle Paul is teaching us in his comments about the church as the bride of Christ. The passage is very short, but should be read slowly and thoughtfully.

Finally, I say a few words about the most important mystery for the individual Christian, the mystery of the indwelling of Christ as the hope of glory or spiritual deliverance by the power of the indwelling Christ (Colossians 1:26-27; 2:1-15). Apart from the eternal destiny of believers in Jesus (heaven instead of hell), believers in Jesus still have to live while on the earth. Each has to face a variety of temptations and challenges from within the person and from others and circumstances. The mystery Paul mentions here is that Christ also lives within the individual believer, and it is the indwelling Christ that enables the believer to live a God-pleasing life, regardless of circumstances. It is hard to imagine anything more significant than that for the believer in Jesus Christ.

In this musing I said a few words about six mysteries of the New Testament. I hope your appetite has been whetted and you will look into these mysteries (and the others of the New Testament) so that you can benefit from knowing the reality that they reveal. That will enable you to be more successful spiritually if you apply that knowledge than your life would be otherwise. My hope for each who reads this musing is that person knows Jesus as Savior and lives a life which pleases God.

Musing 120: Balaam
(initially posted April 25, 2017)

This morning as I was reading in an English translation of the Septuagint (LXX, a Greek translation of the Old Testament made a couple of centuries before Christ; it probably was the primary Old Testament for Christians and many Jews of the Diaspora during the first couple of centuries after Christ ascended into heaven). Not too long ago I decide to read through the Septuagint; I had only read parts of it before.

Today I came to Numbers 22-24; the passage that deals with Balaam. Many people know that Balaam's animal spoke to him in human language, rebuking him for beating her when she was saving his life. That incident is unique. Nowhere else in Scripture does an animal speak in human language; but that is not what struck me this morning, struck me so hard that I feel impelled to share it in a musing even though it would have to be a second one for the day since I do not want to exclude any already in the queue for the rest of this month. I hope you think what I share here is worth my posting this second musing today.

Balak, the king of Moab, was worried. Israel under Moses had moved to the north of his territory (on the east side of the Jordan River across from Jericho) and had defeated both the Amorites and the forces of Bashan. Previously Moses had asked Moab for permission to pass through its lands peacefully and that permission had been denied. Now Balak was frightened. So he turned to Balaam for help.

Balaam lived quite a way from Moab (in Mesopotamia along the Euphrates River – but some think Pethor was near the Jordan instead of the Euphrates); his reputation as one able to bring God's blessings or curses on people apparently was widespread. Balaam was firm in stating that he could only say what God revealed to him, whether to bless or curse; therefore he blessed the Israelites instead of cursing them as Balak wanted. However, Balaam did something that is mentioned later (Numbers 31:16) that the New Testament notes. Jesus in His letter to the church in Pergamum said Balaam told Balak to entice the Israelites to idolatry and fornication with Midianite women (Revelation 2:14). Peter and Jude both warn people about the false teachings of Balaam.

As I read the core of the story about Balaam this morning, I was struck by several things. First, I think that the direct interactions between Balaam and God, as described in Numbers 22-24, was more direct and more extensive than described in the Old Testament for anyone other than Moses. That amazed me; I had not noticed that before in reading the Old Testament, nor have I seen that point addressed specifically in commentaries or Bible dictionaries. The extensive interaction between Balaam and God struck me since he was not noted as a prophet from God, merely as someone whose blessings or curses seemed to come about.

My reaction to that insight was to realize that God's ways of working are far beyond what I might image, more extensive and more complex than I might expect. Too often I, as most of the people I know, limit God in our conception of how He might act. So let us be careful not to impose on God the puniness of our expectations about Him; but let us rejoice in His wise and creative ways of working in and with people. William Cowper's 1774 hymn published in the Olney Hymnal and now known as *God Moves in a Mysterious Way His Wonders to Perform* captures this truth beautifully. The lyrics are well worth reading (as well as listening to this hymn that is seldom performed today).

Second, I was struck by the implication that Balak, king of Moab, in keeping with his time thought God was merely a local deity and moved Balaam from one place to another as he sought to get Balaam to curse the Israelites. Throughout ancient times it was common for people to have such limited concepts of God that they associated God with a geographic location or attachment to a people. The idea of a God so great that He created all that is and is in total control of all that is was outside the scope of consideration for most people in ancient times, and still seems hard for people to comprehend outside the truth of the Bible. Many Christians also seem inflicted with that limitation. I think many of the doctrinal debates within the church come from people just emphasizing part of Biblical truth; for example, on one side of the free will/God's sovereignty debate are those primarily emphasizing God's sovereignty (often called Calvinists) and on the other side are those emphasizing free will (often called Arminians) while the Bible seems to emphasize both sides fully. Such doctrinal disputes are easily resolved when we realized that truth about the infinite God revealed in the Bible is not limited to the constraints of finite reasoning but may include aspects of truth that seem to contradict one another.

That's a heavy thought. It is something of a by-product from my reaction to the story of Balaam. He was a man who interacted with God amazingly, but failed to connect with him for salvation. At God's direction, he blessed the Israelites, but in his greed and avarice he told the enemy of God's people how to mess up the people of God. Opponents to Christianity are as clever in their resistance to God's work and able to corrupt it as happened from Balaam's advice; so we should beware.

Musing 121: The Return of Christ (initially posted on April 26, 2017)

At the ascension of Jesus into heaven, two men dressed in white suddenly appear and tell those who had watched the ascension of Jesus, "Men of Galilee," they said, "why do you stand here looking into the sky? This same Jesus, who has been taken from you into heaven, will come back in the same way you have seen him go into heaven." (Acts 1:11)

Jesus will return, but when that will happen is not something God has chosen to reveal to people. Jesus said this specifically to those present at His ascension just before He ascended into heaven. During the week before His crucifixion, Jesus had told His disciples this previously. No human knows that, not even the angels, only the Father of Jesus know when that will be. (Matthew 24:36) The Apostle Paul wrote the Thessalonians that the day of the Lord will come like a thief in the night (1 Thessalonians 1:2); hence Christians should live so that they are ready for Christ's return, whenever it may be. Paul leaves the impression that it could occur at any time. So be ready for Christ's return all the time.

While there are some things that the Bible tells us about the return of Christ, it's timing is not one of them. However, if I Google the "return of Christ" I find web sites with labels like "Seven Prophecies that Must Be Fulfilled Before Jesus Christ's Return" and "Fourteen Signs Announcing Christ's Return." Some people foolishly ignore the plain words of Jesus that tell us that only the Father knows when it will be. Don't be like them.

Throughout the history of the church, some have predicted when Christ would return or when the Rapture would occur; the Rapture being the taking away of Christians from the earth in association with Christ's return. This kind of foolish prediction has even been done in our times.

Many have been blessed by Christian music and religious programs on Family Radio over the years. However, one of the three founders of Family Radio, Harold Camping, foolishly predicted the return of Christ wrongly four times: September 1994, then March 1995, later May 21, 2011, and finally October 21, 2011. Wrong everytime. Two millennia ago Jesus said no one would know when He would return, as noted above. When you encounter one who gives a specific date for the return of Christ, draws parallels between our times and how things will be when Christ returns, or in some other way tells you that His return is near and we can know it will be soon, put that person down as deluded. Jesus can return at any time, perhaps before you finish reading this musing or perhaps it will be hundreds of years (or more) in the future.

The first coming of the Christ (the Messiah), though addressed in a number of prophecies of the Old Testament, was not properly understood by Biblical scholars of Jesus' day. Likewise I think it is likely that many will misconstrue what the Bible has to say about the second coming of the Christ. Scripture indicates that the return of Christ has multiple aspects and may take some time to work itself out as it reveals itself. Probably the return of Christ begins with the Rapture (1 Thessalonians 4:13-18 and 1 Corinthians 15:50-54) to remove the church (believers in Jesus Christ) from the earth prior to God's dealing with the earth in conjunction with Christ's second coming.

Instead of trying to organize the various scriptures related to Christ's return in the limited space of a musing, I want to emphasize the reality of Christ's return, its imminency (at any time), and the importance of being ready for His return. Wise people know Jesus as Savior and live in ways that please Him awaiting His return. Anything else is foolish and hazardous.

For nearly a thousand years (since Joachim of Fiore in the 12th century), some have thought the book of Revelation portrayed the whole of church history (that approach to interpretation of Revelation is often called "historicist"). In the past couple of centuries, and especially among those who approach the Bible dispensationally, Revelations 2 & 3 have been taken as letters to the seven churches indicated but also as a prophetic indication of church history. Then the rest of Revelation is taken to refer to things associated with the return of Christ.

Unfortunately I think that way of dealing with Revelation 2 & 3 is faulty. Certainly Revelation 2 & 3 contains letters to seven churches in southwest Turkey at the time. Churches similar to those seven can be found in every age and they have valid application as examples of churches. However, to try to map church history to the seven churches in their order requires a distorted view of church history. Most who take this view will identify the current era as that of the Laodicean church, the last one with its luke-warmness that Christ detests. To take that view requires one to focus on the Western church in Europe and the U.S., not the whole church. The 20th century saw more Christian martyrs than the total of the previous 19 centuries. Those with the view mentioned seem oblivious to such reality, and they seem unaware that the center of vibrant Christianity appears to be moving from the U.S. to Asia. Unfortunately, you are likely to encounter many fine Christian leaders holding that distorted view of Revelation 2 & 3.

I hope you are looking forward to the return of Christ and strive at all time to be ready for His return.

Musing 122: Is It Racism?
(initially posted April 27, 2017)

Racism is slippery, hard to pin down and has multiple connotations. Some consider belief that a particular race is superior or inferior as racism. Others use racism to imply a particular race is more likely to have particular biological and behavioral characteristics. Others associate racism with hatred or intolerance of another race or other races, and equate it with racial discrimination.

Evidence makes each of these connotations for racism appropriate. For example, average IQ scores from various groups show racial differences. Of course, there are many high and low scores by people of every race, but in IQ tests of a sizeable population the average score by race follows the same pattern as average IQ test scores from a different collection of people. Likewise, some diseases are more common in particular racial or ethnic groups than in others (e.g., cystic fibrosis, sickle cell disease, or Tay-Sachs disease).

There are similar trends in criminal behavior, with violent crime rates for one racial group being several times higher than for other racial and ethnic groups. Some try to excuse that group's excessive criminality by claims of poverty and past discrimination against the group; but falseness of that explanation is evident when crime rates for that group are compared with crime rates for an ethnic group poorer and more discriminated against than the group with excessive criminality (i.e., native Americans are poorer on the average and they have been discriminated against more than any other ethnic group in the U.S., but their violent crime rates are similar to those of most ethnic and racial groups). Only the racial group with excessive criminality has great potential to change itself, outsiders have little capacity to do that; unfortunately leaders of that group appear to tolerate its behavior.

There are many examples of discrimination, both negative and positive, in our history, both recent and older. Some only think of negative discrimination as racism, but positive discrimination when a racial or ethnic group is shown favoritism is also a form of racism. Most positive discrimination has a negative impact on others. For examples, numerous studies show Affirmative Action gave favored applicants to elite universities the equivalent of a 200-300 increase in SAT score relative to those from other ethnic groups; that harmed some better academically qualified by preventing their acceptance at those universities.

With this introduction to illustrate the complex, elusive nature of racism, I ask about a couple of situations, Is it racism? I leave it to the reader to decide the answer.

In judicial efforts to redress segregation in public schools, the judiciary used statistical analyses to demonstrate inequality of education in public schools for blacks and whites. Court mandated busing was one of the tools used by courts in this endeavor during the past half-century. However, look at how the courts react to police using similar statistical analyses to guide use of police resources most effectively to reduce crime and promote public safety. Instead of applauding police for wise procedures, some courts label the process racial profiling and prohibit it. That seems somewhat hypocritical by the courts, and perhaps is some form of racism by the courts. What do you think? Is it an instance of racism?

Police drew upon statistics about demographic backgrounds of those more likely to be involved in criminal behavior than others; then they based where they patrolled, who they gave more attention to, etc. upon that data. This is exactly what retailers and advertisers do. They promote their products to those more likely to want and use them. It is what a fisherman does when he fishes where the fish are biting. But the courts did not like it because it gave extra attention to the racial group whose criminal behavior is far greater than that for any other ethnic group. So, who is being racist in this? The courts? Or the police?

Reverse discrimination (as it is sometimes called) is as much racism as regular discrimination. Both are wrong.

Many white religious groups were criticized half a century ago for lack of racial and ethnic variety in their services. Since then, formerly white religious groups are far more likely to be diverse ethnically and have participation that is similar to the ethnic proportions of their communities. However there are two religious groups which generally are not so diversified ethnically. One group is a religious organization (church or something else) whose services are not in English. Typically only those fluent in that language participate in that group's activity. The other group comes from historically black churches. Few of them reflect the racial or ethnic distribution of the communities in which they are located. So the question arises, Is this racism? As noted above, I leave the answer to that question to the reader.

Some may find this musing disturbing, and others may be agitated by it. My objective is to stimulate careful thought about the subject of racism.

It is a multifaceted reality that is hard to grasp properly. It exists in many ways beyond the simple way it is usually portrayed (especially by the media). Only as we come to grips with the totality of racism and deal with it realistically are we likely to make much progress in overcoming the racial turmoil and disruptions of our society. If we fail to deal with racism more effectively than we have, I fear that our nation's progress will be severely hindered. That would be bad for everyone.

Positive behavior change of an ethnic group generally has to come from within, with primary responsibility for that on the group's leaders. Thank you for your attention to this unpleasant subject.

Musing 123: Rest
(initially posted April 28, 2017)

The Biblical concept of rest is not well understood; yet it is of vital importance. As noted by Hebrews, the rebellious Israelites under Moses angered God so He refused to let them enter His rest and they all died during the exodus wanderings before the people entered the Promised Land (Hebrews 3). Then the writer of Hebrews encourages recipients to believe and obey so that they might enter God's rest (Hebrews 4).

In Matthew 11, after denouncing cities which failed to repent after hearing Him and seeing His marvelous works, Jesus speaks to the Father (verses 25-27) and without any indication of those to whom He addresses these words, Jesus says "^{28} Come to me, all who labor and are heavy laden, and I will give you rest. ^{29} Take my yoke upon you, and learn from me, for I am gentle and lowly in heart, and you will find rest for your souls. ^{30} For my yoke is easy, and my burden is light."

Earlier in Matthew 11, disciples of the imprisoned John the Baptist came to Jesus to ask if He were the One. After they left, the passage says Jesus began speaking to the crowds about John. Perhaps the crowds were still there when Jesus denounced the cities of Chorazin, Bethsaida, and Capernaum. Perhaps they were still there when Jesus spoke to the Father and then said the words cited above. We do not know. Usually there were a number of people around Jesus most of the time. So it is possible that the Twelve, other followers of Jesus, and curious on-lookers were present when He invited people to take His yoke, learn of Him, and receive His rest.

We have a hard time understanding rest. Many think of rest as simply not being involved in activity. That is what parents usually mean when they tell a child it's time to rest. They want to child to lie down or sit quietly instead of romping about.

Rest of a spiritual variety in the Bible is contrasted with the normal activities of life in order for the one in rest to have a special relationship with God. Let's look first at what Jesus said (shown above) and then consider what the writer of Hebrews said in light of that, after which we will glance at other things in the Bible about rest.

Jesus offered rest to those consumed with daily life; He said the prerequisite for His rest was to take His yoke and learn of Him. An animal that is yoked has a job to do, as the people of Jesus' day understood. They used animals that way; most of us have never put a yoke on an animal and put the animal to work. **The rest Jesus offers comes from serving Him!**

Think of other things Jesus said about those who would come to Him. Jesus demands to be first in the life of one who follows Him, as noted in Luke 9:23-27, 57-62 & 14:25-33. This involves such commitment to Jesus that one denies self, accepts whatever Jesus wants the person to do (takes up one's cross), and follows Jesus, obeying Him. Such is not idleness nor lollygagging. It is not limiting one's movement to no more than a specified number of steps, as ancient Jews did on the Sabbath. Nor is it just avoiding normal work or entertainment on the day of worship, as many Christians have done. A person in God's rest enjoys a close relationship with Him and relies upon the wisdom and power of God's Spirit to perform the things God wants the person to do.

How different that is from the idle condition that most people associate with rest. **The rest Jesus offers refreshes and invigorates; and it comes from trust in Him and obedience to Him.** Certainly that is the connotation of spiritual rest the writer of Hebrews had. Those who missed God's rest did so by not trusting and not obeying Him; so the recipients of Hebrews are urged to enter God's rest by belief and obedience.

Genesis 2 says God rested after six days of creation; basically that meant God stopped His creative activities. It did not mean He was tired; nor did it mean He did nothing (He sustained His creation as He has continued to do since it was created). However, God used that seventh day in which He rested as a paradigm for people. He called it holy, a special time for people to relate to Him. Later He made it part of the Ten Commandments and it became the most obvious characteristic of the people that He chose to be the people from whom the Messiah (the Christ) would come. Jewish observance of the Sabbath set them apart from the rest of the world. At the time of Christ, the Roman Empire basically employed an eight day cycle called the market week; not the seven day week of the Jews.

Christians, in the new covenant with God through Jesus (in contrast to the old covenant of God with the Jews, given to the Jews through Moses) are freed from the rituals of the Mosaic Law. However, most followers of Jesus use a seven day week, and most worship on the first day of the week in celebration of Christ's resurrection. Unfortunately, most Christians in modern America do not focus of a weekly day of rest to draw closer to God through obedience and full attention on the Lord; all they do is attend worship services for an hour or two on Sundays. Hence, few manifest the rest Jesus offers.

Musing 124: Spiritual Carelessness (initially posted April 29, 2017)

Spiritual carelessness occurs whenever one does not pay close attention to what God has said. By that definition, both I and most of the people I know are guilty of a lot of spiritual carelessness. Unfortunately we often are unaware of how dangerous such behavior can be. This musing may help you to be more conscious of the dangers of spiritual carelessness.

Think of things the Bible tells us, things we believe God wants those who claim Jesus as their Savior to do. For example, Christians are told to constantly rejoice, pray, and give thanks (1 Thessalonians 5:16-18). How many people who belong to Christian churches do you know who are grouches, frequently are complaining and being bitter, or obviously not praying given what is coming forth from their mouths? Most of us think nothing of such; it's just the way people are, even those claiming to follow Christ.

Could God take a different view? Moses was a great man of God. He was used to free the Jews (probably a couple of million of them, counting women and children as well the 600,000-plus adult males) from slavery in Egypt and lead them for forty years; but he was not allowed to go into the Promised Land. The reason that Moses was not allowed to enter the Promised Land is shocking. In Numbers 20:2-13, we read about a miracle that God worked through Moses at Meribah. Because Moses struck the rock for water to come forth from it instead of merely speaking to it as God instructed, God said Moses would not go into the Promised Land. WOW! Who would have expected that? What a severe consequence of what appears to be a very small bit of spiritual carelessness.

To see something similar in the New Testament, look at what Jesus says in the Sermon on the Mount. Just after presenting the model for praying that we call the "Lord's Prayer," Jesus says "[14] For if you forgive others their trespasses, your heavenly Father will also forgive you, [15] but If you do not forgive others their trespasses, neither will your Father forgive your trespasses." (Matthew 5:14-15). How dangerous it is to hold a grudge, to be unforgiving when wrong has been done to you! Most of us tend to ignore this warning from Jesus when we are offended by someone.

Perhaps you begin to appreciate the dangers that can come from spiritual carelessness. The writer of Hebrews recounts the sad fate of adult men who left Egypt under Moses (only two of the 600,000-plus made it into the Promised Land – the rest did not because of their unbelief and disobedience) in chapter 3 and follows it with encouragement to believe and obey in chapter 4 so one can enter God's rest. That is the way to avoid adverse consequences of spiritual carelessness: believe and obey. The refrain of an old hymn (from 1887) captures this truth superbly: "Trust and obey, for there's no other way To be happy in Jesus, but to trust and obey."

Unfortunately few sing that insightful hymn today in our churches; and also unfortunately spiritual carelessness seems to abound in our churches today. Neither you nor I can do much about the way others behave, but we can impact the way you and I behave. We can be conscious of the dangers of spiritual carelessness and apply the Biblical solution for avoiding its consequences.

Yes, you are right. We have to pay attention to what the Bible says, and then behave as if we believe God really means what He says because He does mean what He says. So simple even a young child can do it. The question is, Will you and I do it?

Musing 125: Publication of The First Year of Pace Musings (initially posted April 30, 2017)

With this musing, I have posted 125 musings since my first one on April 26th last year. I am preparing to publish them as *The First Year of Pace Musings*. If my plans work out as I intend, that publication will be available inexpensively on Kindle or other electronic venues. I hope to have it available also as a print-on-demand book at a not-too-high a price. When the arrangements are settled, which I hope will happened sometime in May, I will post information about it here with a few musings. That will enable those who see the musings when they are first posted to get the collection of them in a single place.

As I prepared the material for publication, I was reminded that I have covered a lot of topics. I hope insights I have presented have been helpful. I have been told that I made people think and consider things differently than they had previously. I am glad for that. Usually that helps a person to have a better perspective about an issue.

As you know, I have permitted individual musings to be shared and given to others without limit; however, I have not made that offer for the collection of musings when they are published. I have made the collection available at such a low cost that anyone who wants a copy can have one. I certainly will not object if someone buys a number of copies and shares them with friends.

At this point, I assume I will post more musings from time to time. The future will show if that happens.

The rest of this musing addresses a very different topic.

The rest of this musing is an appeal to leaders of the black community. You, leaders of the black community, have potential to do what no one else is likely to be able to do. Only you, leaders of the black community, have much potential to transform the black community. If you believe, as I do, that black lives matter, the black community must be transformed. It is unlikely that the black community can be transformed by those outside it, and perhaps even you who lead that community cannot transform it. Perhaps there is something intrinsically corrupt in the black community that makes it far more inclined to criminal behavior than other races and ethnic communities; I hope that is not the case which is why I urge you to make concerted efforts to transform your community.

A great deal of attention has been given to the few hundred black people a year that are killed by police (both proper killings of criminals involved in crime and some killings that may be inappropriate – the number of blacks killed by the police each year is usually ¼-1/3 of the total number killed by police during the year). However, I hear little about the 8-10,000 black people a year who are murdered annually, and over 90% of them are killed by black murderers. It seems to me that anyone who really believes that black lives matter would give much more attention to what kills thousands a year than to what kills a few hundred at most in a year.

The black community consistently (year after year) has higher rates of violent criminality than any other ethnic group, even than ones which are poorer and have endured as severe (or worse) discrimination than blacks (such as Native Americans). Somehow this bad behavior by blacks has never become the top issue for leaders of the black community, and until it becomes their top issue so that they try hard to change it, I do not expect the bad behavior of the black community to change much.

There is another behavior in the black community that costs many black lives each year, many more than even the murders of black people by black murderers. The high rate of abortions by black women prevents births of ("prevents births of" is an euphemism for kills) hundreds of thousands each year; many times more than the 7-8,000 black murder victims of black murderers. Perhaps if the leaders of the black community were to give a great deal of attention to this, the behavior of the black community might change so that so many women would not feel compelled to abort their child because the one who impregnated her was unwilling and unsuitable to live responsibly with her and be a real father to the child. If leaders of the black community really gave that subject a lot of attention perhaps as many as 100,000 fewer black babies would be aborted each year.

There are some in America who delight in the huge number of black abortions. They like that it keeps the black community from growing larger and they feel it reduces future crimes and welfare payments; statistically they are right. But I have a different point of view because to me black lives matter as do the lives of people from other races and ethnic groups. I hope leaders of the black community share my view in that.

No one outside the black community has potential to change either of these bad behaviors, but perhaps you as leaders of the black community could transform the black community so that it did not kill so many blacks. I hope you will try.

If you have read this, please pass it on to any you know who is a leader of the black community.

— The End —

CPSIA information can be obtained
at www.ICGtesting.com
Printed in the USA
BVOW10s2041180717
489651BV00008B/144/P